HIDING
IN **HIP HOP**

ON THE DOWN LOW IN THE
ENTERTAINMENT INDUSTRY—
FROM MUSIC TO HOLLYWOOD

TERRANCE DEAN

HIDING
IN HIP HOP

ATRIA BOOKS

New York   London   Toronto   Sydney

ATRIA BOOKS
A Division of Simon & Schuster, Inc.
1230 Avenue of the Americas
New York, NY 10020

First Atria Books hardcover edition May 2008

ATRIA BOOKS and colophon are trademarks of Simon & Schuster, Inc.

For information about special discounts for bulk purchases,
please contact Simon & Schuster Special Sales at
1-800-456-6798 or business@simonandschuster.com.

Designed by Suet Y. Chong

Manufactured in the United States of America

1   3   5   7   9   10   8   6   4   2

Library of Congress Cataloging-in-Publication Data

Dean, Terrance.
Hiding in hip hop : on the down low in the entertainment industry—
from music to Hollywood / Terrance Dean.
p. cm.
1. Dean, Terrance. 2. African American bisexual men—Biography.
3. African American bisexual men—Psychology.
4. African American bisexual men—Attitudes. I. Title.
HQ74.2.U5D43 2008
306.76'5092—dc22
[B]   2007043448

ISBN-13: 978-1-4165-5339-7
ISBN-10:   1-4165-5339-8

For my aunt DeLisa Dean-Betts

and

To all the gay, lesbian, and transgender people
who live out loud, boldly, daringly, and without fear

CONTENTS

DISC ONE

DISC TWO

If it weren't for blacks, Jews, and gays, there would be
no Oscars.

> —Ellen DeGeneres,
> Host of the 2007 Oscar's,
> opening monologue

It is better to live your own destiny imperfectly
than to live an imitation of somebody else's life
with perfection.

> —*Bhagavad Gita*

DISC ONE

1. WELCOME TO HOLLYWOOD

ONE OF THE MOST invigorating things to do at least once in your life is to drive across the country and take in the wonderful views of the great ole U.S.A. I fell in love with life all over again after witnessing some of the most beautiful skylines spread throughout Oklahoma, New Mexico, and Arizona.

It took us two days to drive to Los Angeles from Nashville, Tennessee. I was so excited that the long drive didn't bother me. It was me and my boy, Jacob, from North Carolina.

I was thrilled to be out in the world, seeing the green and brown land, and looking at the blue sky. I was twenty-eight and just released from a correctional facility in Nashville. I spent eight months in prison for stealing a car and was released early on parole for good behavior.

I stole the car years earlier while I was in college in Nashville, and the judge put me on probation. I wasn't supposed to leave the state without permission, but as soon as I graduated from college I hightailed it out of Nashville, and became a fugitive on the run for several years.

The first place I went to was Washington, D.C., where I started working in television production, and then later I went to Wilmington, North Carolina, where I met my boy, Jacob. It was in Wilmington where I was caught and extradited back to Nashville to serve my prison time.

But when I first arrived in D.C., after college, I was broke and sleeping on the living room floor of a friend. I was desperate to make my communications degree work for me. I was fortunate to land an internship with CNN, which I liked. I found what I was meant to be doing. I discovered something that brought me joy, and it was working in television. What so many search their entire life for, I found early.

When I went to work each day at CNN, it was magical. I spent four years in college trying to figure out what I wanted to do, so I felt like the luckiest person in the world to have discovered my passion, something that gave me a purpose. After being there a few weeks, I decided that I wanted to become a producer. They were in control and handled business. People respected them, and I liked the title because it seemed to have prestige attached to it.

I couldn't have asked to get better training for it, either. I was working with the most prestigious news network in the world. I was going places. I became a sponge and soaked up every piece of knowledge about television that I could. I asked questions, I volunteered to do things, and I stood out. I was on a mission to make it in the entertainment world.

After my release from prison I was a free man, but I had a record. I was tarnished. My squeaky-clean record now had a felony conviction on it. In the real world my chances of finding a decent job and making decent money would be even more difficult. With a felony, I knew I couldn't work for a bank or any financial institution. Not even most corporate companies would hire me. I couldn't become a teacher or work for any government agency. My list of options was very short.

But I discovered that in the entertainment industry many people had felony convictions. Many people were criminals. The very thing I loved the most was a saving grace for my life.

In the world of Hip Hop, the more adversity in one's life, the more street credibility earned. And with street cred comes your playing card: dropping out of school to make money (gold card), selling drugs (platinum card), jail term (titanium card), getting shot (the almighty, invite-only black card). I'd been to prison so surely I would be accepted, no questions. Hip Hop artists usually fall into one or even several of these categories.

Now that I was working in the entertainment industry, I didn't worry about my livelihood. I could make money doing something I loved to do. Besides, I didn't have to explain or tell anyone about my criminal past. No one asked. There were no applications to fill out and no human resources department to do criminal background checks. So there was no need to be fingerprinted or provide my social security number.

Being in the clear and not feeling limited, I worked on movie production sets, learning everything I could. I was moving quickly up the ranks from production intern to production assistant to production coordinator. I was on my way toward my goal of becoming a film producer. My name was spreading among production crews because I had a great work ethic. I didn't mind the long hours and going above and beyond my job duties. I wanted this. I needed it. And the hard work paid off with a plethora of job offers.

Jacob and I kept in touch while I was locked up, so I called him as soon as I got out. I had to find out what was going on in the industry and if anyone was talking about me. I had developed a name for myself and I didn't want my arrest to prevent me from moving up in my career. I was determined to make it in entertainment. This was the only thing I knew and I didn't want to lose it.

Jacob was a real cool brother who didn't pass judgment on anybody so I knew I could trust him. He was a down low brother, like myself. Although we had girlfriends and slept with women, we also liked sleeping with men. The women were unaware of our lifestyle.

Jacob let me stay at his condo with him in North Carolina. The place was right off the beach, and it was laid out beautifully. Jacob had very nice taste, and his condo was a reflection of it—big-screen televisions, plush leather furniture, and queen-size beds in each of the three bedrooms. He was making some serious money as a soundman in North Carolina.

He was also one of those brothers who everybody loved, with the nicest disposition and kindest heart. Whatever you asked of him, he would go to great lengths to help you. When I got locked up, he just packed up all my things and put them in his basement. I was very grateful for his kindness and willingness to stick by me.

"Jacob, what's going on? What are people saying about me?" I asked nervously when I called. I had been gone for nearly a year.

One thing about the industry is that any bad news, gossip, or rumor will spread faster than wildfire. But as quickly as they spread, they are forgotten. If you're away from the industry for too long, you, too, can be forgotten. It's true what they say: In this business you are only as hot as your next project.

"Nobody's talking about it any longer," he replied. "It's old news. Besides, this is Wilmington, this ain't Los Angeles or New York where the big boys are."

I was relieved. That meant I could get back in the game and start fresh.

I just needed a place to go. Nashville is cool but, let's be real, it's not a television or film city. I needed to be in a place where I could make things happen.

Jacob let me know he was moving to Los Angeles to continue his career as a soundman for films. I was looking for a new start in life and to begin my career as a film producer. He was driving cross-country and planned to pass through Tennessee. He asked if I wanted to go along with him out to Los Angeles. That was music to my ears.

Before I spoke with Jacob, I had narrowed down my choices to either going back to New York or trying out Los Angeles. I chose Los Angeles. I could hide in a big city. In Hollywood it's all about illusions. I could be anyone I wanted to. I had already lived in New York for a couple of years, and besides, the farther I was away from my family in Detroit, the better. I didn't have a good relationship with them and hadn't seen them in a couple of years.

While I was holed up in Nashville, I was staying at a motel off Trinity Lane. It was one of about six sleazy motel spots for truckers, druggies, and prostitutes, but I had my freedom and I knew it was temporary.

Being locked up makes you appreciate the small, simple things in life. Once I knew Los Angeles was my way out, I knew it was a sign from God. I just knew it. I could feel this was my chance to start over.

The motel was twenty dollars a night. My cousin Cynthia wired me some money that I had stashed at her home in Detroit. Damn, that six hundred dollars was right on time. It wasn't a lot in a city like Los Angeles, but I'd lived off less than that before.

When I lived in D.C., I barely had money because the internship with CNN did not pay. I had to live off money I made from a part-time telemarketing job. The only thing I could afford to eat were Snickers bars and potato chips. That was my meal every day for lunch. For dinner, it was whatever pieces of chicken and pasta I could find for less than five dollars.

I was excited that I had some money to help me move to Los Angeles—I was desperate to go.

One thing I needed to take care of before leaving Nashville, however, was getting my parole transferred to Los Angeles. I was going to be on paper for two years and I definitely didn't want to be in Nashville all that time. I wanted to get as far away from Tennessee as possible. Being a black man with a felony in the South and trying to get a job was like going to an all-white college and trying to convince them you did not get in because of affirmative action. It ain't going to happen.

In order for my parole to be transferred to Los Angeles, I had to prove I had a place to live and a job.

A good friend of mine, Sandy, had recently moved to Los Angeles to pursue her career as a producer as well. She knew about my sexuality— she was one of the few people with whom I shared my deep, dark secret. I actually had no choice but to tell her.

Sandy is very attractive and has humongous breasts and they are very hard to miss. When we met I fought hard not to stare at them as they spilled out of her top. After a few months, she came to me and said, "You're gay aren't you?" I looked at her, perplexed. I had never before been approached so forthrightly by anyone asking me about my sexuality.

"Naw, why you say that?" I asked.

"Well, most men can't keep their eyes off my breasts when they speak to me. But you never stare at them while you're speaking to me."

Although she was right, I was simply trying to be a gentleman and not make it obvious. We joked about her breasts, and I confessed to her that I was bisexual. I told her that I was still attracted to women, but I liked sleeping with men. After that, she would grab my hand and put it on her breasts, or she would grab my head and push it inside her cleavage. "I'm going to turn you straight," she would joke with me.

I called Sandy and asked if I could stay with her. I let her know that if I had a place to live in Los Angeles there was a strong possibility I could get my parole transferred. "Boy, you better bring your black ass out here." She laughed. "You know you always have a place wherever I am."

I met Sandy while I was in D.C. working on a Warner Bros. film called *Shadow Conspiracy*. It was directed by George Cosmatos and starred Charlie Sheen, Donald Sutherland, and Linda Hamilton. I would often run into Charlie Sheen and Donald Sutherland at the production office. They were extremely friendly.

Mr. Sutherland was a tall man who towered over most of the other actors. In Hollywood most male actors are very short. He had a commanding presence with his white hair and piercing eyes. He was very sophisticated and refined. Even with his leisure attire he wore a blazer.

A real gentleman, Mr. Sutherland once asked me to get flowers for all the women in the production office. He wanted to let them know how much he appreciated all their hard work.

Charlie Sheen was a handsome man, but was short and small in stature. When I visited the film set, I would often see Charlie joking around with the crew. But later in the evening, I would see him in the hotel lobby surrounded by beautiful women who looked like models. Charlie was definitely a player. The smile on his face was a dead giveaway.

Working on the film also garnered me some attention from the hotel staff. The film's production office was located in the Wyndham Hotel. A few of the male front desk employees would flirt endlessly with me. Ironically, all the men were black, and there were no women at the front desk of the hotel, or maybe I just didn't notice. I think it was the latter because I found the men to be very attractive, but I was careful not to let on I was paying them any attention. I didn't want to blow the cover on my sexuality. The less anyone knew about me the better.

Every day when I ran in and out of the hotel to do errands, the men would try to make conversation. I was always cordial and exchanged pleasantries with them, but I wasn't going to let on that I was interested in any way. Even so, one brother did catch my eye. He was definitely an attractive man—tall, with a caramel complexion, beautiful lips, and an athletic body. When I first saw "Calvin" I assumed he was very straight. Nothing in what he said or did gave me any indication he was a down low brother.

Calvin was pursuing a career in acting. He was a model and had done a few commercials in the D.C. area. He really wanted to break into acting. On the few occasions when I had time to talk, he and I would discuss my goal of becoming a film producer and his desires to become an actor. I must admit that I was smitten by him. He had an engaging personality and an inviting smile. Whenever I came through the hotel's lobby, I would see his handsome face and broad smile from behind the counter. He'd nod toward me and I would nod back smiling.

I became aware of Calvin's motives. He wanted my help getting a part in the film. I liked him and didn't want to be shallow, so I bought Calvin a book, *The Artist's Way,* that many actors swore by as they pursued their careers. I figured if Calvin read it he would become motivated and make moves for himself. Sure enough, he loved the gift, but the message was perceived in the wrong manner, and Calvin eventually asked me out. He wanted to hang out and show me around the city. I accepted. But Calvin had an ulterior motive. From his advances, I knew he was willing to do whatever it took to get what he wanted. Well, if he was willing to play the game, so was I.

My part wasn't difficult. I had friends in the casting department and all I had to do was give them his photo and résumé.

I eventually helped Calvin get into the film as an extra, and each time we slept together, he made sure that he put his all into it, as if his career depended on it.

After I called Sandy, I informed my parole officer that I had a place to live.

While waiting to get permission from my parole officer to move to Los Angeles, I came across an opportunity to work as an assistant to one of the executives, "Orlando," for the Stellar Gospel Music Awards.

Orlando was an attractive, older man. Well, he wasn't that old; he was in his forties. He looked like the type of man who was settled down with a family in the suburbs, and he had no idea I had just gotten out of prison. He was impressed with my qualifications and the jobs I had held.

As we prepped for the show, Orlando invited me to dinner. I was game. I had not eaten a good meal since my release. During dinner I would catch him gazing at me. I felt uncomfortable because I knew that look. It was a look I had seen in the eyes of many men when I was out with them. It was passionate. It was lust.

I focused on my food. I refused to let my eyes meet his. I knew if I looked into his soft eyes I would respond. But I also considered how much older he was. Even though he was a good-looking man with a nice build, I just couldn't imagine myself in bed with an older man.

But Orlando continued to flirt with me. He made numerous requests for dinners and invitations to his home, and I would always make up some reason why I couldn't join him.

I was happy when we got closer to the show date because I knew he would be too busy to focus on me.

Working the show, I had the opportunity to meet some of the top gospel artists whose music I sang as a child in church, artists such as Shirley Caesar, BeBe and CeCe Winans, and John P. Kee.

I also got the chance to see how big the gospel industry truly was. People from all over came into town for this event. There were choirs from North Carolina, South Carolina, Alabama, Georgia, Mississippi, and Chicago. Backstage was like a huge family reunion. Everyone was greeting and hugging one another like they were distant cousins who had not seen one another in years.

As I ran around for Orlando, I noticed another scene happening backstage. Men screaming excitedly, embracing one another, and giving air kisses. They twirled around in their choir robes. Some sashayed flamboyantly, waving their hands in the air. I knew those types of men. They were the brothers we whispered about in church. They were the men the ministers preached their antigay sermons toward.

Seeing these men, I was glad to be an outsider. Men like these are called "church queens." They are well known in the church community and travel from one church event to the next. I kept my sexuality a deep secret, like most down low men, and I was not a part of this church circuit. Even though they appeared as if they were not bothered by what people thought of them and they hadn't a care in the world, I hated that they were so flamboyant and was glad I had not become that effeminate. I didn't want anyone singling me out and making fun of me.

After the first day of rehearsals and meeting most of the staff, I finally met "Clifford," one of the producers. He was an impeccably dressed man. When Clifford walked in you would have thought the president of the United States had entered the building. Everyone surrounded him, shaking his hand and hugging him. He was well respected and well known.

I was impressed that Clifford knew many people by their names. He asked about them and their families, and the way he touched them and put his hand on their shoulders, sometimes hugging them, made him appear fatherly. He was compassionate. He cared.

Yet, it was Clifford's interaction with the flamboyant men that made me notice how friendly he was with them. He knew them, personally. They laughed and kee-keed like old friends. He was comfortable with them. There was a familiarity.

Clifford approached me with his broad, dazzling smile. "Who are you, young man?" he asked. His voice was deep and sounded like he was singing when he spoke.

"My name is Terrance."

"Hello, Terrance. What are you doing here on the show?"

"I'm the assistant to Orlando."

Clifford looked at me, puzzled.

"The assistant to my Orlando?" he said as he placed his manicured hand delicately on his chest. His wrist and fingers were dripping with diamonds.

I looked at him, confused.

"Yes, I'm Orlando's assistant."

"*My* Orlando?" Clifford asked again. His hand tapped his chest.

"Yes, Orlando." I was not sure what he meant.

He smiled and walked quickly toward the production office.

As the days went by, I noticed a change in Orlando. He no longer pursued me or gazed at me. He was short with me and spent a lot of time with Clifford. As a matter of fact, they were stuck together like glue. I never saw one without the other.

I asked Orlando if everything was all right. I missed the attention. He assured me everything was fine, but it was pretty obvious what had happened.

I was ecstatic when I got the phone call from my parole officer that the transfer had been granted. I was ready to get out of Nashville. Now all I needed was a job when I got to Los Angeles. My parole officer granted the transfer on the condition that I get a job in thirty days. I knew that wouldn't be a problem. I was going to the entertainment capital. I was going to be in a place where there was an ample amount of production jobs.

While I waited for Jacob to come get me, I killed a lot of the time sitting in the motel room watching television. I didn't want to venture out and get caught up in anything. I only left the room to get food. Shit, I didn't need anything else, and it gave me the opportunity to reflect on my life. This was a new turn of events for me. I no longer had to constantly look over my shoulder wondering when I was going to be arrested. That chapter was over. It was time for a fresh start, a new page in the book. I was going to be on a new path. Maybe moving to Los Angeles would be good for me. It would be a welcome relief from all the drama I'd experienced in my life.

And my, oh my, what a life.

2. WHAT WOULD YOU DO?

THE COLD STEEL was pressed against my temple. I tried not to cry, but the man with the mask on his face kept yelling at my grandmother. "I'll kill his little ass," he screamed as she lay tied up on the bed next to me. The gunman gagged her mouth with my mother's stockings that were hanging on the door.

My four-year-old body shook violently. I had never seen a gun before. The man had already taken my mother hostage in another part of the apartment.

My grandmother was pleading with him with her eyes. She couldn't do anything drastic for fear he'd pull the trigger. He was erratic. He was jumpy and kept pacing back and forth. Every word he spoke he screamed. I flinched each time he moved closer to me and my grandmother. I wasn't sure if he was going to hit me with his fist or shoot Grandma Pearl. Every time he moved I watched him for fear he would raise his gun and just end our lives.

Every weekend, Grandma Pearl came to pick me up from my mother's apartment.

It was a Friday afternoon, 1972, when my grandma knocked on the door. It startled the man who was in the bedroom raping my mother. I could hear my mother crying and pleading from my room. I was crying, hoping it would come to an end.

When I heard the knock I knew it was Grandma Pearl. I cried

louder hoping this would scare the man and show my grandma something was wrong. The man opened the door and grabbed her. He pushed Grandma Pearl into the room with me and tied her up and put the gun to my head.

Once he had us under control, he went back into the room with my mother for what seemed like a lifetime. A few hours later the man was gone. I untied my grandmother, she grabbed me and held me close, and we ran out of the apartment together. I didn't see my mother for a long time after that, and we never talked about it ever again.

I had to live with Grandma Pearl. My mother was out of control. Her life was a mess. She was a heroin addict and prostitute. She couldn't care for any of her children. She tried but she was not emotionally or mentally ready to raise any of us.

My mother, Blanche Gerald, had five children—four boys and one girl. Anthony, George, Jevonte, Sheritta, and me. None of us had the same father, and I never knew mine. I am the oldest, and at the time of the rape, I was the only child. My mother had me when she was sixteen.

Grandma Pearl became my first superhero. She swooped in and saved me. She was invincible. I thought nothing or no one could stop her.

We lived on the northwest side of Detroit, in a relatively average family community.

Our house was a huge tri-level. Compared to my mother's small, one-bedroom apartment, this was a castle. I loved that I had so much space to run around.

It was only Grandma Pearl; her husband, Mr. Charlie McGhee, and me.

In 1967, Mr. McGhee took Grandma Pearl and her seven children into his home. She never married either of her children's two fathers but raised them alone until she met Mr. McGhee. Some would have seen that as the most amazing thing for a man to do. When I came to live with them, all of Grandma Pearl's children, including my mom, had moved away. I soon discovered why.

Mr. McGhee was the meanest, angriest, most hateful man I had ever laid eyes on. He was a pint-sized, scrawny, bowlegged man. His left hand was permanently closed from arthritis. He had a short temper and a sailor's mouth. He didn't tolerate anything. Mr. McGhee cursed at everyone and everything. If you walked into his house and didn't speak he would say, "What the hell, you can't speak, motherfucker? Get the fuck out of my house!" No matter who you were, you had to speak to him when you walked in the house.

And if you didn't move quickly enough when he said to leave, Mr. McGhee went into the bedroom and got his shotgun. "I bet your ass will get out now." Folks would haul ass getting out the door.

On the rare occasions when my friends came over, I had to prep them so they wouldn't get the curse-you-out treatment. To alleviate the drama, I rarely invited any friends over. Everyone in the neighborhood hated Mr. McGhee.

In the kitchen pantry, Grandma Pearl and I had shelves for our food. Mr. McGhee bought his own and kept it separate from ours. I wasn't allowed to touch it without asking.

You couldn't walk on, touch, or damn near look at the lawn. Even though the house was surrounded by a chain-link fence, nobody was allowed anywhere in the proximity of the grass. That was his pride and joy. Mr. McGhee loved his manicured lawn. No one, and I mean no one, not even me, could cut or mow the lawn. He was the only person allowed to touch it.

Mr. McGhee was a bitter old man. He didn't see anything good in anybody. According to him, everyone was evil and up to no good. Mr. McGhee would often tell me not to let the left foot know what the right foot was doing, and not to trust anybody.

When people tried to reason with Mr. McGhee or if he felt threatened in any way, he would yell, "Hold on, motherfucker, just hold on." He would run into the house and grab his shotgun and stand on the porch like the character in the movie *Walking Tall.* "Come on now, motherfucker. What you got to say now?"

When he and Grandma Pearl argued, Mr. McGhee called her everything from a low-down, dirty dog to a trifling, no-good, shiftless son-of-a-bitch. I couldn't bear listening to him yell at her. I hated him. He spoke to her like she was nothing. I never understood why she didn't go toe-to-toe with him and fight back.

Grandma Pearl would just stand in front of him with her petite cocoa brown frame while he ranted and raved.

She always kept calm. She never raised her voice. She would often say, "You can't argue with fools. Kill them with kindness."

I wanted to grab Mr. McGhee's shotgun and show him what it felt like to bully people.

Mr. McGhee never cursed, yelled, or screamed at me. I never understood why. Mr. McGhee always put me on a pedestal. He and Grandma Pearl would brag and boast about me. They encouraged and pushed me. They made me feel special.

I was a quiet child. There were no other kids around at the time, and I didn't have my brothers and sisters. When I went to school, Grandma Pearl and Mr. McGhee were both at work. He worked for the Ford Motor Company until he retired a few years later. Grandma Pearl held a job as a pharmacist's assistant at the local drug store. After school I would go to her job, get the key, and go home alone. I had to grow up fast.

Grandma Pearl and Mr. McGhee were both alcoholics. They would drink heavily, and I mean put it down—E&J, Crown Royal, and Hennessy. After binging on the alcohol, Mr. McGhee would start an argument.

I got used to it. After all my prayers that he would die and go to the devil went unanswered, I came to learn that evil needed kindness in order to live. The darkness couldn't survive without the light. Mr. McGhee relied heavily on Grandma Pearl for everything. She dealt with everything related to the house. She paid the bills. When he needed someone to take him shopping, to the barbershop, or on hospital visits, she did it all. People only wanted to deal with her. She was the mediator. Mr. McGhee needed her.

They didn't hit or mistreat me. They made sure I was clothed, fed, and went to school each day. They just weren't ready to be caring for a young boy in their old age. They wanted to live out the rest of their days partying and enjoying life. Unfortunately, I wouldn't be the last child to land on the doorstep at Grandma Pearl and Mr. McGhee's house. My brother George and a host of young cousins would come to live with us.

Grandma Pearl was a stickler for education, and it pleased her that my teachers liked me. They bragged about me to Grandma Pearl. They were impressed with my reading and writing skills. She would always tell me, "Don't let anyone tell you what you can't do."

I loved Grandma Pearl and everything I did was to make her happy. My mission in life was to make her proud of me. I performed well in school and she would compliment me. "You are special. You have a purpose."

Grandma Pearl made me feel like I could accomplish anything. She encouraged me to go out and see the world. Whenever the school or church had trips out of the city, Grandma Pearl made sure I went. She wanted me to see life outside Detroit.

She also made sure I did my homework and read books. We had a small library in our house that included a complete encyclopedia set and a book on etiquette by Amy Vanderbilt. I remember that book well because her name sounded rich and cultured. There was also a host of black authors like James Baldwin, Ralph Ellison, Iceberg Slim, and Langston Hughes in our collection.

In school I was far more advanced than the other kids, and it brought me a lot of attention I didn't like. I hated when teachers singled me out in front of my classmates. I didn't think I was any different from any other kid. I liked going outside for recess, laughing and joking around, playing sports. But the attention from teachers brought on the attention from the girls. I knew girls liked me, but when I started receiving preferential treatment, the girls became my new interest and friends. I wasn't sure how to handle it. My aunts and uncles always joked with me about girls and who I liked, and if I had a girlfriend. I hated being put on the spot with their inquisitions. Being an only child for a while, I was used to being alone and no one invading my privacy.

In the fifth grade, I was sent to do an errand with a female class-mate, Renee. I was always chosen by teachers to leave the classroom and do things around the school for them because they trusted me.

While we were walking in the hall, Renee smiled. "Can I go with you?"

I looked at her like she was crazy. "You *are* going with me."

"No, I mean can I *go* with you?"

"You are going with me. What are you talking about?"

"I mean, can I be your girlfriend and you be my boyfriend?"

I looked at her and she was serious. I knew girls liked me, but she was bold.

"Naw, I don't want to go with you." She wasn't pretty enough. I had my eyes on another girl in my class.

I played a lot of sports with the local boys in my neighborhood. There were mainly five of us—Bruce, Royce, Drew, his brother Earl and me. Whatever the sports season was, we were outside playing it—football, baseball, and basketball. We were all around the same age, but I was the tallest. I sprouted up. I drew more attention because I was tall, slim, and cute. Our crew did typical boy stuff. We would often venture through the neighborhood looking for things to do.

Most times, though, I was alone. I loved being by myself—reading, writing, listening to the radio, watching television without any inter-ruptions. I liked to live in the fantasy world I created where my mom was a doctor and my dad was a banker and we lived in a huge house in the suburbs. That is what I fantasized about.

However, in reality, my mother came to visit me at Grandma Pearl's after being dropped off by strange men. She was dressed like a pros-titute, which was little of nothing. I hated when my mother came to Grandma Pearl's house looking the way she did. Everyone—our neigh-bors and my friends—would notice her. You couldn't miss her. I hated and loved her at the same time.

My mother was absolutely beautiful, stunning. She was statuesque, standing at about five eleven, with caramel-colored skin, almond eyes, and a shape that had men tripping over themselves. She knew men fawned over her. She knew how to trap them with her words, a seductive glare, and her amazing body parts.

I loved when she and I were alone. When she dressed like a normal mom, with jeans and a blouse that covered her breasts. She'd take me to the store or the park and we would laugh, talk, and just hang out. But then the men would stop her on the streets. It irritated me how the men stared, gawked, or tried to touch her. I would pull her hand and tug at her so they wouldn't have time to talk to her.

My mother reminded me of this biblical story I'd heard as a child about how there were these beautiful Amazonian women bathing and lounging on earth in a garden of paradise. When the angels from heaven saw them, they were taken aback by their beauty and came down from heaven, took them, and had their way with them. God was so furious that he cast the angels out of heaven and gave them over to the devil.

Whenever I saw my mother, I always thought that one of the angels in heaven had seen my mother and came down and did the same to her.

Other times when my mother came to Grandma Pearl's, she would casually sashay into the house as if she had just been there the day before, when in actuality it had been weeks, sometimes months. She would go into the kitchen and grab what was cooking, go downstairs in the basement, and after a few hours, emerge and go into the bathroom, locking herself in for another few hours.

I hated going in the bathroom when she finished. It reeked of acidic, burning flesh. The smell of heroin stung my nostrils. They would flare from the pungent odor and I would hold my breath as I quickly relieved myself.

My mother would then sit in the living room and mumble through her drug-induced stupor. She would promise me she was going to buy me something new like clothes or toys. She would ask me about school and what I had been doing. I would ramble on about how great my teachers were, how much I really liked school, and how my homework wasn't really that hard. I would always look into her eyes for a glimmer or some sign that she cared. I wanted for her to say something like, "That's good, son. I am so proud of you. I love you." But I got nothing.

All I got were the many promises that she never kept. As much as I always wanted to believe her, I knew she wouldn't keep her word.

This pattern with my mother taught me never to trust anyone. Never to trust people, because even though they will make you promises, they will not follow through. To this day I have a problem with people who make a promise to me. Maybe Mr. McGhee was right when he told me, "Don't trust *anybody*."

3. MORE THAN I CAN BEAR

WHEN I WAS THIRTEEN, Grandma Pearl felt I needed to be around my family more, especially the boys. She wanted to make sure that I learned something from the men and boys in my family. But it wasn't only her idea, it was my aunts', too. Because I liked reading, writing, and doing creative things, they felt I should be around boys doing boy things. Even though I hung out with the guys in my neighborhood and was actively involved in sports, they still thought it wasn't normal that I sat in my room reading and fantasizing. So, on the weekends I would go to an aunt or uncle's house to be around other boys.

I had two aunts, Lisa and Priscilla, and two uncles, Johnny and Andrew. My grandmother's other two children had already died.

Aunt Lisa moved a few houses down from Grandma Pearl. She had two daughters, and I would often go there to visit. She was hip and fun.

Aunt Lisa also had a colorful host of friends—gay men, drag queens, and transvestites. Whenever she brought them over to Grandma Pearl's house I would get nervous. I had never seen men in dresses. They were dramatic and over-the-top. Their hair and makeup was impeccable, but their huge muscular bodies stuffed into their dresses and large feet crammed into high heels made me uncomfortable.

I wondered what possessed them to dress like that. But they were jovial, loud, and happy, and always seemed to be having a good time.

They'd say to my aunt, "He is trade, honey. That little boy is trade." However, I misconstrued the word *trade* for *tray*. For the next couple of weeks, I hoped they would come back again and explain what *tray* was, because whatever it was I didn't want to be it. I later learned that *trade* was a term gay men used to describe thuggish, masculine men who were not necessarily gay. They were generally the thug boys who hung out on the street corners, or guys who were very masculine and romanticized by gay men.

My saved and sanctified aunt Priscilla made sure I got right with God. I went to her house every weekend. She and her husband, Eddie, had seven children and they were all members of the Pentecostal Church of God.

Pentecostals believe in living at the church. We were there beginning at eight in the morning for Sunday school, followed by the ten o'clock morning worship, which lasted until three in the afternoon. Then we came home, ate dinner, and went back for the seven o'clock evening service. I would be pooped out by Monday.

I liked going to her house, and this is where my routine for church began. Since they had so many kids, we had to wake up by five in the morning to start getting ready. That was way too early.

I was actively involved in church. I was in the youth choir and youth ministry, and was an usher. I was taught that we were servants of God and we were to let ourselves be used by him for his glory.

But being in the Pentecostal church wasn't just coming and hearing the word of God, it was a praise service all day long. People would speak in tongues, get the Holy Ghost, and fall out of the pews and into the aisles. The Spirit would move through the building, and everyone would be yelling and screaming. This was all I knew church to be.

The minister was this huge man in the pulpit, shouting at the top of his lungs about the glory of God and all his righteousness. Everyone was in awe of him. He would tell us each Sunday how God spoke to him and gave him the word. God spoke to him and told him he was to be a preacher. He told us how he followed God's direction and that we all were sheep in the pasture and he was our shepherd.

I believed every word he said and sat in astonishment listening to him. Whatever he said had to be true because he said God told him. But I wondered why God spoke to him and no one else. I wondered how God's voice sounded. Was it loud and booming or soft and melodic? I would silently pray for God to speak to me. I asked him to tell me why I had the mother I did. Why was I born into this family? But I mainly wanted to hear his voice. I would hide under my covers and peek over the blanket, looking around the room, waiting to hear something. Nothing. I heard absolutely nothing, but it didn't stop me from praying and asking to hear it.

On other occasional weekends, I went to my uncle Andrew's house. I enjoyed going there because he and his wife partied the entire weekend, and Grandma Pearl partied right along with them. Just as she did with Mr. McGhee, Grandma Pearl indulged in her drinking with Uncle Andrew and brought her fifth of liquor to his home. When they depleted the bottles they headed right over to the liquor store and got more.

Uncle Andrew had four boys and one girl. His boys were more like my friends I hung out with in my neighborhood. They were rough and liked to play hard and they lived a hard life.

Their house was a small outhouse. Man, it was tiny. It had two small bedrooms, a living room with a huge boiler in the middle of it, a bathroom you could barely turn around in, and a kitchen barely big enough to accommodate the stove and refrigerator. All six of them were crammed into that little, bitty house. But they loved one another.

Uncle Andrew's house was always loud with the radio and television blasting and the adults all talking over one another. But it was there I learned to love soul music. The radio blared music by The Four Tops, The Temptations, The O'Jays, Teddy Pendergrass, Lionel Richie, and Marvin Gaye. Hearing those songs today always makes me think of when I was a child.

My grandmother didn't listen to the radio a lot, but if she did, it was news programs. My aunt Priscilla didn't play any secular music in her house. That was the devil's music. It was gospel music or some preacher's sermon coming from the speakers all day. However, Aunt Lisa's home is where the seed of Hip Hop was planted in my brain.

It was in her living room I discovered her album "Rapper's Delight" by The Sugarhill Gang. When I heard that song it was like a light had gone off inside me. The words and lyrics dripped over me like I was being baptized by holy water and filled with the Holy Ghost.

From that moment on I fell in love with Hip Hop. I yearned for the music by artists like Father MC, Big Daddy Kane, Afrikka Bambatta, Roxanne Shante, and Run-DMC.

I'd sit in my room with my tape recorder next to the radio waiting for hours for the DJ to play one of their songs. Especially Run-DMC's "It's Like That," and Afrikka Bambatta's "Planet Rock." I loved those songs. I would record them and sit another couple of hours transcribing the lyrics to paper. Then I would grab the hairbrush and play back the songs, lip-syncing along with the music in front of my imaginary audience as if I were live in concert.

Back then it was important to go to school rhyming the words of the hot new rap song. People *oooh*ed and *aah*ed when I could recite the words by memory. The long hours of rewinding the tape recorder after every other phrase really paid off.

I really enjoyed the weekends at Uncle Andrew's because it often meant we kids had a lot of freedom. They would leave us alone or have the next door neighbor come and sit with us. Sometimes they didn't return until the next day, and Ramone, the man who babysat, would stay the night with us.

Ramone was in his twenties and not an attractive man. He was rough looking, as if he had lived a hard life. He had an amazing, muscular body, but his face was not that appealing. He looked like an orangutan. He had a large nose and lips and severe acne on his face.

Every time I spent the weekend at Uncle Andrew's, the boys were in one room and my little girl cousin, Kristy, was in her parents' room. In the boys' room there were three beds. The two youngest boys, David and Alex, shared a bed. The older boys, Andrew Jr. and Carl, had their own beds. Whenever I spent the night, I would sleep with Carl.

One night while we were sleeping, Ramone came and laid in the bed between Carl and me. I immediately awoke. My heart was beating fast. I didn't say anything.

Ramone was fondling my cousin Carl. I saw Ramone pull out his own humongous, hard dick and play with it. He then grabbed my hand and put it on his dick. I was freaking out. I didn't know what to do. I just held Ramone's huge, massive dick in my hands. He then started fondling me. He did this to Carl and me at the same time.

One thing Grandma Pearl taught me was to never, ever let anyone touch me inappropriately. If someone touched me, I was to tell someone. Find an adult and tell them. I didn't understand it growing up. When people tell you things to watch out for, you never think it's going to happen to you. I knew this was inappropriate. It was not right.

At first my dick didn't get hard, but Ramone kept massaging it until I finally got an erection. This went on for a good fifteen minutes. I just held his dick and he fondled Carl and me. He then sucked off Carl and had him do the same to him. He didn't make me. I was glad; I didn't want to do that. Besides, I didn't think it would fit in my mouth.

The next day Ramone was gone. Uncle Andrew and his wife had come home early that morning, and Grandma Pearl drove back home.

I was waiting for Carl to say something, but he didn't. I was so confused about what happened, and when Carl didn't say anything, I figured maybe I should just keep quiet. I didn't want to embarrass him, or me, so I just kept it to myself. It was our secret, but I hoped that an adult would find out because it was killing me to hold on to it.

A few months went by, and my grandmother had the itch to party and also felt it was time for me to visit my cousins and Uncle Andrew. Again, they left the house to pick up some liquor, went to a party, and left us alone with Ramone.

We fell asleep, and Ramone found his way once again back into bed between Carl and me. My heart raced; I knew it was going to happen again. He was going to make me touch him. I blocked it out and thought of something else. But this time he decided to perform orally on me. I hated it. I didn't like his mouth on me. What he was doing turned me off. He tried jacking me off and sucking at the same time.

I was only thirteen and this was my first sexual experience. I didn't ejaculate because I was so focused on not liking the experience. All I kept thinking was that I wanted this ugly-ass man and his huge lips off me. I hated hearing his slurping sounds as he sucked my dick. I stared at the ceiling praying that it would be over soon. No matter how hard I prayed, it seemed like it took him forever to stop.

To this day, oral sex has not been something I am fond of. For most men, receiving oral sex turns them on more than intercourse. I have met many men and women who promise they will give me the best oral service, and yet, I haven't been able to fully enjoy it because I relate it back to my experience with Ramone.

Once Ramone had finished with Carl and me, he went back into the living room. I pulled up my underwear and couldn't go back to sleep. I wanted to turn and look at my cousin but I was afraid to look in his eyes. I just turned on my side and glared at the wall. This was wrong. I had this gut-wrenching feeling in my stomach. I hated that I couldn't get up and shower and wash Ramone's touch off me. I just lay there feeling awful. I couldn't understand what would make him do this to me. I thought of how and why he did it. I hated him. I asked God why this was happening to me. I thought about Carl, and how Ramone probably had been doing this to him for a long time.

The next day Ramone came over to my uncle's yard. Smiling at us, he went to talk with Carl. I didn't know what he was saying, but the sight of him made me angry. He disgusted me, and while my uncle, his wife, and Grandma Pearl were in the house, I pointed at Ramone and yelled, "He touched me, he touched me."

We were outside in the yard—my cousins, their friends, and me—and I didn't care who heard me. I knew I had to say something. I had to speak up for Carl and me. I had to stop Ramone before he did it again.

Ramone's eyes lit up. I ran into the house screaming, "He touched me. Ramone touched me last night." I told everyone in the house what he had done. My uncle leaped from the couch and ran outside, with his wife and Grandma Pearl sprinting behind him.

I don't remember what happened afterward, but I do know that I never saw Ramone again and he never babysat for my cousins, either.

No one said anything about the incident. No one came to me and asked me anything. I'd hoped someone would tell me I wasn't wrong for speaking out. I needed for someone to comfort me because a huge cloud of guilt and disgust filled me. As much as I tried not to believe it wasn't my fault, my head filled with thoughts of doubt that maybe I had brought this onto myself. Maybe I deserved what had happened. I'd been too friendly with him when he wanted to talk. We'd wrestled and played with him like he was a kid. I should have kept up my guard around him because I didn't know him.

For a long time I didn't go to Uncle Andrew's house. Grandma Pearl stopped partying as much with them. Carl and I never got to talk to each other about the experience. It turned into a faded memory. Carl later became a big drug dealer in Southwest Detroit, and was killed. He got into a fight at a bar with someone over drug money, went to his car to get his gun, and when he returned to the bar he was shot.

I continued to go to church with Aunt Priscilla. I prayed and asked God for answers. I hoped the minister would tell me God spoke to him and wanted me to know everything was going to be all right. At night I continued to ask God to speak to me. I begged him. I needed to know what I should do with the guilt and pain I was feeling. I wanted God to call me to the ministry. Maybe that would help me. Maybe then I could hear his voice, be delivered from my pain, and help his people.

I started to think about men more. After the ordeal with Ramone, it was like something crept into my consciousness about sex and I questioned my sexuality. I wondered if I was gay, a sissy, or a punk. People in my family and boys in the neighborhood often used those words. I sometimes used them too.

I wondered if the boys in my neighborhood knew, because when we joked around and called one another fag or gay, I felt as if they really knew what had happened to me. I wondered if I had this big red x marked on my head letting everyone know I had been molested by a man.

Since I didn't go to Uncle Andrew's anymore, I found refuge with my own homeboys. I hung out more with them. One of the guys in our crew, Earl, had a well-sculpted, muscular body for a young teenager. His muscles were like those of an adult man. He was very attractive, too, light-brown skin with curly hair and a body that wouldn't quit. But the elevator didn't always go to the top, if you know what I mean. He was cool and he lived with both of his parents and, just like us, he was a latchkey kid.

One day the crew was outside in front of his house laughing and joking when I looked at him and noticed how attractive he was. Before the molestation by Ramone, I had never paid him any attention, not sexually.

He was fine. Damn, he was good looking.

All of our parents had a rule. No one came in the house when they were not home. And they meant no one. I dared not bring anyone in Mr. McGhee's house. I was too afraid of what he would do.

Somehow we ended up in my boy's house. All of us. The entire crew. But before long, everyone was out of there except Earl and me. We ended up in his bed, under the covers, naked. I remember his muscular body feeling warm. We were both excited. Our breathing was hard and heavy. We were all over each other, kissing, caressing, and grinding our hard dicks together. Then all of a sudden we stopped. We looked at each other and jumped out of bed like we knew it was wrong. But I think we were both more afraid of our boys finding out. After that we pretended like it never happened.

4. THE BEAUTIFUL STRUGGLE

AS A TEENAGER, your body, voice, and world naturally changes. However, when you are in a dysfunctional environment, you feel like you are the only one going through what you are experiencing. As I grew up, men and women noticed my physical changes. I sprouted in height to six feet tall. My body trimmed but I maintained my thick thighs and butt. Girls always wanted to touch my butt. I hated it. I didn't have pimples like most teenagers, and my face remained smooth and youthful. My voice deepened. I was complimented on my nice smile and pretty eyes. Everything about me changed and people commented on them, out loud. I heard them. They were suggestive and inappropriate remarks for me to hear.

One time I was on my way to school, and it was cold outside. I was bundled up in my parka, hat, and gloves with my backpack slung against my back and waiting at the corner for the light to change. A married man who I had seen in the neighborhood was standing next to me on the corner.

"Hey," he said, smiling.

"Hey," I responded.

"On your way to school, huh?"

"Yeah."

"Cold out, huh?"

"Yeah."

Come on, light, hurry up and change, I thought.

"Damn, you grew up to be tall and sexy. I'm sure you're warm, too."

I ignored him and quickly walked across the street, leaving him standing there. I didn't know what to say or think. I was already confused and questioning myself after being molested by Ramone.

Another time, I was outside with my crew when June, a girl in our neighborhood, came up to me, grabbed my hand, and led me into her house.

June was a teenager like us but had a body like a grown woman. She was what the women in our neighborhood called fast. She was too grown for her own good. And just like everyone in my crew, she was a latchkey kid. She lived with her mom, who was never home.

June led me to her bedroom, pulled off her clothes and underwear. I immediately got an erection seeing her naked body. She had beautiful big breasts and smooth, brown skin. Her vagina was hairy. I stared at it. June put my hands on her breasts. My dick was so hard it hurt. She pulled me on top of her and guided my dick inside her. After a few humps and pumps, she moaned, and the juices released from my body.

I was scared and nervous. I didn't know what had just happened, but it felt wonderful. I had never had intercourse before. I was thirteen, and June took my virginity.

I was especially scared because my come was all over her vagina. I was still dripping when I pulled out.

June told me not to worry about it. She got up and cleaned herself. I stood there, dick still hard, trying to make sense of what had just occurred.

When she came back, I wanted to do it again. June's body looked delicious and she felt warm and juicy. I liked that feeling. We had sex two more times. My dick just wouldn't go down.

We had sex almost every day after that. June liked that my dick didn't go soft after our sessions. I could keep an erection and didn't grow tired. I became June's personal sex toy. She taught me what she knew about sex. We experimented and tried damn near every position. Some were too painful for her, but we enjoyed every minute of it.

One day my mother had stopped by Grandma Pearl's after being gone for nearly two months. You never knew when she was coming. She just showed up. Unannounced. This time she didn't leave as she often did but stayed around for a few days. Now that I was older, my mother and I never really spoke; I didn't have much to say to her. It's difficult trying to have a conversation with someone who is high on heroin. The drugs made my mother talk randomly about anything. The subject constantly changed, and she couldn't focus because she was always nodding off.

I just didn't understand why she had abandoned me. I couldn't comprehend how a woman could up and leave her children and act like we were some incidental part of her life she wished she hadn't experienced. I never understood why she never said she loved me or showed any affection toward my siblings and me. By this time there were four us.

I was on my way out the door, and my mother was sitting in the living room, snacking on her favorite meal—Argo Corn Starch. My mother craved the white ingredients and would sit and eat an entire box. I thought she was crazy. I mean, who in their right mind ate starch? I never understood it; I figured it had something to do with the drugs.

Before I made it to the door, my mother stopped me.

"Where you going?" she asked.

"Outside with my friends," I said, agitated.

"Come here."

When I walked over to her she sniffed around my neck, chest, and lower body area.

"You having sex?"

"What? Naw!"

"Boy, don't lie to me! I know you're fucking that fast-ass girl down the block. I'm not stupid. I'm your mother and I know you. You're walking and acting different."

That was the first time my mother noticed anything about me. It boggled my brain that she knew I was having sex. I couldn't understand how I was walking and acting different. Things seemed normal to me. But it took sex, something she was familiar with, for her to notice that her own son was growing into a teenager.

As a young boy, I didn't really have a clue what my mother did. I didn't understand her clothes and makeup, or why so many different men with fancy cars dropped her off. It was not until I became a teenager that I found out my mother was a prostitute.

I grew to despise her even more. I didn't want her coming around embarrassing me in front of my friends. Even when I hung out with my friends, I avoided areas where I knew prostitutes walked the streets—especially Woodward Avenue, the long, vast street that went from north to south, dividing Detroit between the east and west sides. It was known for its sex stores, theaters, and women of the night. I prayed that neither I nor any of my friends would spot her out there, parading up and down the ho stroll looking for a trick. I thank God no one ever saw her.

I didn't want her as a mother. She'd left. She'd walked out the door, abandoning her motherly duties. Drugs were more important to her, and I felt it. She didn't spend any time with any of her children. We were left at the doorsteps of relatives to care for us, and they had their own problems. They complained how they couldn't afford to feed another mouth or didn't have room for another body. I hated them for that. I thought family was family. If someone needed assistance, you reached out and did what was necessary. My aunts and uncles knew my mother had a drug addiction. They knew that we needed guidance and support, but more important, that we needed to be shown love.

Every day, I hoped my mother would be delivered from her addiction. I hoped that she would come and save her children, and we would all live happily together. I fantasized about a mother who was respectable and caring. But she was my mother, she was who she was, and nothing changed.

By the time my other siblings came along, Grandma Pearl couldn't manage a house full of babies, so we got split up. To avoid putting us into the foster care system, my brother Anthony lived with his father and grandmother on the east side of Detroit. My brother George and I lived with Grandma Pearl. My sister, Sheritta, lived with my cousin Donna. It bothered me that we all were separated.

My brother George was a handful. He was angry and hurt. He, like I, didn't understand why our mother wasn't around.

George was a bully, often fighting in school and even cursing out his teachers. He had a serious temper and anger problem. If anyone made any snide comments about him or anyone in our family, he would haul off and start swinging. And God forbid if there was something he could pick up and use as a weapon. If he was in attack mode, the best thing to do was to get out of his way, because he wouldn't stop until someone pulled him off you or he saw blood being drawn.

George often ran away from Grandma Pearl's house, searching for something or someone to love him. Grandma Pearl couldn't handle him, and no other family member wanted to take on an angry and emotional child. So George ended up in group homes for boys. He had several stints in and out, breaking out of them and making his way back to Grandma Pearl's.

Eventually our neighbor Mrs. Hughes took him in. She was the nicest and sweetest woman, just like Grandma Pearl, and had her own family. But she told my grandmother that George could stay with her, which made him happy.

One summer when I wasn't too busy running errands for everyone in the neighborhood, I grabbed two books from Grandma Pearl's library, Ralph Ellison's *Invisible Man* and Iceberg Slim's *Mama Black Widow,* which I read several times over. I had not heard anything about them nor did I know who these authors were. But after reading those books, I discovered that there were others who understood what it was like to be different. It helped me to see that no matter who or where you are in your life, difficult circumstances happen to everyone, and those events can make you feel like you don't matter in a world full of people.

Going to church with Aunt Priscilla every Sunday, I figured God would have a handle on the situation. I got baptized and turned my life over to Christ; I was doing everything to make my life right with God. I prayed and asked God for my mother to be better. I asked for him to protect her and deliver her from her drug habit. I wanted to be delivered from my sinful thoughts about men. The preacher warned in his sermon that thoughts could be impure, and I was having impure thoughts about boys.

As a teenager, everything for me was trial and error. I watched the adults and did what they did or I read books on a subject to learn more. I hated that I didn't have a father to explain to me the things I was going through. I longed to have a father to talk to or even to chastise me. I needed discipline, a strong hand. Since I had no real direction, I tried to figure out things on my own.

There were some subjects I just didn't feel comfortable talking about with Grandma Pearl. Although she made herself available, I didn't know how to talk with her about the feelings I had for boys. As a matter of fact, I didn't talk about it with anyone. How do you tell the people you love that you have feelings for someone of the same sex? How do you articulate those desires? All I ever heard from anyone, male or female, was, "Men who like men—it ain't natural. God is going to deal with them." So I bottled it up and swallowed my voice. I already felt I didn't deserve anything. People like me weren't special or worthy.

5. MY LIFE

I KNEW I WANTED to leave Detroit. I hated it there and wanted to get to New York City where everything was happening. As a matter of fact, I had planned to run away just as soon as I graduated from high school. I wasn't going to tell anyone; I was just going to buy a plane ticket and leave. Fuck them all.

I had to get to New York because in all the books and magazines I read, everybody was cool and hip there. It seemed like everybody wore Adidas sneakers, Calvin Klein and Levi jeans, and Kangol hats. But most important, all the rappers lived there—LL Cool J, Run-DMC, Father MC, KRS-One, Big Daddy Kane—and their music was something I could relate to. It was young and for us. It was Hip Hop. In New York, everybody was somebody and I felt it was someplace I needed to be.

In the fall of 1982, I entered Detroit Central High School. When I got there the school officials told me I was going to be part of the honors program. It was one of the best things to happen to me, affording me the opportunity to do lots of things in school. But I always knew that even though I studied, teachers from my elementary and junior high years gave me A's and B's because I was well-behaved. I shut my mouth and did my work. I became invisible. I learned how to hide in a classroom full of kids.

I had a great time in high school, jumping right into the swing of things and becoming involved with a lot of activities and events. I became freshman class treasurer, sophomore class vice president, Mr. Junior, and, in the fall of 1985, I was voted homecoming king.

I seemed to find my rhythm. I knew to keep quiet about my feelings for other guys. I dated girls, got along well with my classmates, and stayed on top of my studies. Life was moving smoothly. When I won homecoming king, my family celebrated along with me. They were proud of me. It felt good to make my grandmother happy; she kept pushing and encouraging me.

But everything came to a screeching halt, and the party ended quickly. I was sitting and talking with my grandmother when Aunt Lisa and my mother came by. My first reaction was to get up and go to my room like I always did when my mother visited. I tried to have no communication with her, to just shut her out of my life, as she did with my siblings and me. When I was forced to acknowledge her, I would bark hello at her. She didn't care because she was too high to notice.

When my mother and Aunt Lisa sat at the dining room table, something registered to me that this was serious. They were not smiling or joking like they usually did. Aunt Lisa was always in a light mood and things never seemed to bother her. Her life always seemed like a party, but now she had a frown on her face. I glanced at my mother, who looked as if she was carrying something, something very heavy that she wanted to drop off and then keep moving to get past.

A worried look swept across my grandmother's face. She knew her children and she knew when something bad was coming. She would always tell me, "If it ain't one thing, it's another." Then she would go to the kitchen cabinet, open her Crown Royal bag, pull out her pint of liquor, and get her "a little nip."

This time there was no getting a little nip. There was no pint of liquor nearby. She picked up her cup of coffee and took a sip.

Aunt Lisa took my grandmother's hand, looked her in the face, and told her that my baby brother Jevonte, who my mother had recently given birth to, had been born with the AIDS virus. This meant my mother also had AIDS.

I blacked out and I didn't hear anything else my aunt said after that. The only thing that kept echoing in my head was that my mother had AIDS.

6. MONEY, MONEY, MONEY

THE NEWS ABOUT MY MOTHER spread through the family quickly. Everyone was stunned. We had heard of AIDS, but we did not know what it actually was or how you got it. I just knew I wasn't ready to handle what it would do to our family.

My mother didn't have insurance, so she relied upon the mercy of the city to take care of her. No money, no real treatment. Our family was not prepared for the financial blow.

That's when I realized the importance of money. This was a world of the haves and have-nots. No one in my family had any financial resources. What my grandmother had, she managed and budgeted wisely. Yet our simple lifestyle was definitely reflective of her meager resources.

I tried not to focus so much on what was going on inside my tiny bubble. I knew I couldn't tell anyone about my mother having AIDS. This was a family secret.

No one in our family really discussed it, but I often overheard my aunts and uncles whispering about my mother and the disease. "She's really sick. She can't eat and drink in my house anymore. What about the kids? She can't touch them because maybe they will get it."

Hearing these comments hurt me. My mother had become an outcast and yet she was still my mother. As much as I didn't want her in my life, there was nothing I could do about it. She was mines. I didn't want to face my family; I wanted to disappear and go someplace else. I asked God again, "Why was she my mother? Why did she have to get this disease?"

The more I questioned, the fewer answers I got. I would just look at her to see if there were any tell-tale signs. She didn't lose any weight. She still had her bodacious figure. I didn't want her to eat at our house anymore because I thought I could catch AIDS from her. The times I got close to her, I would simply stare at her, wondering what the disease was doing to her; I wanted to know how AIDS was affecting her. But she never let on and she never acted any differently. I never saw her cry or heard her complain. All I knew was that AIDS was this scary new disease that nobody seemed to have any answers about, and one day my mother was going to die from it. That was what I hated most—I knew my mother was going to die. I would no longer have a mother, and that was an absolute.

I resorted to drinking. You name it, I was drinking it: Cisco, coolers, Bacardi, and gin. A friend introduced me to 151 rum and that became my drink of choice. I drank after school with my friends; I drank on the weekends at home. I would stop by the liquor store and get a half pint or pint of liquor, drink in my room until I fell asleep, and then hide the liquor bottles and throw them out in the neighbor's trash can. It was party time, and I was drowning my sorrows. I didn't have to think about my sexuality or my mother and brother suffering from AIDS. When I was high, my sexuality was a moot discussion; it didn't exist. Nor did my mother. She was nowhere in my fantasy world. Whatever problems I had simply disappeared in my drunkenness.

I convinced Grandma Pearl to let me get my driver's license. Bad idea. I became a drunk driver. At times, I couldn't remember how I made it home. I learned quickly how to mask my alcoholism. I had great examples to learn from: Grandma Pearl and Mr. McGhee. I learned what not to do when I watched them drink; not to stumble, slur my words, or act silly. I remained cool, calm, and collected; I was a master at masking my drinking.

I didn't stop praying though. I would get on my knees in my room and I would pray, "God, I know you love me and that you answer all prayers. You know my heart and all I ever want to do is to serve you and do right in your eyes. Continue to use me for your purpose. You know I struggle with my sexuality. I have asked that you take away those tendencies. Please, please, please help me to be delivered."

I prayed for this every day and night. I only wanted to serve God, do right in his eyes, make my family proud, and not be gay. Praying to God for deliverance was something I was taught as a little boy. If you needed God to do anything for you, just send it up in prayer and he will answer it. That's what I learned from Grandma Pearl, my aunts, and the preacher who damned everyone to hell if they were not following God's word.

Yet my feelings for men began to filter through the prayers in my senior year of high school. I was attracted to a fellow classmate. Dude was fine. He was captain of the basketball team and I had never really noticed him until I glanced toward him one day in math class. His tall, lean, muscular body lounged at his desk and his huge hands rubbed his fresh face. His smile gleamed, and when he spoke his voice resonated throughout the room. His presence made me unaware of anyone or anything else. At that moment he was my everything.

Each day following, I tried not to stare at him, but when he wore his fitted Levi jeans I couldn't help but notice the bulge in his crotch. When he was called to go to the chalkboard, his back would be to us and I saw that his ass fit perfectly in his jeans. I loved when he wore his basketball shorts to class. My gosh, he had the most amazing legs. Nice fat, toned thighs and muscular calves. I fantasized about everything I wanted to do with him.

Although I thought about him constantly, I chalked it up to the idea that I was going through a phase. I had heard that most young people go through a phase where they're infatuated with someone of the same sex at one time or another. Yet my infatuation never ended.

After our senior class prom, I took my date home and drove in my tuxedo to Mike's house. He was a junior and we were best friends. And he was someone else I had the biggest crush on. I *thought* I just loved being around him but I loved his company. We talked about everything. We did everything together. We had so much in common, except that he was very much into girls and I was very much into him.

Mike was attractive. He had long eye lashes, and his hair was wavy all over. He constantly brushed it to sculpt the waves so they formed around his head. He was tall and had a nice, slim body. All the girls flirted with him.

When I arrived at Mike's home, it was after two in the morning and his mom let me in. For me to show up at their home unannounced was not a problem, especially this night. She knew it was my prom, and in her eyes, I was coming to hang out with my boy and to tell him all about the night.

I went straight into Mike's bedroom where he was sleeping. I woke him up. He rolled over in his basketball shorts with no shirt on. Seeing Mike's bare chest sent chills through me. It was then I knew for sure I liked boys, especially him.

I told Mike about the prom and all the fun I had, but I was really fantasizing about him. I wanted to tell him, but I couldn't; it would have ended our friendship. Besides, the next day, Mike was coming with a group of us to Cedar Point Amusement Park in Sandusky, Ohio. I would have all the time in the world to be with him. But in the meantime, I had to just settle with climbing into bed with him for the night and hoping our bodies touched.

7. DÉJÀ VU
(I'VE BEEN HERE BEFORE)

THE BEGINNING of my senior year, my guidance counselor called me into her office. "Terrance, you have very impressive grades," she said. "You can attend practically any college you choose."

I had to get away from my family. I didn't want to be around them. I felt they didn't do enough to help me or my brothers and sister. We all were split up and living with various family members. My brother George was in and out of group homes. I was out of control with my drinking. I had severe issues with my mother, the AIDS virus she and my younger brother Jevonte had, and my sexuality. It all left me feeling abandoned. It was clear that George and I were reaching out for something, and none of my aunts or uncles recognized the signs. Leaving Detroit would give me freedom to discover myself.

I applied to three schools—Morehouse College, Fisk University, and the University of Detroit. I got accepted to all three.

In June of 1986, I walked across the stage to accept my high school diploma. It was exhilarating. I was the second male in my family to graduate from high school; my cousin Andrew Jr. was the first. Grandma Pearl, my mother, Aunt Lisa, and Aunt Priscilla all came to cheer me on. It was great having my mom there and I was glad that she looked normal for once. She wore a simple black dress and had her hair pinned up. She looked beautiful. She must have known this was a special day for me because there was no indication that she was high on heroin. She gave me a big hug and told me she was happy for me. However, after the ceremony I didn't see her again for another few months.

They were all proud, especially my grandmother. Everything she instilled and inspired me to do had paid off. I'd accomplished a milestone in my life.

Grandma Pearl put my diploma in the center of the china cabinet, right next to my trophy and sash for homecoming king.

She was even happier when I was accepted to college—the first in my family. I had decided on Fisk University.

Being at a black college was a great experience. The culture on campus was strong, and students were unique in their style. Every day at lunchtime, there was a fashion show on the campus yard when everyone came out to parade their latest gear.

The classes were challenging, and we studied hard. The professors were sticklers who impressed upon us the importance of learning our culture and knowing oneself. We were students at Fisk University, the Black Harvard of the South.

My first year was not excellent. I partied, continued drinking, and barely went to classes. I met one of my best friends, Gerrod, and we hit it off immediately. Proud to represent Brooklyn, he was a true New Yorker through and through. He had a rough exterior, a no-holds-barred, b-boy attitude, and didn't take no shit from anybody.

Gerrod was a sophomore who knew everyone on campus, and everyone knew him. He was infamous for fighting and for screwing practically every woman on campus. He tried to help me settle into my first year at Fisk, but in the fall I was back in Michigan at the University of Detroit. I had not been focused. I didn't get anything done. I had no discipline. I hated being back at home, but I needed to regroup and get my act together.

When I arrived at the U of D I met a few young brothers who were members of various fraternities. I had not thought of pledging a fraternity. I certainly wasn't up for the mental and physical abuse I heard they put their pledges through. But the men of Alpha Phi Alpha Fraternity, Inc. demonstrated brotherhood and unity; they were studious and focused, and I knew they were a fit for me.

Gerrod also pledged Alpha Phi Alpha Fraternity, Inc. at Fisk. He and I remained in contact after I left, and we discovered we were joining at the same time. He kept me updated as to what was happening around the campus. His conversations made me nostalgic for the black university, and I made up my mind that after I joined the fraternity I was going back to Fisk.

8. BREAKDOWN

ONCE I JOINED THE FRATERNITY I finally felt like I was part of a brotherhood; I fit in. We were all proud men. I felt comfortable and well hidden in an organization where men were men. No one would suspect anything about me. I was in a fraternal group. The last thing on anyone's mind would be my sexuality.

After a huge party for our induction into the fraternity, I was standing outside talking with a frat brother when I saw one of the most beautiful women I'd ever seen strolling across the campus. It was Jaslyn, a member of Delta Sigma Theta Sorority, Inc. She was a senior at the University of Detroit and, man, she was fine. She was breathtakingly beautiful. Her almond-chocolate skin was smooth and silky. She was right, oh yes, she was right. A phenomenal body—thin in the waist and thick in all the right places. She had a smile that lit up the night. She was unlike any woman I'd met on campus. Jaslyn was a woman, a lady, and sophisticated.

My frat brother introduced us, and we exchanged phone numbers. We started dating immediately and I fell head over heels for her. I knew that if I could love any woman, Jaslyn was the one. I had thoughts about marrying her. She was everything I imagined in a woman.

Jaslyn lived alone, and I often spent the night at her home. The first time we had sex, it was mind-blowing. We showered together, and for the first time I performed oral on a woman. I had vowed I would never do anything like that, but with Jaslyn I wanted and needed to taste her. She tasted sweet and I loved it.

After we finished in the shower, we went into the bedroom where we made love all night long. Her body shivered and shook from the long lovemaking session because—me, being the energizer bunny—I couldn't get enough. Although she begged for me to stop, she begged for me not to stop. I was thankful for all the sexual practice I'd had with June; I knew a woman's body and I was determined to let Jaslyn know that.

For the next few months we were seen everywhere together. Everyone on campus knew we were dating. We were the "it" couple, and I reveled in it. I was the man and no one could question my sexuality. I thought that I had been cured, that I was no longer gay. I still had desires for women. I'd thought that once I started liking men I would no longer be attracted to women. But that wasn't the case. Maybe I was bisexual. Whatever I was, I was just happy to be in love with a woman, and when I was with Jaslyn I didn't think about a man. God had finally answered my prayers. I was feeling good, really good.

Being with Jaslyn made me feel like an adult, like I had matured. It was my first real college relationship, and I couldn't have been happier. I loved that she carried herself like a lady and that she was always put together. Her hair and makeup never overpowered her true beauty. I thought about her all the time. When we were apart, I wished we were together. Seeing her each day lit a fire in my heart. Jaslyn had invaded the cold place where I refused to let anyone in like a warrior conquering a stubborn leader. She revived me with her tenderness, soft kisses, and gentle touches. I longed for the moment when we were lying together in her bed with her soft, silky skin resting on top of me. I didn't want to let her go; I held on as tight as I could.

Jaslyn shared her sentiments with me as well, and wrote me notes and letters expressing her love for me. She hated when I left her apartment, and whenever we reconnected, she let it be known she was happy to see me. She felt protected by me—I wouldn't have let anything happen to her.

I received a phone call one day from one of Jaslyn's sorority sisters who told me that she needed to speak with me. I found it odd but went to meet her anyway.

"Terrance, I hate to tell you this," she started, "but Jaslyn is cheating on you."

"What?" I looked at her like she was crazy. "What do you mean?"

"She is seeing this Que at the University of Michigan." A Que is a member of the Omega Psi Phi Fraternity, Inc. "She's been going up there to see him for the past couple of weeks."

I just looked at her; I couldn't believe my ears. No, not Jaslyn—she was my world, my everything. This was the woman I was going to marry. She couldn't, no she wouldn't do this to me.

"I'm sorry, Terrance. But I really felt you needed to know." She reached over and gave me a hug. "I felt you deserved to know."

And like that, an empty sinking feeling crept into my stomach. My world fell apart. I couldn't wrap my mind around Jaslyn cheating on me; it seemed impossible. I struggled to make sense of the words, and then an incredible feeling came over me. My head ached, then my heart, and I felt like I couldn't breathe. My body went completely numb.

I figured maybe this was a sign that it was not meant for me to be with women. I thought perhaps being with a man wouldn't be this difficult and heartbreaking. This was my first time experiencing something where my feelings were involved. I had invested time and energy in a relationship with a woman, and as much as I'd thought about men before, when I was with Jaslyn I didn't have those thoughts. Now, everything I questioned about myself and my sexuality seemed to make me even more confused.

Maybe I wasn't bisexual as I had thought. Maybe I was gay, simply a gay man hiding in a heterosexual world.

I called Jaslyn and confronted her.

"So you cheating on me?" I said straight out. I didn't want to play the guess-what-I-know game. I got straight to the point.

"What are you talking about?" Jaslyn said, obviously caught off guard.

"I already know about the Que at the University of Michigan you're fucking, so don't give me the bullshit like you don't know what I'm talking about."

"Who told you that?" She was upset.

"Why does it matter? I thought we had something special! I thought I meant something to you." I was pissed.

"You do mean a lot to me. It's nothing serious between him and me. I am so sorry, Terrance. Please . . . I am so sorry." She was crying.

"Well, thank your sorority sister because she's the one who told me. I don't want nothing else to do with you. It's over." I slammed down the phone. Damn! I was overcome with a sense of disappointment. I'd wanted her to deny it, but she hadn't.

She apologized, but it was too late; the damage had been done. I had let a woman into my life and she lied to me. She was unfaithful and untrustworthy. I didn't understand how she could tell me that I meant something to her but cheat on me. How could someone you love hurt you intentionally? It would become a pattern in my relationships. My mother, my first real relationship with a woman, had laid the foundation.

I sulked for months after the relationship with Jaslyn ended. I couldn't eat or sleep and I continued drinking. I hated being alone again. I didn't want to be without Jaslyn. I thought about picking up the phone and calling her, but I resisted the urge. Although she called me, I couldn't find it anywhere inside myself to forgive her. She'd betrayed me. She'd hurt me terribly, and it was something I felt was irredeemable.

I counted down the days until I could leave Detroit to return to Fisk in Nashville. I didn't want to be there anymore. I wanted to escape to a place where I knew I wouldn't see her face, or expect her phone call. Jaslyn was no longer a part of my life and I didn't want any reminders of her.

Right before I left Detroit I discovered Jaslyn's sorority sister told on her because she wanted me.

When I returned to Fisk in the fall, I started dating a freshman named Tiffany, a petite glamour girl from Ohio. Damn, she was gorgeous. Our relationship was fun—we enjoyed each other's company and spent a lot of time talking. It was an easy relationship, but I was reserved about opening myself to someone again. I didn't want to get hurt, so I protected myself by building a wall around myself. Eventually, during the school year Tiffany and I ended our relationship because I couldn't get what Jaslyn had done to me out of my head.

This time at Fisk I studied and did well in my classes. I learned what it meant to be a student at a prestigious institution where many of my predecessors, such as W.E.B. Dubois, John Hope Franklin, and Nikki Giovanni, had studied. I was part of a family, the Fisk family, and that's what the administration ingrained in each of us.

Gerrod was excited when I returned, as were my other friends Fred and Cooper, who were both down low men like myself, although Fred had a girlfriend on campus.

We would sometimes sneak out on the weekends and hang out at Fred's boyfriend's house. Fred seemed so much more mature than the rest of us. For him to have a boyfriend while in college seemed so adult to me. His boyfriend was a student at neighboring Tennessee State University. I enjoyed hanging out at his house because we could go there and not be judged.

Gerrod introduced me to his line brother, Vincent. In black Greek fraternities and sororities, your line brother or sister is the person or persons who you pledge with into the same organization. The term comes from when we stand and march in a single-file line during the pledging process.

Vincent was also a native of New York from Queensbridge. A smooth brother, a short dude with a cocky build, he was fly. He dressed the part. His gear was on point and was always sharp. But it was Vincent's demeanor that made him personable. He was laid-back, cool, calm, and collected. Nothing fazed him. As with Gerrod, everyone on campus knew Vincent, and he was well respected.

Vincent and I became friends just as quickly as Gerrod and I had. The three of us would become lifelong best friends. We were the three musketeers and you could always find us together.

One day while I was talking with some friends, I noticed a beautiful young woman on campus. I had seen her before, but this day she caught my eye. Charmaine was a sophomore and she was on point. A slim, beautiful, brown-skinned sister with a short fly haircut, she too was from Detroit.

I rolled up on her and introduced myself; I knew I had to have her. She had an innocence about her, something pure. I liked the way she smiled at me; it made my heart flutter. Charmaine had class and style. I liked that about her. It added an extra element to her buoyant personality.

Instead of taking my time with Charmaine, I dove in head first. I was wide open for her. But I also wanted to prove to myself that I was still attracted to women. I desperately didn't want to be gay. I hoped the men I fantasized about would go away. I hoped being with Charmaine would help me with that.

Charmaine and I dated for several months. When we went home for semester break she introduced me to her family and friends. She made sure I met everyone. There wasn't a person in her house she hadn't told about me. For some reason though, I thought it was a set up. I felt she was only doing this so I would think she really liked me. At any moment she was going to dump me and make a fool out of me. Jaslyn had done the same thing. I met everyone, yet I was played like a fool.

Instead of waiting on Charmaine to break my heart, I broke hers. I went to her dorm room one night and told her I couldn't do this anymore. I didn't even give her any explanation. I just said I didn't want to be in a relationship any longer. It was my way of running from who I was. I was struggling with my sexuality and trying to overcome a heartbreak. I had hoped that being with Charmaine would be some type of a cure. It wasn't.

Charmaine then came to my dorm and confronted me in front of all the men on my floor. "Why the fuck are you doing this?" she yelled. She was hysterical. I was caught off guard; this was my first time seeing her this angry. "I don't believe this. You're not even man enough to give me a reason. I hate you!" She stormed out of the building.

I stood there and didn't even respond. I didn't even run after her. Charmaine was right and she deserved better. I wasn't man enough to tell her the truth. One of my friends walked up to me and put his hand on my shoulder. "Damn, man, what did you do to her?" I went into my room and sat there wondering why this had to be my life. After college, Charmaine moved to Atlanta and became one of the city's biggest socialites, entertaining dignitaries and celebrities.

The year went by quickly, too quickly. Vincent graduated in May of 1990, and it left me with a bittersweet feeling. I hated that he was moving on without Gerrod and me, but I was excited that he was getting his degree. It instilled in me hope and possibility. Seeing Vincent do it let me know that it was also possible for me. However, my junior year would turn out to be one of the most devastating times of my life.

As my sophomore year ended, I decided to tell Gerrod about myself. He would be the first person I opened up to and told about my desires. We had become so close I felt horrible hiding my secret from him. I was nervous as all hell when I told him.

"Hey, Gerrod, I need to tell you something," I said to him. "It's really important."

"Yeah, what is it?"

I took a deep breath. My hands were shaking, my mouth was dry, and before I knew it the words flew out of my mouth. "I like dudes."

"That's what you had to tell me? So what, who cares? Man, you still cool with me," he told me. "You're still my brother. If somebody got a problem with you, then they got a problem with me." Gerrod was not bothered by my sexuality.

Hearing that from Gerrod made me feel good. For the first time in a long time, I felt comfortable. This created an even closer bond between us. It was the first time I had a real honest friendship with a straight man.

9. CATCHING FEELINGS

BEFORE I RETURNED to school for my junior year, I had what I think of as my first sexual experience with a man. Kelvin lived in my neighborhood, and I'd only known him casually. Whenever I came home from school, I would see him on the street talking with the other men in the neighborhood, and we would often speak. When he spoke, it seemed like he beckoned his voice from deep within his belly, because I could feel the bass of each syllable of every word. And there was something about him that intrigued me. He was an old-school player. The women in my neighborhood said they knew he was a bachelor because of the many different women they saw coming and going from his house.

When he walked, he had a slight pimp in his step. His right hand would slip behind his back and then gently swing forward. I always felt like he was watching me, his eyes following me as I walked by. No matter where I saw Kelvin, his disposition would change and he would become extremely excited to see me.

He was a snazzy dresser and meticulous in his appearance. He wore creased blue jeans and collared shirts with casual suede walking shoes. I could tell he took care of himself—he had an amazing body for an older man, and his bald head and massive, manicured hands turned me on.

Kelvin made me feel like he believed in me, and often asked me about school and how I was doing. He seemed to have a real interest in me making something out of myself. "You're not like the rest of the knuckleheads around here," he would say. "You're going places. You're going to be somebody." Those words made me feel good—I liked hearing them from him.

I went to visit him one day, and he invited me into his bedroom. I had never gone any farther than his living room so I was nervous. There was no conversation between us about sexuality, but there was obviously some sexual tension. In the bedroom, he lay on the bed and pulled out his hard, fat dick and masturbated in front of me. I was turned on, but didn't know what to do, so when he finished I just left his house. This went on a few more times.

Finally, one evening he asked me to join him on the bed. He slowly took off all his clothes and then mine. He neatly folded them and placed them on the chair next to the bed.

I was shaking when he touched me, but he took his time, and was gentle. Kelvin kissed my body from head to toe, sending chills all over me. His lips were unexpectedly soft. His massive hands caressed me, stroking my dick. He lay on top of me and I felt the heat rush from his body. I took a deep breath and captured his odor; he smelled clean, like fresh soap. We started grinding like we were doing a slow dance together. Our bodies were in perfect rhythm and he felt good. We kissed, and when he parted my lips with his tongue I tasted his minty breath. He sucked my breath each time our tongues met and released it so I could capture him in my own mouth.

Kelvin took my hand and placed it on his erection. He wanted me to hold him, and I felt the weight of his thickness as it throbbed in my hand.

He turned me over on my stomach and spread my cheeks. He stuck his tongue inside me, and my breathing stopped for a moment. It was the most orgasmic feeling I had ever felt.

After what seemed like an eternity of unrelenting pleasure from Kelvin eating my ass, he put a condom on his fat dick and tenderly entered me. I felt a sharp pain and my body flinched. He caressed the back of my head and kissed me. I had never experienced such an excruciating pain in my life, but I wanted to know what it felt like to have a man inside me.

He slowly inched inside until I was comfortable and relaxed. After a while, his gentle strokes were not as painful, and I was surprised that he was able to fit his entire dick in me.

After we finished having sex I didn't say anything to him; I put on my clothes and left. I was overcome with guilt because I felt what I was doing was wrong, though the pleasure made me desire more of it. It would take another few years before I was with another man.

DISC
TWO

10. CERTAINLY

THE DAY JACOB PULLED UP in front of the motel, my mouth dropped open. He was driving his new, blue Jaguar. Being a soundman in North Carolina really paid off for him. We were doing it big; I was going to arrive at my new home in style.

As we drove across country, I shaved my head for the first time. For nearly my entire life I had only sported a fade haircut. It was a marker for me. Shaving my head symbolized my transition of moving forward, and it felt good. This was a fresh start, and I wanted to look and feel different.

After two days on the road, I saw the highway sign welcoming us to California and I smiled. I was both excited and nervous because I didn't know what was in store for me. I was looking forward to this new chapter in my life.

Everything was different, new, and just like I had seen it in the movies. The palm trees, the grass, the hot California sun were almost too perfect. It all looked unreal, unlike anything I had seen before.

My new apartment was in the Mid-Wilshire district, an expensive area well-populated by those aspiring to be in the entertainment industry.

Sandy and I were excited to see each other, and we went to a local Mexican restaurant on La Brea Avenue to grab some takeout food. We spent the night catching up as she gave me the lay of the land. In the few months she'd been in Los Angeles, she had quickly learned the ways of the city.

She landed a prime studio position in the Warner Bros. production management program, which was designed to help people learn the ins and outs of film production while getting on-the-job training.

A studio job is one of the hardest jobs to get in Los Angeles. If you land a position at a studio, it's because of one or two reasons: who you know or who you fucked. Sandy knew someone.

La La Land, as people call Los Angeles, is laid back and full of beautiful people. Women flaunting perfectly tanned bodies with silicon breasts. Men with workout physiques and coiffed hair. Nearly everyone is a vegetarian or vegan. Protein shakes serve as meal replacements along with diet pills and other drugs to keep you from gaining any weight. Everyone's a model, actress, producer, director, or screen writer. You have to wear your title on your sleeve, and the exchange of business cards is as common as a handshake. Simple introductions go from your name to what you do for a living. Everyone is looking for their next big break or contact, and if you're not someone who can help them—"it was really nice meeting you."

Coming from the East Coast, I quickly had to train my ear for the slow, dragging gangster drawl of West Coast rap. My appetite for anything from the east was like a splash of Coke in a glass of dark rum. I barely heard any East Coast music and as much as I missed New York, I had to quickly adjust to my new home, and its sounds.

I also got a real introduction to West Coast rap from Power 106, KJLH 102.3, and 92.3 The Beat. No matter what radio station I tuned into my ears were filled with lyrics from Ice Cube, Snoop, Tupac, Mack 10, Xzibit, DJ Quick, and Dr. Dre.

During the first few days, Sandy showed me around town to help me get familiar with the area. The Santa Monica Pier was full of bright, festive lights and vendors selling handmade jewelry, art work, and celebrity pictures.

We ventured to Rodeo Drive in Beverly Hills with its couture stores like Gucci, Chanel, Armani, Cartier, and Tiffany's. Definitely for the wealthy, it was a great get-away from the crowds, and later I would drive through the neighborhoods and admire the multimillion-dollar homes, imagining owning one of them and having big, elaborate parties.

The black communities of Leimert Park, Baldwin Hills, Compton, and Inglewood were filled with young kids running in the streets. Young black men hanging out on the street corners in front of the stores. A black church on nearly every street with a barber and beauty salon perched adjacent to it.

Baldwin Hills was the black version of Beverly Hills, with big, exquisite homes. A few black celebrities live in this area because it reminds them of home in the South and Midwest, yet it is still rich and elegant.

At the top of Baldwin Hills, you can see all of Los Angeles, neatly tucked in at the bottom of the hills.

We drove to Compton and Inglewood, but I never ventured into those areas alone again. They were farther and deeper in the city of Los Angeles. I had not learned how to navigate the city and I didn't want to get lost. I knew some parts of those areas were extremely dangerous. Since I was not from those areas, I wasn't too keen on visiting them without someone who knew them. They were known gang territories, and wearing the wrong color or making sudden moves could get me killed.

Sandy and I made a stop in Leimert Park to visit Carol, a friend of hers. They'd met when Sandy first got to Los Angeles looking for work, and Carol was also a transplant. She had recently moved to the area seeking the Hollywood lifestyle, and worked as a writer's assistant on the television show *Friends*. I was in shock because I had never met a black person who worked on a set of a television show in such a highly sought-after position. Many aspiring screenwriters long for this type of position. But also, *Friends* was a show that very seldom featured any black actors. The thought had never crossed my mind they would have any black production crew members, let alone a black writer's assistant.

On the weekends, Carol worked on her own independent film. She was making her directorial debut with a short film about a woman who was conflicted over two men after she discovers her boyfriend cheating.

She was working with a small crew of people who were also aspiring actors, producers, and filmmakers. It was great seeing young black people making their own independent film. They were inspiring and gave me fuel to get on my hustle to find a job soon.

During breaks, we were introduced to the crew and actors. Three of them had been living in Los Angeles for over five years. Most people who live in Los Angeles are not from there; nearly everyone is a transplant from somewhere else. During my time there, I only met five people who were Los Angeles natives.

While conversing with the crew, I noticed one of the actors. He was playing the role of the boyfriend of the main character. He was very attractive not only to me, but to everyone there. Everyone was eyeing him. He could have been a model. His smooth, clear, and cocoa-brown complexion was perfection. Everything seemed delicately put in place.

We glanced at each other a few times before we were introduced. When we were face-to-face I was taken aback. He'd had a nose job. It was not noticeable until I was close to him, and I tried not to stare and make it obvious, but it was my first time seeing someone with a nose job, especially a black man. I figured he noticed me looking at it because he seemed to be a little shy and nervous as he watched my eyes go from his eyes to his nose.

"Clay" told me he had been in Los Angeles for three years and had already done some commercials and was a regular on a popular daytime soap opera. It was then I realized I had seen him before. I was not a fan of daytime soaps, but I saw a few of them from time to time. Clay was on the soap for a short while, but he now wanted to get movie roles.

We made some idle chitchat, but it was obvious we were aware of each other's down low status. The way we danced around our conversations of places to hang out and things to do in Los Angeles made it apparent Clay was avoiding certain details. There were people around and I knew folks were listening even when they appeared not to be. We didn't get the opportunity to talk long, but before we ended our conversation Clay smiled and told me he was sure we would see each other again. With that being said, I knew we would. It was only a matter of when and where.

I spent the next few days in Los Angeles job hunting and calling Sandy's contacts. Also, I needed my own place and a car. In Los Angeles, not only is a car imperative for getting around, it's a statement of who you are. It's almost a rite of passage to have a good car. Your car must say who you are and what you do, but more important, it has to make people take notice of you.

In the meantime, I was hoofing it on the bus. Sandy would occasionally let me use her car, but it was a stick shift and I didn't know how to work one and I didn't want to get stuck in the infamous Los Angeles traffic struggling with a stick shift.

Living with Sandy quickly became crowded with four other people joining us in a one-bedroom, one-bath apartment. Sandy's then fiancé, Kel, came out from D.C. Then Alexis, the niece of critically acclaimed author Gloria Naylor, drove in from New York, followed by Bill Bellamy's ex-girlfriend Yvonne, a pretty girl who knew it and you couldn't tell her any different. I knew we were not going to get along. She came to Los Angeles to pursue her acting career.

We were *really* living *The Real World.* Alexis, Yvonne, and I shared the living room floor with our makeshift beds, while Sandy and Kel slept in the bedroom. Ironically, we never saw one another during the day. But at night, we had the best of times sharing our stories, dreams, and aspirations. We all had moved to Los Angeles seeking fame, fortune, and the glitz and glamour we'd seen and read about in the magazines. We were one big family, and just like most families you have the siblings who don't get along. That was Yvonne and me.

All we heard was Bill Bellamy this, Bill Bellamy that. I swear I felt like I knew him personally as much as she talked about him.

I was glad when I came across a job to make some money. The plan was to save as much as possible for a down payment on my own place.

I was called to be a production assistant on the set of a porn movie. I didn't mind. It was a job paying five hundred dollars for the weekend.

The producer and I met near his offices in Santa Monica, and he wanted to fill me in and also to make sure I would be comfortable around a bunch of naked actors. Hell, I was getting paid to look at dicks for the weekend. I certainly didn't have a problem with that.

A few minutes after our meeting, I was introduced to the actors. There was one fine, short black brother who was in the movie. He had an amazing body and beautiful dark skin. He glided over to me, and his huge hands swallowed mine. "Henry's" deep voice was rich with a southern texture, and he still had his southern hospitality. After our introduction, I was looking even more forward to working with him. I was definitely interested in seeing his acting skills on screen.

After his short-lived porn career, Henry worked as a stunt double for a few black action stars, but he later went on to make a name for himself costarring in many major films with Paramount and Warner Bros. He never married, but has been a lover of many Hollywood actresses. His charming, smooth personality has always been one of his greatest talents in scoring roles and bed partners.

Henry was really cool, but I couldn't understand why this good-looking man would be in a porn movie. He didn't have to sell his body like this. If he needed to earn some cash I was sure there were other ways to do it, but I gathered this was his way to make fast money and help his then burgeoning career.

Most aspiring actors who move to Hollywood think their good looks or talent will get them in the door and onto the big screen. Unfortunately, it doesn't work that way. I've met and know of many actors who are struggling to pay their bills, rent, and car note. Most of them are bartenders and waiters because those jobs allow them the flexibility to go on auditions during the day. It's a hard and sad fact, but as much as you may think you're the next best thing to hit Hollywood, there are also hundreds daily who move there with the same attitude. The competition is fierce.

The producer of the porn picture asked if I could drive with Henry to Palm Springs where filming was to take place. It was my job to bring him to the set; over the weekend we would share a room together. I smiled on the inside. Neither of us had a problem with it. I can truly say that the job was getting better and better, and of course, I was going to be a true professional. Maybe I would get the opportunity to prep him for his all-important scenes.

But right after I landed this job, I received a call from the Star Temporary Agency in Beverly Hills. They specialized in placing people with television and film experience at various entertainment companies in the city. They had a long-term assignment for me with Orion Pictures. I was to report the next day first thing in the morning, to be the temporary assistant to a senior executive at Orion.

I was excited. I got two gigs in my first week in Los Angeles. But, damn, I couldn't do the porn movie because of the conflict. I handed over the job to my boy, Jacob, but I made sure he filled me in on all the juicy details of the shoot, especially Henry's endowment. Even though I wasn't going to be there, I still wanted to know all about his performance.

Although my job was temporary with Orion Pictures, all I needed was to get my foot in the door. I could handle everything once I was inside. Things were looking up for me. I could call Grandma Pearl to let her know that I was doing well and that I had gotten a job.

No matter what I was going through, Grandma Pearl would always provide words of support. She also sent me encouraging letters and cards wherever I was staying. She was my mother and father. She was my foundation and my rock.

Grandma Pearl was the only one who believed in me. My aunts and uncles didn't believe in me or my dreams, and I resented and was angry with them. They had tried hard to deter me from doing a lot of things. When I decided to go to college, they were excited, but they wondered where I was going to get the money and made it clear they were not contributing to my education. Whenever I called home for money there was always some excuse. Either Uncle Johnny didn't have it to send, or my aunts Lisa and Priscilla, who had their own households and children, couldn't afford anything. Grandma Pearl sent what she could, and most times it was twenty or forty dollars.

When I told Aunt Lisa I was going to pursue a career in entertainment, she tried to persuade me to get a "real" job, something stable with benefits. Being the first one in my family to go to college and the first one to leave Detroit to pursue something other than a job at one of the car factories, I had something to prove and I wanted to let them know I was going to be successful with or without them.

I was still dealing with the pain, hurt, and betrayal I felt. With the exception of Grandma Pearl, they abandoned me. If they didn't want to help me, I was fine with it. My mission was to prove them wrong.

I arrived at Orion Pictures at eight thirty sharp the next morning. I sat at a desk in the small cubicle right outside the door of my boss "Rob." It wasn't until after nine that Rob called to let me know he was out of town on business and would be returning later that week. He gave me a few directives on things to do for him. He sounded cool, laid back, and easygoing. I liked that. I loved working in stress-free environments.

Throughout the day Rob called in to check on me and to retrieve any messages. His office wasn't buzzing with a lot of traffic, but I found things to do to keep myself busy. I managed to introduce myself to the rest of the staff in the department, who seemed pretty cool and laid back as well. There were only six of us, and I was the only black person in my department. When I had to deliver things from my boss to other departments, I noticed there were practically no other black men in the company. Nothing new to me; I had worked on many television and film sets where I was the only black person.

It wasn't until I had to deliver something to Accounting that I met another black person who would become a very good and dear friend. When I first saw Kathy, I was blown away by her beauty; I had never seen a woman so beautiful in my life. Kathy is a cross between Halle Berry, Beyoncé, and Lisa Raye. She's absolutely stunning, with a bodacious body, long flowing hair, amazingly golden skin, and beautiful, light brown eyes. She seems unreal—the type of woman you dream about. When men see her, they do triple and quadruple takes.

Kathy and I immediately hit it off. We did lunch together that day and every day after. We talked about everything from where we grew up and how we got to Los Angeles to what our dreams were and our past relationships. Well, she talked about her relationships, and I just listened. I learned early on to be very leery of telling women about my sexuality. Although they are generally cool with it, they sometimes have a tendency to tell everyone, because you have now become their new, gay best friend.

I didn't identify with being gay and I certainly wasn't going to admit to having sexual relations with men. Besides, this industry is not too keen on supporting the homo boy, especially if he's black. It is no secret there are many gay men and women in Hollywood, but you dare not openly discuss the topic. Although in all appearances it seems like it's acceptable and tolerable, there is an understood "Don't Ask, Don't Tell" policy. It's taboo to talk about a celebrity's sexuality in public, and even behind closed doors you have to be careful what you say and to whom you say it. The Hollywood circles are small, and information will get back to an individual faster than you can get it out of your mouth.

I was smart enough to know that at the top of the ladder was the old boy network, which consisted generally of older white men. It's a network for the priviledged, those with certain qualifications and pedigrees. They assist one another in moving ahead, share resources and promote their own. They love to talk about their wives, children, and girlfriends on the side. If they like you, they invite you into their elite world. Until I got in the circle, I was going to play it smart and on the down low.

When Rob returned, he called me into his office to meet me in person. Rob looked really young to be a bigwig at a studio.

When I first saw Rob I knew he was gay. His mannerisms were a dead giveaway. He frequently gestured with his hands when he spoke and then put them on his hips and spun on his heels, sashaying around the office. He seemed almost childlike, as if he needed someone to take care of him, though it had to be done his way.

I had to make it clear I didn't care that he was gay. Gay men can read when a man is uncomfortable around them, and sensing that makes them leery of you. It's almost like you have something to hide yourself. And I was hiding. Having just moved to Los Angeles, I certainly didn't want my secret to get out. I was on a new journey, and the less people knew about me the better.

Sitting across from Rob, I felt uncomfortable because he was staring at me, trying to read me. On the down low, you learn how to make yourself unreadable. You learn to play dumb and be evasive about various things, especially things relating to your intimate relationships.

We talked in depth about what my role would be as his assistant and what he expected of me—arranging his schedule and appointments, answering the phone, and getting the weekly film distribution schedule. It wasn't anything I couldn't handle.

The next several weeks seemed to fly by. Rob traveled a lot, so I had a lot of time to hang out with Kathy at the office and check on other job opportunities. I was still a temporary employee and needed to keep my résumé floating to find something permanent.

One day when Rob returned from a trip, he called me into his office. "Terrance, I need to speak with you about something very important." I was nervous. With so little work, maybe he had to let me go.

"Close the door behind you," Rob said as I walked into his office. I sat across from him and waited anxiously. "Terrance, you have been doing a great job here. How would you like to have the position as a full-time employee?" I was in shock.

"Yes, of course I would like to be a full-time employee," I said excitedly.

"Well, the position is paying $27,000 a year. So, if you're okay with that I already told Human Resources I was going to make you an offer."

I was happy with the salary. It didn't matter at all what the pay was. I was just happy to have a permanent job.

I went to Human Resources to fill out the paperwork, and it was made official. I was made a permanent assistant at Orion Pictures, with my first gay boss.

Working became even more fun and exciting after I was hired permanently. Rob often treated me to lunches and dinners, movie tickets, and little perks from the marketing department, like T-shirts or hats for the films we released.

Orion Pictures was considered an art house film company, so many of our films went to those types of theaters across the country. These films were generally dark in humor or drama. During the time I was there, we released the movies *8 Heads in a Duffel Bag, City of Industry,* and *Ulee's Gold.*

One evening, Rob invited all the employees to his home for a pre-Thanksgiving dinner. His house had a gated entrance and a long, winding driveway lined with lots of trees and bushes. It was decorated like it was out of the pages of *Country Living* magazine. The fireplace was burning, and over the mantle was the head of a deer. The rooms had vaulted ceilings and huge bay windows.

After dinner and dessert, I went into the kitchen to get another drink while everyone continued to talk, and a few minutes later Rob came in behind me. We were the only two in the kitchen at this time.

"Terrance, I'm going to New Orleans next week," Rob started. "Can you suggest some hip and happening gay bars in the area? Or, if you have any friends down there, maybe you can hook me up with them?"

At first I looked offended. I was trying to keep up my façade. *What the fuck, are you serious? What makes you think I'm gay and why would I hook you up?* I thought. But I said, "I'm sorry, I don't know anything about that."

"You know what, Terrance, you can cut the act." Rob looked at me. "I know you're a closet case. I knew when I met you that you were gay. Why do you think I hired you? I thought it would be great to have a gay assistant. Someone who was good in the office, but also resourceful in finding gay clubs and other things to do while I'm on the road."

I tried to hold on to my demeanor but I let out a forced laugh. My cover was blown. I could continue trying to pretend or just be honest. Time seemed to stand still as I stood in the kitchen sipping the drink.

"You're so crazy, Rob," I said jokingly. He put his hand on my shoulder. "Terrance, it's okay to be who you are. I'm not going to tell anyone about your secret."

Yeah that's easy for you to say, you got this big-ass house. I'm trying to get where you are, I thought. As much as I wanted to be free with my sexuality, I just couldn't. I still felt the need to hide. Things were different for me. He was white and I was black. His community was more accepting of his sexuality. It's hard as hell to be an educated, smart, and attractive gay black man in the black community.

We don't discuss sex and sexuality in our community. It's taboo. Try to bring up the topic of sexuality and you will get shot down. No one wants to talk about it. If someone is gay in our family we whisper about them. Even though everyone knows, our families don't want to know the details. We don't openly discuss it nor do we tell everyone.

I've often heard people in white families say that they have a gay child and strongly support him or her. Or that they have a brother or sister who's gay. "We love them no matter what," they say.

You'll rarely hear people in a black family say anything about their gay child or sibling. Many of us are disowned by our families. Sure, it happens in the white community, but in the black community it's a sin before God for a man to be attracted to other men. The black churches and ministers preach emphatically on the despicable lifestyle of a gay man. As a young man growing up in the church there wasn't a Sunday where the minister didn't say something negative or derogatory about gay men and women.

Many nights I cried, praying to God, asking and pleading with him to take away my sinful homosexual thoughts. Man, I wanted to be straight. I wanted to live my life as a heterosexual man with a wife and kids, but I couldn't shake my urges for men. I knew this would be my burden for life.

I had met many gay men who had been shunned by their families. They were put out on the streets at an early age, their mothers and fathers refusing to speak to them. They had become outcasts. Some had suffered severe abuse from their parents who tried to beat the homosexuality out of them. Others, forced into therapy, were told it was a phase they were going through. They needed to have their heads examined, and maybe the psychiatrist could find the reason and cure. I just learned to keep my mouth shut and for good reason.

I had yet to meet an openly gay black man in the entertainment business, let alone in Hollywood and in a powerful position. In order for us to get jobs as actors or working behind the scenes, we had to remain tight-lipped. Black men are often seen as objects of desire because of our reputations of sexual prowess and a fascination with our penises, but we are only acceptable in the heterosexual world. No one wants to associate with you if you are gay, especially other blacks, for fear of being found guilty by association.

In Hollywood there is no place for openly gay black actors; they are shunned. I remember meeting a few black actors who were on the down low. When they came out for casting calls for some of the movies I worked on, the producers would whisper about them after their audition. "Didn't he come across as gay?" or "He looks a little too soft for this role." Despite their being good actors they often lost out on roles.

Later my friends would ask me how they did and what the producers thought of them. I couldn't tell them the truth because I didn't want to hurt their feelings. I just told them that they did a good job, and it was a tough call because there were a lot of good actors who came in.

I've also found that in general the white gay community tends to be more accepting and tolerant of gays in the business. They have many resources such as support groups, agencies, and communities where they support one another.

I have yet to find a black gay community where men live, shop, and support one another. Most major cities have white gay communities such as Chelsea in New York City and DuPont Circle in Washington, D.C., but men of other ethnic and minority groups have to sneak around, ducking and dodging into dark clubs off the beaten path in order to be with other like-minded individuals.

After the party, Rob never mentioned my sexuality again. It was as if we had never discussed it. I continued to play the straight role as much as I could, but I knew I had to be more on top of my game. I was pissed that he discovered my secret. I knew what I had to do, I couldn't let people get close to me. I hated myself for being vulnerable.

It was important for me to continue my double life. One for my career and the other for myself—the real me. Only I didn't know who the
real me was. I was so accustomed to living in multiple worlds I often
confused myself.

As a down low man, I had to make sure people saw me as a heterosexual man; they had to see me with women. They had to think I was
getting an ample amount of pussy. Nothing about me could be associated with the gay lifestyle.

But other down low men had to feel safe around me. It's imperative in the down low world that men associate only with those who are
unidentifiable. People must not suspect them of being gay. They cannot
be effeminate, soft-spoken, flamboyant, or a part of the gay scene. If
they are around someone who's easily clock-able, they dissociate themselves.

With women and heterosexual people, I had to remind myself to
watch what I said, how I walked, what I wore, and who I associated
with because many women had become savvier about identifying down
low men. When I walked, I made sure there was an extra something in
my step—that swagger, that slight pimp most black men have. I would
find myself being conscious of making sure not to say "he" when I referred to someone I was dating or my friends that I hung out with over
the weekend.

I'm glad that I was a Hip Hop head and wore urban clothing, so my
dress made it easier for me to shop. It was the basics: T-shirts, jeans,
Timberland boots, and sneakers. I didn't want to come across as too
fashionable or too trendy in my attire, because when a man knows
more about fashion than most, it brings suspicion to his lifestyle. I had
to be mindful of everything in and around my life. One misstep would
have been the end of my career. Hell, it would have been the end of my
life. I was still not comfortable with being gay.

11. BETWEEN YOU AND ME

AFTER I WAS MADE FULL-TIME, I immediately started looking for my own apartment. I needed to have my own space. I had not been with anyone for well over a year and I needed some sex.

I found a really nice studio apartment in the Mid-Wilshire district on Mansfield Avenue a few blocks from Sandy's place.

It was great being in my own space. I had just turned twenty-nine, and living on my own made me feel mature and responsible, like the adult I was. What a wonderful feeling. I didn't have to rely on anyone but myself, and no one was dependent on me—no pets, no kids, and no spouse.

Although Sandy was cool with me living with her, I really liked living on my own. There is nothing like having your own spot. If I wanted to walk around butt naked, I could. If I wanted to have sex on the sofa, in the bathroom, or in the kitchen, I didn't have to worry about anyone interrupting my flow. Hell, I could yell, blast the radio, and leave a mess if I so desired; I had freedom and I loved it.

I was enjoying Los Angeles, but I missed New York. Unlike New York, stores in L.A. closed early. Rather than on the streets or subways, everyone was behind the wheel of a car. The nightclubs shut down at two in the morning, and it was hard to find restaurants open later than eleven. The streets often looked like a desert after ten. In New York, people were out and about everywhere all the time.

New York is where you make it happen, and Los Angeles is where you wait for it to happen.

I needed a reference from the right brother that would be my ticket into the down low entertainment scene. I wanted to get back into an environment where I felt most comfortable. I had no problem socializing with straight people, but it was comforting to be around other brothers like myself, united in our struggle. We didn't have to put on any airs or act like something we were not. We didn't have to put on a front as if we were fucking women on the regular; we could openly discuss men and those we were dating.

Down low men in the industry are hard nuts to crack—we are very protective of our lives and one another—and the right brother could introduce me to key contacts.

I got two big breaks. My boy Sterling, who worked in the publicity department for Atlantic Records, called and said he was coming to Los Angeles. He would be in town for R&B singer Brandy's twenty-first birthday party, which was being held at the House of Blues. At the time, she was the biggest act on the Atlantic Records roster and had a number one television show, *Moesha*. Sterling came to help manage the media for the party.

He invited Sandy, Jacob, and me to the party and to the set of *Moesha* during a taping. After the show, he took us on the set to introduce us to the cast. We met Countess Vaughn, Sheryl Lee Ralph, Shar Jackson, and Lamont Bentley. They were the nicest group of people. They laughed and joked with one another, just like they were a family, and definitely seemed to enjoy working together. Brandy was especially nice. She apologized that she couldn't stick around because Sterling had her on a tight schedule. She asked us if we wanted autographs and pictures with her, which we had to take quickly because they were rushing her out the door for an interview.

Sandy and I started talking with the crew. We were making connections, looking for the next hook-up to a job in the industry.

I noticed this tall brother standing nearby. He looked extremely familiar, and I slowly walked over to get a good look. It was "Kevin." I'd met him years earlier in Detroit when he was visiting one of my fraternity brothers.

"Kevin? What's up, man? It's me, Terrance." I smiled, extending my hand. He was stunned to see me standing there.

"What's up, Terrance?" he said with his big, robust hand shaking mine vigorously. "What are you doing here?"

"I live here now. I just moved here not too long ago. I'm working at Orion Pictures."

"That's what's up. Man, it's good seeing you."

"Yeah, it's good seeing you too."

"Have you seen much of the city yet?" he asked.

"Just a few places. I've been busy working and I don't have a car yet."

"Well, we definitely have to get up and hang out." Kevin and I then exchanged phone numbers. "I have a lot of contacts in this city, so if you're not happy at Orion I can definitely get you in the circle here. But listen, I can't talk long because they hate to see us standing around not doing anything."

"Thanks, Kevin. I appreciate that," I said.

True to his word Kevin called a few days later and we made plans to meet at Roscoe's House of Chicken and Waffles, one of the joints where entertainment types dine.

Kevin had been living in Los Angeles for almost seven years. He was pursuing an acting career and had appeared in a few blockbuster movies and television shows.

He provided me with a list of people to contact in the industry on various television shows. Kevin was extremely generous and I was grateful for the information. He was definitely a cool brother, and we hung out quite a bit after that. He would often invite me to the set of *Moesha* and introduce me to more of his friends in the industry. He also invited me to his house a few times to hang out.

I often got the impression he was picking me for information. He asked a lot of questions about my background and personal life. Questions about who I hung out with and where I went clubbing and who I knew in the industry.

I don't like people asking me a lot of questions, especially someone I don't know. Kevin was cool, but his questioning made me very uncomfortable. I was cautious with information I provided. I didn't know what Kevin was trying to find out, and only gave him enough information to satisfy his thirst.

But the more I hung out with him, the more I noticed he was the same with other people—very inquisitive. I chalked it up to him being nosy and I knew how to treat nosy people—with a ten-foot pole. I kept them far enough away, but close enough to make them feel comfortable.

Kevin invited me to accompany him to the West Angeles Church of God in Christ, a huge church on Crenshaw Boulevard. I went because I was looking for a place to worship; I had not been to church in a while and I needed to hear some of God's lessons. Everything was going well, but I needed a spiritual environment and to surround myself with spiritual people. I was still struggling with my past and my sexuality. Church was the one place I felt connected.

Kevin was well known in the church. He introduced me to everyone, and made sure we exchanged contact information. "We all need to help each other out in this business. You never know who may be your next boss or resource to get you that job," Kevin said.

I really enjoyed the services at West Angeles. I became a regular and met many show business people there. Although it was understood you don't conduct business while people are praising the Lord, it was another place where we could shoot the breeze.

A few of Kevin's friends decided to make Sunday a potluck day. Most of us were actors, comedians, and industry insiders. Since many of us were new to Los Angeles and missed the family Sunday meals, it was the perfect way for many of us to have a good home-cooked meal. It also allowed for us to get together to network, catch up on one another's lives, and share our dreams of becoming Hollywood bigwigs.

We filled Gwen's house each Sunday. She was a voluptuous woman with a witty sense of humor, and her colorful stories always kept us entertained. She definitely had a way with words. She was a writer hoping to make it big.

I loved going to Gwen's house. With all her dollies, figurines, and patterned furniture, it was homey and I felt like I was in one of my aunt's homes. I just sat back and relaxed, not worrying about anything.

At any given time there were at least five of us sitting around eating and sharing updates of who got cast in a new role for television or a movie like *The Nutty Professor, The Parkers,* and *The Jamie Foxx Show.* It was great seeing everyone get the parts. Their spirits were lifted and they felt hopeful for their future in show business.

But Gwen's success didn't come as quickly as ours. She watched as those who struggled for years landed roles and walked away with lucrative television deals. Many nights she let them sleep on her sofa because they had no place else to go. On the outside, she smiled and was happy for everyone, but on the inside she was hurting; she wanted Hollywood to happen for her too. And it did, many years later when she became an accomplished author. But it would be her winning a huge payoff on an ABC game show that gave her a start, after answering questions correctly on a topic she knew all too well: sex.

Interestingly enough, we all talked openly and casually about sex. I felt more comfortable in her home discussing the topic than any other place I had been. We talked about positions, climaxing, how to please a man, and how to please a woman. In these conversations everyone shared, but I kept my cover and they never questioned my sexuality.

However, it was Gwen's open candor about sex that made everyone feel comfortable. She was quite the connoisseur of the topic. She didn't mind discussing women pleasing women.

"I'm not saying I ever did it, but if times got hard, I wouldn't have a problem with a woman eating me out," she would say and then lie back on the sofa and open her legs.

Her vulgarity made me gush inside; she was abrasive and I loved it.

She revealed what others often thought about but were afraid to say in public.

And she didn't mind sharing her sexual exploits with me. One day I went into her bedroom to get something and couldn't find what I was looking for. "Just look in the nightstand next to my vibrator and dildo," she yelled from the living room. It was a big black dildo, and I didn't want to imagine what she was doing with it.

But she let me know. Gwen and I often spoke on the phone, and on one particular night she had me speechless.

"Let me ask you something," she started. "If a man wants you to play with his ass during sex, what do you think that means?"

At first I was scared to answer. Was she asking me a trick question? I figured she had discovered my secret. Maybe she knew I was hiding my desires for men.

"What are you talking about?" I asked.

"Do you think he may be gay?"

"Well, I don't think so. I mean, just below the shaft of a man's penis and under his balls is an erogenous zone."

"What if he wants me to stick my fingers in his ass and fuck him with my dildo?"

"Who are you talking about?" I asked. She piqued my interest. I was curious to know.

"This guy came over last night, and he asked me to do that to him. It freaked me out when he asked, but I was down for it. I wanted to see how far it would go. Do you think he's gay?"

"It depends. How far did it go?" If he was taking things up his ass, then I surely wanted to know. I figured we could make it a real adventure and I could give him the real thing.

"Let's just put it this way. He loved when I put the dildo in him. He lay there moaning asking me to do it harder. It was hot. I got turned on by it."

I was getting turned on just from her telling me about the experience.

"He's definitely gay," I said.

"You really think so?"

Gwen felt that because she was open to anything, then maybe he was also. He could have been into S&M or some other type of sexual pleasure I wasn't aware of. However, I know if a man likes his ass played with, especially having fingers and foreign objects put inside him, then he has at least experimented with another man. I am sure he didn't just wake up one day and say, "I think I want to have a dildo up my ass."

I decided not to go into a long conversation with her about it. No matter what I said, she would have kept asking me if he was gay, and even though I told her he was, she would have remained in denial. Like many women, she could never fathom how such a masculine, good-looking man who loves pussy could be gay.

There were lots of women I knew like Gwen, who refused to question their men for fear of either knowing the truth or having their man leave them. She would not share with her girlfriends because she didn't want the embarrassment.

I know if my sexual partner came home with a new position or asked me to do something I'd never done before, I would be a little suspicious. Especially if he asked to have fingers and a dildo placed inside him. Where did he pick up this behavior and who else has he been doing it with?

I often wondered why, if a woman thought her man was on the down low, she stayed in the relationship.

When I was in college, I roomed with Johnny, a frat brother from Memphis. I used to call him Baby Johnny Gill because of the striking resemblance they shared in skin tone, body type, lips, and hairstyle. Johnny was fun, cool, and liked to party, something I was always game for. On weekends, he spent a lot of time with his girlfriend, Carla, in her room.

One night, Johnny woke me out of my slumber and said he really needed to talk with me. He had to get something off his chest. He took a deep breath and then he said, "I'm gay."

When he said those words the blood drained from my face. It was hard for me to wrap my mind around what he said. The words hit me like I owned them. They flowed from his lips and into my soul. I was him and he was I.

"Why are you telling me?" I asked.

"Aren't you gay?"

"What? Hell naw!" I yelled. I was lying and I knew he knew.

"Aren't you and Gerrod fucking?" he asked.

I couldn't believe he was saying this to me. Gerrod was my boy, our frat brother. I never thought of him in a sexual way. Sure, he was very attractive and had a nice body, but he was my boy. But Johnny wasn't the first or last person to think something was going on with Gerrod and me; many people thought this because we were extremely close. Hell, he was my best friend. Anything I had was his and vice-versa.

"What about you and Carla? I thought you were in love with her. Does she know?"

"Naw, she doesn't know. I do love her, but I really like men."

I didn't respond. I was still trying to make sense of the conversation and Johnny. I never suspected him of being gay. He had it all, just like the rest of us—a girl, the frat, and lots of friends.

Johnny then proceeded to tell me about his fascination with our frat brother Gerrod and how much he wanted him. Despite how many times I told him that Gerrod was not gay, it made Johnny even more persistent in wanting to pursue him.

Johnny then went behind my back and made sexual advances toward Gerrod and he became fed up and angry over it. Gerrod approached Carla and told her that her man was gay. At first she denied it and then later told Gerrod to prove it.

Gerrod told Johnny he needed to speak with him and invited him to his apartment. Johnny, sensing this was his opportunity, bought liquor, and dressed in his finest to meet Gerrod. Right before Johnny arrived, Gerrod put Carla in his bedroom closet and cracked the door so she could see and hear.

When Johnny arrived, Gerrod took him straight into the bedroom. He then asked Johnny a series of questions—if he was gay, who on campus he was sleeping with, and who else on campus he knew was gay.

As Johnny poured out his heart with the hopes that his revelations would lure Gerrod into bed, Carla popped out of the closet. When Johnny saw her, he sprinted out of the house.

Some Nashville locals later found Johnny near the train tracks in his car. He'd tried to kill himself by taking a bottle of pills and was rushed to the hospital.

Seeing what happened to Johnny made me even more afraid to come out. I didn't want to experience being abandoned again. I wanted to have friends and for people to love me. I felt sorry for him because his secret had gotten out and the whole campus knew. He was officially labeled a gay man.

Gerrod attacked one of Johnny's bed partners and beat him up because Carla was angry and blamed the guy for sleeping with Johnny and trying to make him gay.

Both Johnny and his bed partner left campus that semester. Johnny returned in the fall; his friend didn't. When Johnny returned, he seemed very solemn and not his outgoing self. He looked heavy, like he was carrying the weight of the world. But what was most disturbing to me was that Carla had taken him back. They were a couple again. I never questioned Johnny about any of this and I never spoke to Carla again; I felt she betrayed and set him up.

I tried to make sense of it, but never had a full comprehension of the situation. I could only gather that there were some women who, when they discover their man is homosexual, figure it may be a phase. They are hopeful, in some way, that they can help him turn back and be straight again. Or they look the other way. They simply refuse to believe their man has sexual desires to be with another man. The women take it personal as if it has something to do with them. In actuality, it has absolutely nothing to do with them.

12. LOST ONES

ONE SATURDAY AFTERNOON, Kevin called and invited me to a taco and card party he was attending that evening being given by a fellow actor named "Ella." In Los Angeles, taco and card parties are really big and part of the culture.

When we got to the house, there were already quite a number of people there. Everyone was drinking, talking, eating, and playing cards. A couple of Spades and Bid Whist games were already under way.

Kevin walked me around and introduced me to various actors and actresses I had seen on popular television shows and films like *In Living Color, Martin, National Security, White Men Can't Jump, Don't Be a Menace . . . , Poetic Justice,* and *Higher Learning.* Other guests included executives from the major studios, film and television crew members, and a few theater actors visiting Los Angeles trying to get their big break in Hollywood.

I learned that Ella's place was like a home away from home for seasoned actors, who sought support and comfort in the confines of their acting community. Many black actors create support groups in Los Angeles because of the harsh reality one experiences in auditioning, seeking an agent, and chasing dreams of stardom. Often they are all competing for that one minority role in a film or for roles in the new black film. The support group helps them maintain emotional, spiritual, and mental balance.

Many fresh new actors move to Los Angeles and jump into the acting scene thinking it's an easy feat, when in actuality it's one of the most difficult and challenging careers to take on. Some will tell you about the casting couch, where producers and directors sleep with young, aspiring actors who are desperate to make it in Hollywood. Being in the business and working behind the scenes, I can attest that casting couches do exist. It's not uncommon for a producer or director to take advantage of an aspiring actor by promising a role only if the actor has sex with the executive. Some actors figure it will help their career and they accept the offer. It's not unheard of for a producer to have slept with some of the stars of a film. Many actors are willing to do whatever it takes to get a role, that big break.

The movie industry is a financial business and it's a business of power and control. In Hollywood, it's about who's got the biggest balls, and everyone exerts their power. Nor is it uncommon for many down low people to use their power to get what they want from an aspiring actor.

I had been to many parties where fresh, new faces were eager to network and get known in Hollywood. Many down low men become friendly with other men to see if they are game for a night of sex. They size up the newcomer, inviting him to other industry parties. They offer to show him around town to help him get acclimated to the city and introduce him to key people in the business. The actor is impressed with the number of contacts a down low brother has and the invite-only parties with superstars.

If he doesn't respond to the passes from a down low brother, he gets dropped and word is spread quickly among us that he's off-limits. For an actor with no inside contacts and no introductions to major parties, his career can fizzle out just as quickly as he arrived in Los Angeles.

Ella was a jovial and lively woman—quite short, dark skinned, and robust with a hearty laugh. Her hair was cropped short, styled similar to Toni Braxton's. Ella reminded me of the big sidekick girlfriend you have who everyone loves and who keeps you laughing. I recognized her because she had a recurring role on a few major television sitcoms as the witty and smart-aleck coworker. She also starred in a few commercials for household cleaners that were running at the time.

"Do you play cards?" Ella said with a hearty laugh.

"Yeah, I play cards."

"No, do you play Bid Whist?" She stared at me.

"Naw, I don't know how to play Bid Whist, but I'm a good Spades player."

"You black and don't know how to play Bid Whist?!" She laughed. Nearly everyone playing cards turned around.

"Come on, follow me," Ella said as she grabbed my hand and led me into the kitchen.

"Do you drink?" she asked as she made me a taco.

"Yeah, I drink. I'll take a rum and coke."

Ella was very motherly and made sure I was taken care of.

After making me a taco and my drink, she took me on a tour of the house. People in Los Angeles love showing off their homes. They are validated by their material things—homes, cars, clothes, and plastic surgeries.

Ella had a nice brick Tudor home, very popular in Los Angeles. It was decorated with tons of black art—masks, drawings, and sculptures. With its colorful interior, it was definitely designed to make guests feel comfortable. Throughout the house, she had lots of framed photographs of herself with other celebrities and family members.

A slim woman with dreadlocks who was taller than Ella came up behind us. She kissed Ella on the lips, told her to hurry up because they were getting ready for another card game, and then went back into the dining room. I tried to hide my shock, so I smiled like it was nothing.

"We've been together for several years and we bought this house together," Ella said as she picked up from the table a picture of them hugging. "She truly brings me joy. I haven't been this happy in a long time." She smiled.

It was then I realized everyone at the party was on the down low. It was coming together for me. These were people I had either heard about or suspected were gay. All of them were chilling at Ella's house, enjoying one another's company. They were "family," and I was being introduced to them. That was why Kevin had been asking me so many questions. He was trying to figure out if he could bring me into the fold and if I could be trusted.

When you are introduced to the down low clique, the person who brings you in is responsible for you. They are like your sponsor. So they interview you beforehand without you knowing it. Your integrity and moral character are being judged. It takes a lot of consideration before you are invited into the exclusive club. In the down low clique, we have to make sure that you will not run and report it to the media, gossip magazines, or to your friends. We have to make sure you have an allegiance with us and that you will go down for us.

Kevin did his job well. He got to know me and spent a lot of time with me. I was familiar with how things worked, but he never let on about his own sexuality. Although I had suspected after a while, I just kept it moving because I was on a whole other mission.

Some of the popular actors and actresses at the party were in relationships or married. Outside the confines of the house you would never have suspected them of being gay.

I had recognized a few from church. A couple I had noticed were very attractive brothers, one of whom was a popular print model. I had seen him in ads for sports gear in *Men's Health* and *GQ* magazine.

It felt good to be among people who were similar to me. As much as I struggled with myself, trying not to accept that part of me that liked men, I had finally found a place where it was okay to be me. I no longer felt concerned about fitting in and could simply be myself. We all had something in common and we were able to be our true selves without any criticism. Despite the world and the industry shutting us out because of our sexuality, we were able to laugh and have a good time.

Being on the down low I knew how it felt to be on the outside. I was constantly being a different person in different environments. Whatever the situation called for I learned to adapt.

When I was around straight men, I talked the talk—cars, sports, women. Though a part of me still lived in that world, and I was able to be a part of it, I still felt like an outsider because I could never be my true authentic self there.

For so long, I had pretended for other people. I, in essence, had become an actor, just like my newfound friends at Ella's house. We all were in the performances of our lives, keeping our sexuality a secret to keep our livelihoods, and keeping the outside world from finding out so that we could be accepted by our family and friends.

Some of the actors at the house knew the importance of keeping their down low status quiet. Once rumors started circulating about them in the press, they got married. Some started dating other celebrities. They had to quickly dispel the rumors or they jeopardized the movie roles and sitcom series they had.

"Jazz," a nice-looking brother, had women swooning when his character as a hard-working married man graced the television screen. His hit show marked a milestone because of its accurate portrayal of African-American family life. Jazz's sexy masculine appeal was very close to his personal persona. A world-class charmer, he had done some modeling but then caught the acting bug and his career took off. He had a warm spirit and the kindest heart. Jazz would go out of his way for anyone.

When he was around the public, he didn't mind signing autographs for the legions of women who adored him. His sex appeal broadened his fan base to include gay males. However, the rumors started to circulate. Was he gay? And who was he dating?

Soon Jazz introduced me to a longtime girlfriend. She started appearing at different social events with him. They walked the red carpet, stopping and posing for the cameras. They were the perfect couple and then they were married. The rumors stopped and his career continued to blossom with him landing a plum role as a compassionate bad ass on a hit network television drama series.

The world doesn't want to know that their favorite actor likes sleeping with other men. Especially women, who want to keep the fantasy of one day meeting and sleeping with their favorite star. As soon as the rumor starts of a male celebrity being gay, they begin dating a plethora of women. They suddenly become tied to someone. If you can fool the world, Hollywood will be there for you. As soon as you can no longer fool the world, Hollywood abandons you.

Besides, the entertainment business is all about illusions, especially in Hollywood. You keep your discretions discreet. As long as you are on the down low and no one suspects a thing, you can do whatever you please, like each one of us at Ella's house.

I was invited to sit in on a Spades game. Everyone started to warm up to me and ask about my time in Los Angeles and what I had been up to. They were letting me know I could relax and be myself.

More and more people came to the party throughout the night. The house was full of people. Some had gone into the backyard and others continued playing cards. A man came into the house wearing a motorcycle jacket and helmet. When he took off the helmet I immediately recognized him. It was Clay, the guy I met who starred in Carol's independent film.

He smiled and walked over to my table. "I told you I would see you again," he said, as we gave each other a brotherly dap. Damn, it was good seeing him. He was finer than I remembered. Without a doubt I was not going to let him get away so easily this time. I was definitely going to hook up with him.

After I finished my hand of cards, we took a walk in the backyard.

"It's good seeing you," he said, smiling.

"It's good seeing you as well."

"What's been up with you?"

"Well, I got a job at Orion Pictures," I said.

"Damn, that's great," Clay said. "You just got to Los Angeles and you already got a gig. Let's have a toast." We both raised our Corona beer bottles.

"To a new start and new friendships," he said, looking into my eyes.

"To new friendships," I said. *I'm going to fuck him,* I thought to myself.

"So, have you met anyone yet?" Clay asked.

"Just this one kat who I ran into when I first got here, but I haven't seen him since," I said, obviously flirting.

"Well, that's unfortunate. Maybe I can help you in looking for him?"

"I would really like that." I smiled, taking a sip of beer.

Kevin came outside to let me know he was leaving. Clay and I exchanged numbers to keep in touch. We then gave each other another dap. "I'll call you soon." He grinned at me.

"I hope very soon."

Clay called a few days later and we hung out at his house. He took me around Los Angeles, but we mainly hooked up for sex a few times. Clay's schedule was so busy we didn't spend a lot of time together.

The times we were together it felt great to finally lie with someone. Pleasing yourself is satisfying, but not gratifying. I was looking forward to climbing in bed with him. As fine as he was and with that amazing body, I knew our sex was going to be off the chain. I was sorely disappointed. Clay's body fulfilled physically a need that I had, to lie naked on top of each other, letting our bodies rock in sync, but that was it. His performance was less than stellar. I was looking for bells and whistles and he gave me crickets. There's nothing like a poor-performing man in the bedroom, and on camera. I only hoped that when he auditioned for roles he was more enthusiastic.

Clay was emotionally distant and removed as well. I couldn't connect with him, but I knew it was because he was afraid of someone finding out about him. He let me know on many occasions how he was very discreet about his sexuality. No one knew and he wanted to keep it that way. He was also extremely private about his life and didn't open up too much about anything. If I asked about his family, he was vague, only mentioning he had a mother and father. Whenever we were out and ran into someone he knew, he kept the introductions and conversation brief. We were always in a hurry to get someplace else.

Clay was more paranoid than I was, but that's how life is for a down low man. You don't want to run the risk of someone finding out and then outing you to others. I've seen many men who, once they were outed, became reclusive and depressed; their lives were crushed. Some even contemplated suicide.

I gathered that if Clay were outed, he would have felt as if his entire world had ended. His body was his livelihood. Women desired him and he couldn't afford for his biggest base of support to turn on him. He needed to be a sex symbol for them, for them to believe he was a real ladies' man. Without them, he wouldn't have anything. His career would be over.

I rarely saw Clay at other down low gatherings because he was often away traveling for modeling jobs. I did catch him on the daytime soap opera he was a regular on as well as a commercial.

While meeting men who were celebrities and studio executives at these parties, I had an opportunity to see how vast the infiltration of down low men was in the entertainment business. I'm not just talking about black men either. I attended many down low parties in the Hollywood Hills with white men too.

Once you have an entrée into the elite world of gay Hollywood, you are accepted in places you didn't know existed. Men who have secret love affairs have separate homes and apartments, and separate phones strictly for their romantic flings. No one ever suspects a thing and they go to great lengths to keep it that way.

Secrets are a big part of the down low life. Every move we make is calculated. We have to keep track of everything we do and say. More important, we have to make sure everyone around us is convinced we are purely heterosexual men.

It's a lonely life because we never get to fully love just one person. Our emotions are all over the place. We go from one bed to another seeking satisfaction, maybe love, or something else missing in our lives. I desperately wanted to be loved. I wanted to know what it felt like to have someone love me just for me.

I craved intimacy and companionship. Going from one lover to the next helped me to satisfy my sexual desires, but I mentally checked out when I was with men. I had to force myself to not let my emotions get involved because when dealing with another down low man I knew there could never be a relationship.

My life was complex. I was confused most times. When I wanted to come out I feared rejection by my family and friends. I was afraid I wouldn't go far in my career. I didn't want to be an outsider. I didn't want to be alone. I saw gay men as loners who were depressed and hated their lives. I didn't want to be that. I wanted to love my life.

Down low men do not think it's possible to be in a relationship with another man. They do not identify or see themselves as gay. For a down low man, it's all about the sexual connection, the intimacy. Having another man touch you, hold you, and kiss you the way you want.

Many people argue that down low men are gay. True as it may be, I consider there to be three types of down low and gay men: down low, gay down low, and gay.

A down low man, in most cases, is in a relationship with a woman. He's comfortable with having sexual relationships with both sexes. He likes the comfort, softness, and tenderness of a woman, but he also likes the hardness, strength, and feel of a man. Most often, he considers himself bisexual, if anything, but will never openly admit it. If he is asked if he's gay, he will say no. He doesn't believe his behavior is that of a gay man. Also, he does not socialize or hang out with gay men. No one suspects him of sleeping with other men. He has just as many friends on the down low as he does who are not. His down low associates are unreadable men who no one would suspect. A down low man hangs on to his masculine persona and wears it as a badge. Many married men, celebrities, rappers, and men in prison identify with this behavior.

I remember one down low brother I met who was a street thug with a reputation for his hard-core bravado. "Just because you fucking me don't mean I'm a bitch. I ain't no bitch. I'm still a man," he told me as he puffed up his chest and mean mugged me.

He, like so many other down low men, consider the sexual act of penetration to be the determining factor of their down low status. If a man is the giver in the act (the top), he doesn't consider himself gay because he is not the one being penetrated.

Down low men consider those who are penetrated (bottoms) as gay, or the girl in the relationship. If they are the receiver, as in the case of the thug, they go to great lengths to keep it quiet because they do not want anyone to discover they like receiving dick. If a down low man likes being penetrated, he will overcompensate in his machismo and will let the man know up front that he is not a woman or bottom. They are still down low, they just like being the receiver. They can still go home to their wives or girlfriends and have sex with them without any problem. It's just their sexual gratification comes from being penetrated.

A down low gay man is a man who no longer sleeps with women, however, he keeps his sexuality a secret from family and friends. He still finds women attractive, but he will not allow himself to become emotionally or physically involved with one. He knows what he likes sexually and being with a woman will not satisfy his sexual desires. He may like the company of a beautiful woman, but sleeping with one is not on his mind. He is also conscious of the ramifications of getting emotionally or romantically involved with a woman. He doesn't want to play with a woman's feelings and would rather not have sex with her, to protect her and himself. He's aware that he likes men and continues to sneak around with others like himself. Although he primarily sleeps with men, this type of man does not identify with the gay lifestyle. If he is asked if he is gay, he will most often say no, depending on who's asking. If it's someone who he doesn't want to know about his sexuality, he will definitely say no. If it is someone who he feels extremely comfortable with and knows relatively well, he will say he finds women attractive, but prefers to sleep with men, not admitting he is gay. Also, he rarely goes to a gay club and he's not well-known or connected to the gay community.

A gay man is someone who identifies himself as such and lives his life openly. He's out on his job, with his parents, and friends. They all know about his sexuality and preference to be with men. This type of man has no desire to sleep with women. He knows he has an attraction for men and only sleeps with them. A gay man seeks to be in an emotionally committed relationship. They are aware of self and proud to be gay.

Someone who identifies himself as gay socializes and interacts with other gay men in the gay community. He has no problem with someone asking him if he is gay and will admit his desires to be with a man.

It takes a lot to get to the stage of being a gay man. You have to love and accept yourself. Despite what others think of you, you have to put yourself first. I had a problem with that. I didn't love myself, and, being abandoned by my mother, I didn't feel loved. I didn't know who my father was and didn't know what it was like to receive love from a parental figure. With an extended family that was not affectionate, I often found myself wondering what love was and how it felt.

I knew I was not a gay man. I generally fluctuated between down low and down low gay. I knew I had feelings for women. I had sex with them, but I never dated a man and a woman at the same time. I didn't want to string a woman along, especially physically. Once a woman is attached physically it's hard to break the relationship. I didn't want to hurt another person emotionally. I had been through that and I knew the pain of heartbreak.

Besides, I grew up in the church where I learned that homosexuality is a sin. If you're gay, you die and go to hell. People hate you. God hates you. Who in their right mind would want God to hate them? I surely didn't. I had to get the gay thoughts out of my system, and religion became my way to fight my urges for men.

Lastly, I continued to meet other down low men who were confused like me. Many of us are emotionally and mentally damaged from our religious upbringings, misinformed communities, or conservative parents. I was from a family where gay was not a topic of discussion. Sexuality was never brought up in my household or many of the homes of the down low men I met. Our existence became sneaking around and covering up our secrets. When I had sex with men I felt guilty afterward. I had been told it was wrong, that it was immoral. It was so good, but it was so wrong. I hated myself for having the desires I craved. I asked God the questions, "Why me? Why do I have to be gay? Why does it have to be so wrong?"

I wished that a pill existed I could take to make it all go away. I prayed to God that I would wake up and all feelings for other men would be gone. But no matter what I wished, it remained inside of me.

13. LAST NIGHT

MY OTHER BREAK into meeting a down low brother came when Karen, a producer at E! Entertainment Television held a Christmas party at her house.

The party was filled with industry types. Karen walked me over to the small crowd of people seated near the dining room. She introduced me to a few of her coworkers who were also producers.

"Hey, what's up, man, I'm 'Charles.'" He was an attractive, short, dark-skinned man, and very, very sexy. He appeared to be around my age.

"What up. I'm Terrance," I said, extending my hand. I didn't immediately recognize him, but something told me he was somebody I should probably know.

"What do you do?" Charles asked.

"I work at Orion Pictures."

"Oh, that sounds cool." He flashed a smile. "I'm a singer/songwriter," he said proudly.

"That's cool," I responded. "You wrote any songs I would recognize?"

"Probably not. I got a few songs being pitched to a few major artists right now. My producers are working to get me on their albums."

"Good luck to you," I said. I had met many men who were on the verge of breaking into the industry.

"Thanks, man. But I'm also working on my own music. I've been going to the studio working on my demo. I'm about to get a record deal."

"You're doing it, huh?" I said, trying to figure out if he was a down low brother.

"Hell yeah I'm doing it! I'm too talented not to be signed."

He had a strong personality and was extremely confident, which I liked. Charles was also funny and loved to talk. As we sat and talked about different people in the industry we knew and places we had been, I became more and more intrigued by him. It was the way he spoke and how he said things. Charles knew he was going to be successful. He was certain of it, and it turned me on.

"Things are definitely happening for me. I want to marry my girl, but we're taking a break right now. I want to make sure I'm doing the right thing."

"It's always safer to be sure than to be sorry later," I replied, disappointed. His swagger was turning me on, and I was hoping we were going to hit it off. The way he looked in my eyes when he spoke, as if I was the only person in the room, made my guard come down. I was now standing in front of the wall I had been hiding behind. I felt an erection coming on. I was ready to lie with him just from his conversation. He was literally talking my drawers off.

"I just got to figure out how to let all my honeys know I can't be freaking them on the regular."

"Oh?" My ears perked up. I began to imagine him with the women, the things he was doing to them and how he was freaking them. I wanted to be a freak with him.

"Yeah, man. I got these other two women I've been seeing and damn, they are some freaks. I can't let them go."

Although I was caught off guard with his candor regarding his sexual relationships, I wanted to know the details. He said he felt comfortable talking with me. I wanted him to narrate what he did to them like the many erotic stories in *Hustler* and *Playboy* magazines I had read as a young boy. Just as I felt reading those stories back then, I was now yearning for a sexual release with him.

We talked practically the entire night. It didn't bother me because I'd already met the people I'd wanted to meet, and we exchanged business cards in order to keep in touch.

People started leaving the party and I tried calling my friend Sandy to come pick me up. "I can take you home," Charles offered. He had to drop off a few people who had ridden with him to the party. I agreed, but it seemed like an eternity dropping off the other three people.

Why didn't he drop me off first since I lived the farthest away from the party? I thought. But I didn't say anything, and soon Charles started driving in the opposite direction of my house.

"Hey, Charles, you okay?" I asked to make sure he remembered he had to take me home.

"Yeah, I'm cool."

"Okay, because I live in the opposite direction."

"Yeah, man, I was wondering if you wouldn't mind staying at my spot. I'm really tired and I'm not too far from my house."

"All right." My mind was racing. I wasn't sure what was going on but I was going for the ride.

Charles's bi-level loft apartment was huge and spacious. The loft upstairs overlooked the entire first floor.

I took a seat on the sofa in the living room while Charles checked his mail and phone messages. He offered me a glass of juice and turned on some of his music for me to listen to. It sounded good. He wasn't great, but he was good. While I listened to the music, he went upstairs to his bedroom and changed clothes. Charles came downstairs in a pair of gray, cotton, thin military shorts and a wife-beater. I tried not to notice, but he had a great physique and he wasn't wearing underwear, as his dick was bouncing in his shorts. And from the looks of it, he was definitely packing some meat. Man, if only I knew what the deal with him was. I wanted to leap all over him.

I kept looking straight ahead and just glanced at him from time to time. I didn't want to give off any signs that I was enjoying the view of his body, and I made sure he was not watching when I did so.

Charles told me he was in the military reserves and spent one weekend a month on call. He had been doing it for over ten years. But he was most excited when he talked about his music. He loved to sing and had acquired a small, local fan club. He showed me lots of pictures of him with various celebrities and women at different clubs he performed in.

What is his deal? I kept thinking. *Why is he being so friendly?* But most important, *is he a down low brother?* He kept talking about the women he was sexing. Usually I would have had him pegged by now, but he was throwing me for a loop with all the talk about his girls. I had come to the conclusion he was straight and he was trying to make sure I knew it.

Charles sensed I was tired so he said I could sleep in his bed. I followed him upstairs to the bedroom and he gave me a T-shirt to sleep in. I took off my clothes and got into bed. I was really tired. It had been a busy day at the office. I was so glad the next day was Saturday and I could sleep in.

As I got comfortable, Charles pulled off his wife-beater, turned off the lights, and got into bed next to me. My heart started beating faster. I wasn't sure if it was a ploy or if we were about to have sex. He didn't say anything. I was lying there on my back, with my eyes open.

Not long after he lay down, he seemed to be asleep, but I was still awake. I was confused. Was he waiting for me to make the first move? Did he want to do something sexual, but didn't know how to say it? Maybe he was so comfortable in his sexuality, being in bed with another man didn't bother him. I was too afraid to move or say anything. I was thinking so damn much, I thought myself to sleep.

When I woke up the next morning we were in a spoon position. I was behind Charles and he was under me. I moved away from him. My dick was hard and I hoped he didn't feel it. I wasn't sure what was going on and I wasn't about to be accused of something I was not trying to do.

Charles stretched and turned over to face me. He smiled and said, "I knew that you wanted me at the party last night." My heart started beating faster. My dick got harder. He leaned over and kissed me. That was all I needed. He grabbed a small toiletry bag filled with condoms from under his bed and the entire day we made love throughout the loft. We had sex in the bedroom, on the steps, in the kitchen, on the counters, in the living room, on the tables, and in the bathroom on the sink.

Our bodies were intertwined sitting on the bathroom sink. It was intense. The heat between us made our bodies sweat. He reached behind us, turned on the faucet, and splashed our bodies with cool water. The water spilled from our chests onto our crotches, down our backs and onto the floor.

We managed to let each other loose only long enough for Charles to have me stand on top of the toilet. He squated below me and sucked the now steamy hot water as it dripped from my body. Each time his mouth found a new place to explore, I experienced a volcanic eruption pour from me as I held on to the shower rod for dear life. We graciously took turns sexually gratifying each other.

It was the best sex I'd ever had. Charles was good. No, he was superb. I swear sex had to have been his hobby. I finally met someone who loved sex just as much as I did. Charles knew how to please a man and he knew how he wanted to be pleased.

From that day on we spent nearly every day with each other. And every day sex was involved. I forgot all about the women he was sleeping with. How could he have time to see them when we were spending so much time together?

Charles took me to various spots throughout the city he liked to visit like Hollywood Boulevard, the mall in Culver City, and the observatory in Griffith Park. We went to Marina del Rey, Long Beach, and Venice Beach. We dined at discreet, off-beat places where he knew we wouldn't run into any of our friends from the industry.

On a few occasions, Charles invited me to his performances. Women stood at the edge of the stage swooning for him. They'd be gazing up at him and singing along.

At the end of the show, Charles rushed out of the venue to avoid the women waiting for him. At times, he would even introduce them to me, but tell them we had to run. And no one ever suspected a thing. Even the woman he was planning to marry never questioned our relationship. When I met her, I couldn't believe that he was cheating on such a beautiful woman. *What the hell is he thinking?* I thought. She had an amazing body, long, luxurious hair, and legs that wouldn't stop. We even had a few drinks together. I felt uncomfortable around her because I knew I had to maintain the façade that Charles and I were just friends. I didn't want to slip up and say anything to cause any suspicion. Even when she asked me if I had a girlfriend, I lied and told her that I was seeing a few girls, but nothing serious. The more drinks I had, the more relaxed I got. Before long, we were all laughing and sipping it up. She was such a sweet woman and had an amazing wit about her, but I knew when we left I was the one going home with him.

Charles had us all whipped; we were wide open for him. If he had said the sky was purple, we would have believed him. I know whatever he told his girl about our relationship, she believed.

I knew many down low men who lied to their women about their male friendships. Often the other man, I was introduced as their boy, distant cousin, or industry contact. Women felt comfortable around me. Nothing I did or said let them know that I was sleeping with their man.

Charles revealed to me that most of the women at his shows were previous bed partners. I knew, like they knew, how awesome he was in bed. They were hoping to be chosen for another night with him, and later, while we were at his place sexing it up, his phone would ring nonstop throughout the night.

14. DIRT OFF YOUR SHOULDER

EVERYTHING WAS GOING GREAT in my life. I had a job, my own place, a relationship, and I was far away from my family. They couldn't get to me, and I chose not to reach out to them. I had decided they didn't deserve to be a part of my world since they had left me hanging at critical times in my life.

It was nearing Christmas and our entire department was called into the office of the president of Orion Pictures. We all filed into the huge office overlooking Century City Mall.

The president applauded us for all our hard work as a dedicated team and then said, "Orion Pictures has been bought out and it will no longer exist. You will all be receiving severance pay at the end of the week. This Friday will be everyone's last day in the office."

We all looked around at one another in shock. No one said a word. He thanked us again for all our hard work, and told us to be excited about the future. He pulled out a putter from his golf bag, stood up, pretended to be swinging at a golf ball and said, "I'm going to get some relaxation and go see my daughter this weekend." We all walked out of his office in disbelief.

Was this really happening? I wondered. *I am getting severance pay and I just got hired two months ago. This is truly a blessing.* Sad as it sounds, I was thinking about the money. I couldn't have cared less about the job, because I felt I could always get another one.

That Friday I picked up my regular paycheck and a severance check for $7,500. I was ecstatic. The first thing I was going to do was buy a car, which I needed badly. I was through with riding the bus. I also needed to find another job, but I had enough money to hold me over for a few months.

I took the bus to a car dealership in Burbank and drove off the lot with a 1995, white, two-seater Honda CRX. I had always wanted a two-seater car since I was little boy because they seemed sporty, flashy, and rich. And this car was sharp and fast.

A few days later, I got calls about possible jobs from Jimmy, a guy I had met through my boy Jacob, and Alexis, who I lived with at Sandy's apartment. Alexis was attending an entertainment conference in Washington and said she would take my résumé to hand out.

Jimmy was a native Californian and an aspiring singer. Talk about a brother with some pipes. Jimmy had a smooth and silky, old-school sound like that of Donny Hathaway. He worked at Motown Records and he let me know there was a position available as the assistant to Suzanne de Passe.

I jumped on both opportunities. Alexis took my résumé with her to the entertainment conference and Jimmy hooked me up with an interview at Motown Records.

I went to the interview to meet with the legendary Suzanne de Passe, the woman who had discovered the Jackson Five. I was thrilled. Mrs. de Passe was just as beautiful in person as she was on television. She was professional and direct in describing to me the qualifications she needed in an assistant. Near the end of the interview Mrs. de Passe said to me, "Terrance, I have no doubt you will be very successful. You are a very bright young man." And even though I didn't get the job, her words left me feeling invincible.

Mrs. de Passe's office did refer me to Benny Medina of Handprint Entertainment. Benny was looking for an additional assistant in his offices.

On the day of my interview, I ran into "Cortez," a well-known actor I had met in New York, whose sister was a good friend of mine. As a teen, he had his own television sitcom for a short while, and as an adult, he did a few other sitcoms for network television. He found his success when he started producing television projects.

"Hey, Terrance, man, it's good seeing you. What are you doing here?" he asked as we embraced.

"It's good seeing you, too. I live out here now," I said. Having him that close brought back memories.

Running into each other was quite a surprise for both of us. Cortez looked just as good as I remembered; he still had a boyish grin and the most beautiful dark eyes. We had spent a lot of time together when he was in New York, and being around him always made me feel flustered. His laugh and his touch were all that I needed to feel good.

I met Cortez when I was new to the game, and to me he was a seasoned veteran. He'd been on television, lived in Los Angeles, and hung with other celebrities. He was very low-key, and being a celebrity didn't go to his head. That is the thing I really liked about him. When I was around Cortez and his friends, hanging in their world, he never put on any fronts. I couldn't have asked for anything else.

"What are you doing here?" I asked.

"Benny and I are discussing him possibly managing me. I'm working on a new comedy show and we're working out the kinks. What are you doing here?" he repeated with a big grin on his face.

"I have an interview with Benny."

"Word? Hold up, I'll be right back." Cortez went into Benny's office. A few minutes later, he came out and told me that he spoke with Benny and told him to strongly consider me for the position.

After a short meeting with Benny, I knew we wouldn't work well together because he was dramatic, demanding, and over the top. His diva attitude was in full effect and I didn't want to be in the line of fire.

I couldn't get out of Benny's office quick enough; it was too chaotic with people everywhere. The phones were ringing off the hook, and the girl answering them looked flustered. I got a good glimpse of what my life would be like working with Benny.

Cortez was in the reception area when I came out and I thanked him for putting in a good word for me.

"How did it go?" he asked.

"It went well."

"You know I'm going to look out for you. When can we get up? I want to see you."

"Call me. It would be great to get back up with you." I smiled as we exchanged information. We did have some unfinished business.

Once I was out the door I felt a sigh of relief. The irritability and anxiety I'd felt in Benny's office was gone. During the interview it seemed like every two minutes he had to answer an important call or someone was knocking on the door interrupting the flow of our conversation.

But working with Benny could provide access to many contacts. This was the man who created Will Smith, Tyra Banks, and Jennifer Lopez's careers. Benny is the man in Hollywood. He's well respected and well known. Working with him would open many doors for me. I truly thought about how this could benefit my career. After working with him for a year or two, I could practically write my own ticket in Hollywood. But I also knew what I had to do. I immediately called the office when I got home. "I wish to thank you for the interview and the offer. Unfortunately, I will be unable to accept the position at this time. I don't think I would be a good fit for you."

15. HOMIE/LOVER/FRIEND

ALMOST TWO WEEKS had gone by when I got called for an interview as a production coordinator for *The Keenen Ivory Wayans Show.* Alexis had given them my résumé at a conference in Washington a few weeks back, and they wanted to meet with me immediately. Alexis really looked out for me. That was a true blessing.

After a few interviews, I landed the job as the production coordinator of on-air promos for *The Keenen Ivory Wayans Show.* Buena Vista Television, a division of Disney, was producing the show. I was going to be working directly with Keenen to produce promo spots for various markets in the United States.

Keenen's hit television show, *In Living Color,* had catapulted him as a comedic genius. He also made several movies that were box office hits. Keenen and his family had become a viable entity in Hollywood.

While working on the show, I got to meet his brothers, Shawn, Marlon, Damon, and his sister, Kim, who came to the set regularly. They were the nicest group of people. They always spoke to me when I saw them. Keenen's siblings were very supportive of him.

I learned a lot by being in Keenen's presence and listening to him. He was direct, professional, and he knew his shit. Keenen didn't take any mess from anyone and he knew how much he could get away with. He knew how to play the game. The Disney executives were all older white men and women. It seemed like they were intimidated or afraid to approach him most of the time. Keenen often joked that they would send me, the black guy, to get him to read the promos because they figured he and I had more of a connection. It worked and I noticed how Keenen often treated them when they came on set. He let them know he was in charge and, if they were banking on him to have a successful show, they'd better let him do what he knew how to do best—his comedy.

But the executives needed Keenen to cooperate because his show was new and it was hard to book guests to appear on it. They pleaded with Keenen to ask his celebrity friends to make appearances, which would make the job of the talent bookers easier. However, most of Keenen's friends were other black celebrities, and the talent bookers often had no idea who they were. I came to learn it was important for blacks working in the business to acquaint themselves with both black and white actors and actresses, though whites working in the business often didn't concern themselves with many black actors.

It was obvious whenever the talent bookers posted their weekly and monthly bookings on the show board. It was often filled with white actors who I, along with quite a few crew members, didn't recognize. It was my job to research them, to call the studios, and get promotional clips. It was from these clips that I learned about an actor. Then I would have to sit with the editor doing the promos and point out the actor we were using for the ad.

Whenever black actors were pitched for bookings, it was always like pulling teeth to get the talent bookers to understand who some of the most prominent black actors were. Although some were big among the black audience, it's all about numbers and ratings, and who's watching and tuning into the show. It's about advertisers and dollars. If an advertiser can't see a return on their investment, then they pull their ads.

Disney was concerned with Keenen's appeal to a broader audience. They wanted him to translate to white people in Middle America. His show needed to do well in areas like Iowa, Kansas, Oklahoma, and Missouri. It became important to book white actors on the show for Middle America because they want to see people like them.

Oftentimes we had to tone down Keenen's sketches in the edit room because most of the scenes were ethnically offensive in humor. Keenen needed to appear as a friendly, warm, and inviting host. The over-the-top antics he's known for had to be heavily edited so as not to offend certain viewers.

While working for Keenen I forged a relationship with a freelance producer from the same studio lot working on another show. "Edwin" was a natural-born hustler. He had an impeccable work ethic and was on top of his shit. I was thoroughly impressed by his style.

Edwin was mature for a twenty-year-old. I had to remind myself that he was still a kid. He had a pure innocence about him, but he was a hot, hot mess.

I learned that Edwin liked to dress in women's clothing and makeup. He was a transvestite. Although he liked to dress as a woman, he had no desire to be one.

Edwin taught me a lot about his world. He educated me on down low men who liked men who dressed as women. These brothers enjoyed the illusion that they were sleeping with a woman, yet had the equipment of a man. It was a world I had never known existed.

Edwin informed me that many actors and rappers solicited transvestites, especially those who were not easily recognizable as men in dresses. The prettier you were, the more likely you were to date a celebrity, and Edwin was pretty. He had golden skin with oval eyes due to his Caribbean, Spanish, and Asian background.

What he taught me were lessons I would never forget, and one that I refer to to this day: no matter how much you may think you know a person, you really don't know them at all.

I also made a lot of friends on the *Keenen* show. It was good to be working with so many young black people who were producers, writers, and key decision makers. We hung out a lot together after work at restaurants to shoot the breeze and talk about the show. People often brought along their significant others, and we got to know one another well. I would bring Kathy to keep my cover.

Although I was close to a few of the crew, I was still not comfortable in sharing my sexuality. I had witnessed how they treated an openly gay coworker. Once he let everyone know he was gay, the jokes began behind closed doors. I didn't want to experience that type of ridicule.

It's really hard to keep lying and remembering the lie you tell people. They want to know who you are dating, how long, where did you meet, and if she's the one. Although I had numerous girlfriends in college and a few afterward, I was a single man living in Los Angeles. In a city where beautiful women are everywhere, people will speculate and question why you're not dating.

I, along with many of my down low friends, had girlfriends or cover girls. Cover girls are close friends who don't mind being arm candy when we need a date for company picnics, dinners, and parties. I had even been to parties and saw down low men with their cover girls. Most times the woman is aware of our sexuality and helps us to keep our cover. She understands the turmoil we experience daily when we are bombarded with the questions, "What did you do over the weekend?" or "How's your girlfriend?"

I hated going to work on Mondays because I knew the questions were coming. I knew people were not being nosy but just wanted to be a part of my life. They were genuine in asking because they wanted to be friends with me. But I couldn't open myself up. It was hard to let down my guard and allow others into my world. It was filled with so much garbage that I didn't want people to discover the trash I was hording.

Although I never told my cover girl Kathy about my sexual preference for men, I gathered she figured it out. She never questioned if I was dating or who I was sleeping with. She knew I was probably uncomfortable talking about my sexuality and she went along with my need to stay secretive.

When Kathy and I were at parties, we danced seductively together. We took care of each other. We knew each other well, and seeing us interact together, no one suspected a thing.

We attended Keenen's birthday party. It was an open bar with food everywhere. A DJ was mixing the latest sounds, but the main event and center of attraction of the party was a huge boxing ring in the middle of the floor. That night we were treated to a boxing match between two women in bikinis.

Everyone gathered in front of the boxing ring to watch, but Kathy and I sat in the back of the club at a table. There were two male celebrity actors standing a few feet in front of us. They didn't notice us because the club was dark. Both men are young and very attractive and have starred in some comedic and dramatic films. One of the actors, "Junior," is a tall, muscular, brown-skinned brother who got his start in television and is known for his comedic roles in films. He never married, but has a couple of children with a girlfriend. The other dark-skinned actor, "Fritz," has been in a few movies and has starred on a popular television drama.

As everyone cheered on the fighters, the two actors occasionally grabbed hands as they stood side by side. The taller actor, Junior, would squeeze Fritz's ass. Kathy and I looked at each other in shock. We couldn't believe what we were witnessing. It also confirmed for me what I, and many others, had thought about Junior. There had been speculation about his sexuality, but now I knew. I was completely surprised about Fritz, however.

Throughout the night, I kept my eye on them; I wanted to make sure my eyes were not deceiving me. They stayed together all night long. They slyly touched hands, and Junior would gently place his hands on the back of his companion. Whenever a woman approached them, Junior and Fritz looked as if they were interested and entertained her with conversation. After a few minutes they would leave her at the bar as they searched out another spot to be alone.

I followed them because I hoped that I'd see them engaging with another down low man I didn't know about who was at the party. However, they just whispered in each other's ear and let out hearty laughs. Watching them interact, I felt like Junior and Fritz were oblivious to their environment, and even though it was crowded and people were everywhere, no one but me paid them any attention. They were able to easily disappear in the crowd. By the end of the night, after sharing a few drinks, the two actors whisked away alone.

I went home thinking about them. I wondered if they were a couple and serious about each other. I wondered if they were in another Hollywood down low circle I was not privy to. I was learning more and more about how deep and secretive the circles were in Hollywood.

Charles and I were still hot and heavy. I was growing more fond of him, spending a lot of time at his house.

One day Charles bought a new car, a Volkswagen Jetta, and we rode around town. I had an urge to ask him about the women he had been sleeping with.

"Are you still sleeping with women?" I asked nervously. I didn't want to know the answer, but I needed to know.

There was a long pause.

"Yeah, I'm still sleeping with one of them."

My heart sank.

"I'm also planning to ask my ex to marry me. I'm ready to settle down."

I felt a knot in my stomach, and my head was swirling. This wasn't happening. How did I not see this coming? Was I that blind or did I just ignore it?

I just stared straight ahead. I didn't want to believe it. I had been played. Hell, he was playing all of us. I couldn't believe I had been such a fool. For the first time in a long time, I felt like I mattered to someone.

"I can't sleep with you anymore. Man, just drop me off at home."

"Terrance, I'm sorry. I really do like you. It's not like I'm sleeping with another man. I'm sleeping with a woman. It's not the same."

I couldn't believe what I was hearing. He really thought it didn't matter because they were women and not men.

"You know I love both dick and pussy. I got to have them both. At least you know who I'm sleeping with."

For the first time since we started the conversation I turned and looked at him. "Yeah, but you're talking about marriage. Did you tell her about me?"

Silence.

I knew he had not told her because she had encouraged him to hang out with me. She'd rather him have male friends than the plethora of females whose names filled his little black book.

"I can't be a part of this love triangle. It's not fair to us. You are the only one getting your cake and eating it too." I was pissed. I had known the situation going in and was naïve to think he wasn't going to get married.

"Come on, Terrance, I'm really sorry. We can work this out. You don't have to be so irrational about this," Charles said as he pulled in front of my apartment building. "Just give me another chance."

"In my rationality I think I'm making the best choice. Go get married, Charles." As I walked up to my front door, he came up from behind and made several attempts to come into my apartment.

"You know how hard our lifestyle is. I really do want to be with you, but you know we can't be together like you want."

"Do you know what I want?"

"You want a relationship. But isn't what I'm giving you enough? Don't you like what we have?"

"You really don't get it. I have real feelings for you and you're not sure what you want."

"I do know what I want. You know we can't be together in the way you want," Charles said. "The world is not ready for men like us. We have to be discreet. We can't be open about ourselves. I don't want people in my business. I don't understand why I can't have you both. I can't help that I love pussy. I can't help that I still have feelings for women. Don't you?"

"Yeah, I do, but I'm not leading people on. I'm not playing with other people's emotions."

"Let's just go inside and talk about this." He smiled at me seductively. I knew this game. I had played it with him before. He figured sex was the best way to resolve the argument.

"I really care about you, but you can't come in," I said, stepping inside my apartment. "You coming in here will only lead to sex. Just go home. I'm for real. I'm not joking." When I closed the door every part of my body was screaming, *What the hell are you thinking? Do you really want to give this up?* Even though I wanted him to leave, a part of me hoped he would knock on the door. If he had pleaded a little more, I would have let him in and we could have talked about it. But Charles walked away.

Although I was proud of myself for ending the relationship, I missed him. I wasn't sure if it was because he was a good man or the over-the-top sex.

I kept picking men who put me second to everything else in their life. Perhaps I didn't love myself enough to let myself be put first. I never thought of myself deserving anything because I felt I didn't come from anything.

16. KEEP MOVING ON

IT WAS SWEEPS SEASON and I began to work longer hours at the *Keenen* show. After work I hung out with my new down low posse or with coworkers. There was a lot of drinking and socializing. I loved it because it allowed me to be numb and forget everything else happening in my life.

One morning, I was running late to the set because I'd overslept from partying the night before. I was rushing to get to work and traffic was heavy. I was at a light making a left turn at Highland and Wilshire when a Ford F-150 truck crashed into me.

I woke up to firefighters, policemen, and the paramedics surrounding my car. I couldn't move.

The ambulance rushed me to Cedars-Sinai Medical Center on Beverly Boulevard, where they kept poking and prodding every part of my body. I was in serious pain and thought something was definitely broken, bruised, or hanging by a limb.

But the doctors found nothing broken or bruised. Miraculously, I didn't suffer any broken bones. They worked feverishly and took several X rays to figure out what happened to my back and why I couldn't move, but found nothing. I was moved to my own hospital room and the doctors informed me they were going to run more tests to find out what the problem was.

The news of the accident spread throughout the *Keenen* set and my coworkers started visiting, sending flowers, cards, and balloons. I felt loved. I didn't realize how much people cared about me. The outpouring of their concern brought me to tears. I didn't realize how many people I'd gotten to know in Los Angeles.

For so long I always felt as if people didn't genuinely care about me. How could they? They didn't really know me. They didn't know my struggles or my family background. I had never opened up and told anyone because I figured they wouldn't be able to relate. No one I knew had a mother who was a prostitute and heroin addict. No one I was familiar with was raised by their grandparents. They all seemed perfectly happy with their perfectly happy families. They shared how they often spoke with their mothers and fathers. They had relationships, be it good or bad, with their siblings. I didn't have any of that. I couldn't just call up my mother and get advice. Most of the time, no one had heard from her or knew where she was. My siblings were much younger than I and lived with relatives. I had no relationship with them.

My friends didn't know the burden I carried about my sexuality. How much I was conflicted and oftentimes wanted my life to end. On most days I didn't want to wake up. I wanted my life to be over. It all started when I was molested by Ramone. I was confused about what happened to me and why I kept thinking of men. Every time I heard the pastor lambasting gays, I wanted for my life to end and then I wouldn't have to deal with my sexuality. I wouldn't have to struggle and try to be what everyone thought I should be. I wanted to be normal like everyone else. I often thought about suicide, but I was too afraid to do it. I was frightened by what I heard from my pastor who talked about those who committed suicide. They didn't inherit the kingdom of God. They went straight to hell. I was already living in hell dealing with my sexuality. I didn't want to commit suicide and live in that misery for eternity. So I just prayed that one day I would just not wake up. Then I wouldn't have to worry about being straight like my friends. I wanted desperately to have what they had. I envied their lives. I wanted to be straight. I wanted normalcy, a steady girlfriend, and kids. Why couldn't my life be simple and easy? Why did I have to carry this burden?

It was odd that during my time in Los Angeles, I got to meet so many people and traveled in many different circles, and yet so few of my friends knew one another. I was so entrenched in keeping secrets they merely became invisible imaginary people. They were, in essence, like my family.

I loved it that my down low friends came by and the ones in New York sent cards and flowers. I was moved by all the sentiments. But I was also upset and angry. I asked Sandy to call my family. Grandma Pearl called me at the hospital immediately. She cried and told me she was praying that I have a speedy recovery and she was happy I was okay. I didn't hear from the rest of my family; I didn't even get a card from them. It made me sad because I thought at least my family would make an attempt to come and see about me, but they didn't.

All the people I met and developed relationships with in Los Angeles filled the void where my family's love should have been. Even though I didn't share much of myself, my friends made me feel welcome in their homes. They invited me to meet their significant others, and I was a part of their lives. All I wanted was to be accepted, for someone to love me, to be liked. I wanted that from my family. I wanted them to be proud of me. I desperately wanted my mother to hug me and tell me how much she loved me. I desperately wanted to have a relationship with her.

As much as my friends reached out to me, I couldn't allow myself to get close to them. I knew the moment they discovered the truth about me, they would desert me. They wouldn't want to be my friend any longer, and I didn't want to risk that.

After a week in the hospital, the doctor's only explanation for my back pain was that I probably tensed at the moment of impact. It caused a back spasm, which prevented me from moving.

One of my friends, Jessie, came and took me home. I asked him to stop by the garage where my car was impounded to see what it looked like, because everyone told me how lucky I'd been to survive.

When I saw what used to be my car, I couldn't speak. It looked like someone had taken the car in their hands and crushed it like a beer can—the entire passenger side was smashed in. If the guy driving the truck had been going any faster, I would not be alive.

My insurance covered everything, but I still needed a car. A co-worker called and told me that he had an extra car and that if I could make the monthly payments, he would let me drive it. It was a new, green Toyota Tercel. I took him up on his offer.

It seemed that no matter what obstacle, tragedy, or pitfall I faced, a blessing always occurred, which drew me closer to God and made me want to learn more about myself. It was important for me to discover and know that I was a child of God and deserved greatness. Yet sometimes it's hard to know what greatness is when you feel defeated and beat up all your life.

For the next couple of months, things seemed to be going smooth again. Then in April I arrived on the set and noticed people seemed different. There was no audience lined up for the taping of the show and the crew was not buzzing around as they normally did when we were taping.

The show had been canceled, and that was it. People had to pack their things and leave the set. Everyone was disappointed. There were no warnings or indication the show was in trouble.

This was my first introduction to the television business, Hollywood style. Shows get canned without any warning. People show up for work one day and are out of work the next. That's the nature of the beast.

But one of the down low brothers set me up with a job handling the production reading for the Warner Bros. film *Message in a Bottle* starring Kevin Costner, Paul Newman, and Robin Wright Penn.

It was a monthlong job and it paid really well. The job was on a ranch owned by the studio and not on the lot, but it was cool because the parking pass they gave me allowed me access to the lot at any time and I was able to visit some of the brothers when I was not too busy at the ranch.

My job wasn't bad at all. I would go by the production office in the morning to pick up the scripts and take them to the ranch. I only needed to make sure the actors had their scripts and any other necessities for the table reads. The readings generally lasted five hours a day. One of the demands of the table reads was that all of Paul Newman's Newman's Own products had to be available to the cast to eat. Each day I had to refresh and restock the refrigerator and table with Newman's Own goods.

The cast would generally arrive around nine in the morning and finish right after lunch. Once they were done, I would head to the lot and meet up with some of the down low brothers who worked at the studio.

Sandy was also on the lot. She was working on a new movie that had some major stars in it. The lead was "Lucas," who is a megastar. No matter what film project he was attached to it was bound to be a box office smash. In Hollywood, he is considered a golden boy and very bankable. However, there were already many rumors swirling about his sexuality, and even though he married, it was hard for him to shake those pesky gay rumors.

"You're not going to believe this," Sandy said when I called her.

"What's going on?"

"Well, the crew is taking bets on Lucas."

"What type of bets?"

"Since we've been filming, his boy 'Kareem' comes by every day and they go into the trailer while we're shooting."

"So what?" I said.

"No, Kareem comes by and they are up in the trailer doing their thing."

"The thing-thing?"

"Yes, the thing-thing," she laughed.

Kareem, a leading sitcom actor, is married to an actress. They both have appeared in movies, but Lucas is the breakout sensation. His boy Kareem, however, found success in television as a leading actor.

The crew's bet was based on how often Lucas's "boyfriend" would show up and how long he would stay. It was like clockwork; Kareem arrived each day at the same time and went straight to the trailer for hours on end. The bets grew larger and larger.

When I moved to Los Angeles and got into the down low world, our circle was talking about the down low circle Lucas and Kareem were in, and which I wanted to be a part of. But it was a hard nut to crack; they were superstars.

But sometimes even superstars slip up, and I wondered why they were not more discreet, working with crews constantly buzzing around the set, who are looking and paying attention even when actors think they are not. I've worked on many sets where I had to deliver scripts or messages to actors' trailers, and many of those actors surely did not practice any decorum. Smoking weed, having sex, and just acting buck wild.

I would later meet Lucas on another project I was working on. He was smooth, charismatic, and charming. Everyone loved him. I know I did. I couldn't help but to fall for him, with his warm smile and personable presence. Lucas didn't need to have his ego stroked and he had no diva airs about him. He made everyone feel like they were special. He spoke to the entire crew and his wife even brought us goodies to thank us for helping them with the show. They were a class act. But I knew the secret Lucas held; he and I were in the family of down low brothers.

One morning when I arrived for work at Warner Bros. there was a brother in the production office. He was fine as hell, scrumptious, with a muscular body that just wouldn't stop. I had seen men like him in magazines, and to see him close up made my heart flutter. He could have been a calendar model.

Our eyes met instantly. It was as if we both were wondering, *Who the hell is that black boy and how did he get a job on this film?* We each nodded what's up. We couldn't talk because it was the early-morning rush, and I needed to get to the ranch. I was hoping when I came back later in the afternoon he would still be there.

When I got to the ranch, I immediately called one of my boys at the studio to find out who this man was. My friend Eric said, "Oh, I see you met 'Marcus.' He is *fine*, ain't he?"

"Why didn't you tell me about him? I damn near tripped coming in the door when I saw him." I laughed.

"I wanted you to see him for yourself. I didn't want to spoil the surprise."

"So what's up with him?"

"Yeah, he's down and part of the family, but he already has a boyfriend."

"Damn! Are they happy?" I asked.

"Yeah, they're very happy together. They've been together for two years. They don't hang out or socialize in many of the circles. I can hear you over there thinking."

We both laughed. I knew plenty of down low, gay brothers like them. It wasn't uncommon or unheard of for a brother not to hang in the down low circles if they were too scared their secret would get out.

Even though we all knew one another, we never disclosed any information about another brother. We knew who to tell or trust with information. We had our code and we stuck by it. You never out another brother, you defend him. When others are speaking about a brother and they ask if you know if he's gay, you deny, deny, deny it.

On many occasions I protected another brother's secret. Sure, I knew the truth, but I was not about to out him. I never revealed if anyone was part of the family. I would simply say, "Naw, I don't think he's gay. He's a cool brother, but he doesn't get down like that." I had been entrusted with a secret.

Just before the actors were about to break for lunch, Marcus walked in the building. I was standing alone in the hall outside the conference room when he approached me with a bright, toothy smile.

We did the general conversation about what we were doing in Los Angeles and what jobs we worked on and who we knew in the business. We talked for about a half hour before he realized that he had to get back to the production office. He asked for my contact information, and we exchanged phone numbers. Marcus and I became fast friends while I worked on the film.

After I finished the film, Marcus and I hung out more and more. He and I became like two peas in a pod. We had a lot in common. We both were the same zodiac sign, Virgos. We enjoyed reading self-help books on spirituality and didn't mind being alone. We also were very private about our lives and did not divulge any unnecessary information. He would become one of my closest friends and someone I could always depend on.

On many occasions Marcus revealed to me how he didn't care what people thought of him. He was often approached by women because of his gorgeous looks. Nothing about him was effeminate or dainty. He loved cars and sports as well as Patti LaBelle and Whitney Houston. He was comfortable with his sexuality, but he didn't broadcast it.

"Terrance, I don't give a fuck about these people. They are not paying my bills and we ain't fucking."

I wanted to develop that attitude. He was bold. I wanted to be bold, but I just couldn't get to that point. Maybe that's why I loved being around him. He was what I desired to be. He was like a big brother to me.

Marcus invited me to various parties in Baldwin Hills. I met his boyfriend, "Gary," for the first time and other down low men—industry executives and businessmen. These parties were my entrée to Los Angeles down low brothers with money. Most lived in mansions in Baldwin Hills and drove BMWs, Mercedeses, Lexuses, and Range Rovers. They were wealthy, held positions in the community, and were involved in church. They seemed perfectly happy. I even dated one for a brief moment.

I loved being around Marcus and Gary. It gave me hope that two men could be in an emotional and intimate relationship. The way they cared and supported one another was inspiring. They went to the gym together, they cooked their meals together, and had date night where they went out to dinner and the movies.

They were affectionate toward each other, kissing and hugging, and

Marcus would often playfully grab Gary from behind and nibble on his neck and ears. "I love you, baby," he would say.

Gary invited me to join them at his mother's home for Thanksgiving. His mother had a full spread on the table for the family. The way Marcus and Gary interacted with everyone was so intimate—the family members completely comfortable with their relationship—and they all laughed, talked, and seemed to have fun. It made me long for a relationship like theirs.

All of the down low men I met seemed jaded to the idea of being in a relationship. They felt like all men cheated, that no man could be trusted. They were only projecting what they were feeling on the inside. They were cheaters and they couldn't be trusted. They were lying and cheating to the women they were with. They were deceptive in leading their women into believing they were heterosexual men who were in love with them. Down low men know themselves better than anyone and if they know they cannot be in a committed relationship with a woman, then they sure as hell can't be in a committed relationship with another man.

17. LIGHTS! CAMERA! ACTION!

ONE OF MY BOYS, "Corey," moved out to Los Angeles while I was working on *Keenen*. It was great to have someone with me from New York. He was an amazing songwriter and singer. A spitball full of fire, Corey could belt out a song and hit every note each time. This ability caught the ears of Death Row Records, who were interested in signing him as a recording artist. Even MTV featured him on their series *The Cut*.

When I first met Corey in New York, I made the trek with him to his showcases and watched the crowds go crazy over his vocal skills. No matter where he went, Corey had a following and it was growing fast. Pretty soon he was opening and performing at places like Chaz and Wilson's and Sweetwater's. He often opened for Jay-Z. This was before Jay-Z *was* Jay-Z.

When I met Corey he'd just finished a Broadway musical, which helped him get signed with "Eli," a popular multiplatinum rapper, who had just started a label at the time.

Eli was a force to be reckoned with. He flew out the gate with his debut album and would become a mainstay in the ever-changing Hip Hop industry, where many rappers are one-hit wonders. He has been hailed as one of the greatest rappers to bless the mic.

When Corey got signed to the chart-topping rapper's label, he spent a lot of time in Eli's home-based studio. On a few occasions when he returned, Corey asked if we could talk. I always figured it was due to the pressures of him being signed to a label and working long hours in the studio. But Corey had much more on his mind. He was caught up in a sexual tryst with his boss, Eli, the owner of the label, the beloved and adored rapper. I didn't understand why he was complaining. Eli was fine as hell and could make his career, and all Corey had to do was suck his dick. That's all the rapper wanted. I was sure there were many young, aspiring rappers who wouldn't mind having that chance.

"So let me get this right," I said. "You're sucking Eli's dick?"

"Yeah."

"How often?"

"It's been a couple of times."

"Does he have a big dick?" I asked curiously.

"Hell, yes!" Corey laughed. "But for real, at first I was scared as hell."

"How did he approach you? I mean did he pull his dick out and tell you to suck it?"

"Well, actually we were alone in the studio. He was on the phone stroking his dick and motioned for me to come over. He pulled it out and looked at me."

"So he already knew you got down?"

"If he knew I didn't tell him," Corey said.

"So he just assumed you were or he was just making a power move on you?"

"Basically."

"Have y'all done anything else? Have you fucked?"

"Naw, we just have mutual masturbation. Mostly I just suck his dick."

Up until that moment I had never heard anything remotely close about the rapper being gay. Eli was a burgeoning superstar who parlayed his marketability into television and movie credits. He even had a promising clothing line. But every man's got needs and Eli's needed tending to.

However, Corey was a young man struggling to make it in the entertainment game, and he was being taken advantage of. The only thing he knew to do was to go along for the ride.

Being young and naïve in the entertainment industry can be a detriment to a person's spirit and morals. You think you're prepared and ready to dive into this industry head first and take over the world. Yet, there are those already in it who are like sharks waiting for the bait, ready to swallow you up and spit you out. When you come away from them you're not sure what hit you and when it happened.

Corey came to Los Angeles because he had landed a production deal with some top music producers who produced music for artists like Missy, Fantasia, Christina Milian, and Tierra Marie. They signed him to their label to write for some major singers. It was very smart of them, too, because Corey was a wordsmith. The way he fused words intricately together to tell a story musically and so eloquently blew my mind.

Corey was always in the studio either working on his own album or writing for an artist, and I stopped by a few times to hang out. It was fun, but the process was very long. But I also hated going because Corey couldn't be his outgoing self. He usually liked to joke and play around, but in the studio with all the men and testosterone he had to be hard. It was important for his career, and he often told me, "They don't know about me, and I don't want to fuck this up." Whatever he needed to do to keep his secret hidden, he did.

Other than that, hanging with Corey was never a dull moment. He was super fun and energetic. He was always singing, dancing, and loved to party. He got plugged into the Hollywood scene quickly, where the music industry was more happening than the film world because of the many young, urban men who wanted to be a part of Hip Hop. Corey also knew a lot of down low brothers there through his contacts in New York who introduced him around more quickly than I had been when I arrived in Los Angeles.

He moved in with Jimmy and I hung out at their house sometimes on the weekends. Theirs was the place to be; everyone stopped by there. No one bothered to call, they just came by. Someone was always at the house.

One day Corey asked me to ride with him to QD III's house. "Who the hell is that?" I asked. Corey explained to me that he was the son of Quincy Jones and he produced the theme music for *The Fresh Prince of Bel-Air.*

"You know I'm down. Let's go," I said.

QD III lived at least an hour away in a gated community in a remote area of Southern California. His house was huge and barely furnished except for the music studio set up.

He was very cordial and made us feel welcome in his home. We laughed and joked for a while. I told him I was new to Los Angeles and worked in the film industry. He was a cool brother, but he was definitely about his music. After meeting QD III and hanging out in the studio with Corey and him for a few hours listening to beats, I went into the living room and chilled with some other guys who were there and played video games.

The music-making process is long and tedious. It takes hours to get the right beat and the right vocals, along with the tweaking, adjusting, and readjusting of beat sounds. I grew tired and was ready to go, but I hung in there for my boy Corey.

There were late nights when I hung out with Corey visiting Club 7969 on Santa Monica Boulevard. The club hosted a ladies night on Tuesday, a lesbian night, and they didn't allow men inside, especially straight men, unless they were accompanied by a group of women. A lot of celebrity lesbian women went there. We often parked across from the club and waited until the women came out. Corey and I would then make our way over to our friends leaving the club, and stand outside talking, laughing, and watching to see who came out.

A few times, I spotted "Asia," a 1990s female R&B singer who had an amazing voice and a number of widely successful ballads during that time. She started as a background singer, but her powerful voice proved she needed to be up front as a solo artist. Her short body was topped with her huge, curly hair. Asia made a number of love songs, and her claim to fame was her rendition of a sexy remake of a song originally done by an '80s icon.

There was a beautiful television sitcom actress, "Daisy," and her actress best friend, "Lisa." These two women have been friends for a number of years and are always together. Daisy had done a number of successful sitcoms and got her start in a Broadway musical. Her multirange vocals were often showcased on one of the sitcoms she co-starred on. She often plays a fiery and feisty character. After meeting Daisy in person a few times at parties, she quickly won me over with her outgoing personality. She was a down-to-earth woman with a lot of humility.

However, I suspected that her best friend, Lisa, a former singer and popular comedic actress, was at the club only as support for her.

There were also a host of WNBA players, but that was nothing out of the ordinary. It's always been rumored that most of the women in the WNBA are lesbians.

On this particular night, Corey and I stood on the sidewalk laughing with one of our female friends who had just exited the club. A few women had gathered around in small groups and were making their way to their cars. All of a sudden we heard a loud commotion a few feet away from us.

"I don't give a fuck!" a curvaceous woman yelled. "She better bring her ass over her!" Everyone turned around to see who was making such a fuss. It was award-winning female rapper/actress, "Sheena." Apparently, she was upset over something concerning her girlfriend. A few girls were holding Sheena back while she yelled and screamed at her female friend. "Bitch, come here! I said, bitch, come here!" The beautiful, shapely woman sheepishly walked over to the female rapper.

We all were shocked at the rapper/actress's behavior in public. I knew I was. I couldn't believe my ears or my eyes. I was dumbfounded as I listened to Sheena rant and rave while she snatched her girlfriend by her arm and pulled her toward the car. The woman was begging and pleading for her to calm down, but Sheena wouldn't hear of it. All I saw were Sheena's arms flailing through the air, as she towered over her girlfriend and shoved her into the car. The woman didn't bother to fight back but just grabbed the car door and slammed it closed.

This wouldn't be the first or last time I'd see or hear about this female rapper/actress attacking her partners. In the many down low circles I ran, I often heard about Sheena physically assaulting her partners. When she made an appearance on Keenen's show, I couldn't imagine her being as violent as I had seen her that night because she was the nicest and sweetest person. She had a striking presence, but it was really her walk that made her appear as if she was pimping.

Whenever Corey and I went to Club 7969, there was always some drama outside. The lesbians didn't play around when it came to their women. The hard-core girls didn't like their girlfriends being looked at by other women, or men. They surely didn't like them talking with another woman. Lesbians are very protective of one another and don't mind fighting for what is theirs.

It was crazy sitting out there watching the scene some nights because I often saw women I never suspected were lesbians. It's one thing to hear a rumor about someone, but when you actually witness it firsthand it seems surreal.

The women exited the club hugged up with their girlfriends, and there was a lot of lip-locking and ass grabbing. Some women held their girls close to them as they headed toward their cars. A few of the girly girls stood in front of the club giving air kisses. They wore revealing blouses and tight jeans or short skirts with heels. Their faces were painted delicately with makeup, and their hair flowed down their backs. The other girls looked just like men, although they had a feminine appearance when in the public eye. They wore baseball caps, white T-shirts, Dickies jeans, and Converse sneakers. They wore their hair short or braided and wore no makeup. They were posted close by trying to get the attention of the girly girls.

The oddest thing about those nights was the number of cars full of men that lined up outside the club. They would try to spit game to the women as they left the club.

"Yo, what up, baby? Come holla at me. I'm a lesbian too." They would stand in front of their cars smiling at the women. Some grabbed their crotches. "Let me hook you up. Come on, I'll be gentle. Don't you want to be in a threesome with me?" The men deserved an A for effort, but the women never responded.

As much as I enjoyed hanging with Corey I needed to stay focused and low-key. I didn't want to be too out there. I was still navigating and learning the culture. It certainly was not New York. Yet, we would spend long nights hanging around the city visiting friends, clubs, and bars. Corey was an entertaining guide. Being with him was like a drug. As much as I wanted to quit, I couldn't.

His energy matched his personality. His small, short body seemed to possess an unlimited amount of vigor, and he was always on the go. No matter the place or time, he had to be there, and I was more than happy to accompany him. When he entered the room, the party started. Each place we visited was filled with people dancing and drinking well into the night. When he got on the dance floor, his bright smile and little body would do all the latest moves and people gathered around gawking at him. He was an attention getter.

Corey introduced me to the Spot, a social gathering for down low men. The Spot was always at a different person's house. There was no formal invitation—you just rolled through—and Corey seemed to be on the pulse of all the happenings.

"Yo, Terrance, what are you doing tonight? Let's go to this Spot in the Hills." Whenever we went to a Spot, there was always a new hand to shake and a new name to remember. "Yo, Terrance, I want you to meet so and so."

There was an insatiable amount of boys. Lots of delicious and available boys. Everyone was friendly and welcoming. I collected numbers and made many lunch dates.

"Let's get together soon," they said.

Each adventure was alluring and intriguing. It was a high, and Corey was my fix. I needed it.

One evening, Corey took me to meet "Lola." I immediately liked her. She was extremely friendly, yet bold and confident. A slim, attractive young woman, her energy was magnetic. She was the female version of Corey.

Lola was an R&B singer/songwriter who had recently moved to Los Angeles from New York. She was a staple on the New York scene, partying with big name celebrities. Her skills caught the likes of super duper producers DeVante Swing of Jodeci, Stevie J, and Dallas Austin. She'd made a noteworthy album, and the critics were eating her up. Her style was hard-edged rap with a little rock and R&B. Her new single topped the charts and was receiving a lot of airplay. Her album was dropping soon. There was no questioning her being on the come up.

We spent a lot of time at Lola's house listening to music, and it was evident from her collection that she was passionate about her music. We listened to everything from rock to gospel. Lola had eclectic taste.

Lola's home was like Corey's where people, mainly producers, continuously came and went. One night, there was a beautiful woman there, and she and Lola were all over each other, cuddling and kissing. I was taken aback by Lola's indiscretion. Although she made no qualms about her sexuality, I didn't think she was into public displays of affection.

Hanging out with Lola and her girlfriend, "Roslyn," was a treat each time. Roslyn was always the seducer and used her feminine wiles to get men to do whatever she wanted. Men would fall all over themselves trying to get to her.

Roslyn was mixed—black, Latin, and Italian. On any given day, she could put any woman to shame. She had an amazing physique with long, black, voluptuous hair cascading down her back. She was paid a hefty amount to travel to the Middle East and Asia to entertain and party with men who made a special request for her. At one time, she was dating the owner of a professional sports team. Whenever we were with Roslyn, we didn't have to worry about anything because we were given carte blanche to everything.

At parties, Roslyn would often ask Corey and me which man we were interested in. Then she would make her way to him, whisper in his ear, smile, swing her hair, and the man would be trailing behind her. Without fail, men would be game for whatever we had up for the night.

On one particular night, we were hanging out at a Hollywood party. Everyone was high or drunk; there was a constant flow of marijuana, alcohol, ecstasy pills, and cocaine. Whatever your pleasure, it was there. I'd already had several drinks and was feeling really nice.

There was a popular, gorgeous actor/model, "Flynn," who was quite friendly and intoxicated. I wanted him. Corey wanted him. Hell, we *all* wanted him. He had been featured in a few clothing designer's campaigns, and graced the pages of many popular magazines such as *GQ, Details,* and *Vogue.* Flynn starred in a few music videos and then later went on to do a few movies. He wasn't a playboy like most male models turned actors who used their good looks to get women.

When Roslyn saw him, she told us he was an easy target. She strolled seductively over to his side, and each step in her come-fuck-me pumps made her breasts bounce in the red silk dress she was wearing. She leaned in to him with her body and whispered to him. He smiled from ear to ear and glanced toward us. I don't know what she said to him but she had him in tow, and he was ready to partake in a rendezvous he would never forget.

We continued partying all the way to Lola's house. Roslyn was as uninhibited in her sexuality as Lola, so it wasn't a challenge to get our guest to strip off his clothes. We were all dancing in the living room, and Lola and Roslyn had Flynn sandwiched between them with their hands all over his body. Flynn then started to strip. He pulled off his black designer T-shirt and slid out of his blue jeans. He was standing before us in his white Tommy Hilfiger boxer brief underwear that was containing a beast of an erection. His muscles rippled everywhere. Flynn flexed and profiled so we could get a good look at every inch of his body. Then his huge hands slowly reached for the waistband of his underwear and he slowly pulled them down. We cheered him on, chanting, "Take it off, take it off, take it off." He was eager to please. He turned his back to us and bent over, allowing us full view of one of the most beautiful asses I had ever seen. I knew it was going to be on and I was ready to pounce on him as I felt my dick starting to grow beneath my jeans. Without missing a beat, Flynn graced us with a full-frontal view as he licked his pink luscious lips, standing in all his glory with his thick, hard muscle standing at attention between his legs. He was even more beautiful naked.

I quickly removed my clothes. I wanted to be on top of him and enjoy our bodies rubbing together. I looked over and saw Lola and Roslyn caressing each other's breasts and kissing passionately. Flynn started sucking on Roslyn's breasts, his tongue flickering around her nipples before engulfing them. Corey and I got in between them, and I fondled Flynn's massive hardness. His erection felt smooth in my hands as I squeezed and pulled on it. He let out a soft moan as Corey sucked his nipples. Before long, we all were taking turns sucking and kissing some part of Flynn. He enjoyed having his muscular body caressed and sucked by us, and it eventually ended with only the two of us stroking each other to satisfaction.

While I worked on *The Keenen Ivory Wayans Show,* Corey and Lola often stopped by and hung out in the green room since Lola lived around the corner from the studio.

I let them know which celebrity was coming on. Some were friends of Lola or Corey, and I would get passes for them to come on the lot so they could catch up. After a few trips, the security guards just started letting them on the lot without a pass, and I often saw them chilling in the green room like they were guests on the show.

Leon, the actor best known for his role as J. T. in Robert Townsend's *The Five Heartbeats,* was scheduled to be on the show. I had already worked with him on a film, so I was accustomed to his aloofness. He was demanding and constantly went back and forth with the director over his scenes. He never spoke to the crew, not even a good morning or good night, and the crew quickly grew tired of his tirades. Everyone wanted to say something, but no one did, and we all anxiously waited for the last day of shooting.

Lola attempted to start a conversation with Leon. "Hey, Leon, how are you doing?" Lola asked, trying to making small talk.

But there was no response from Leon.

"Maybe he didn't hear me," Lola said. She moved closer toward him. "Excuse me, Leon, I'm Lola. How are you?"

Leon continued to ignore her. He only spoke to his publicist. I knew this wasn't going to go over well.

Lola was fuming, and I gave her the "I told you so" look. Corey was crying, laughing, and rolling on the sofa.

Lola then blurted out to Leon and his publicist, "With all the attitude you're giving, you'd think you'd be more successful in your career." Lola marched over to the table where the food was displayed and picked up a chocolate-covered strawberry. She bit into it and then said, "These kids really think they are fierce up in here. If they don't know, they better find out." She snapped her fingers in the air and rolled her head.

Corey and I fell out laughing. I was so happy that someone finally said something to him about his bad attitude.

My boy Jacob called us one evening because he was invited by a very popular and attractive R&B singer to the El Rey Theatre on Wilshire Boulevard—a theater that turned into a popular gay night club on the weekends.

The crooner, "Galvin," who was once part of a legendary R&B group, and who had experienced a brief stint as a successful solo artist, was allegedly linked romantically to an A-list male actor. Galvin'd asked Jacob to join Janet Jackson and him at the club, where they were going to celebrate one of Janet's dancer's birthday.

Galvin invited Jacob because they'd hit it off while he was making a guest appearance on a popular comedy show, where Jacob was the assistant to one of the stars.

Galvin frequently hung out with Janet, but it appeared to me that it was to garner press that they were dating. It would have helped dispel the rumors about his homosexuality, but I doubt if this particular evening would have helped since they were going to a gay club.

In magazine articles, Galvin emphatically denied rumors that he and the A-list actor were dating, but never said that he was not gay. But then again, a down low man will never admit he's gay. At one point Galvin was said to be engaged, but a wedding never materialized.

It was the best night I ever had in a club. When Corey, Lola, Roslyn, Jacob, his boyfriend, and I arrived, we were immediately whisked inside with Janet, Galvin, and her entourage. We were laughing, drinking, and acting a fool up in the V.I.P. section. We all were dancing and grinding on one another and I made sure to grind up on the R&B singer. He was a smooth dancer. His hips gyrated perfectly to the beat. He certainly didn't mind me thrusting on his svelte ass. It was just as hard as the muscles all over his body. Galvin even backed it up a few times, grinding on my crotch. Janet was more subdued and laughed at our antics, but she definitely was enjoying herself. They didn't stay too long, though, because Galvin got wasted and started throwing up. They had to carry him out of the club because he couldn't walk on his own.

Fun times like these in Los Angeles were many. No matter what I was going through or dealing with, the parties, drugs, sex, and the inordinate amount of freedom made me feel like I hadn't a care in the world. Especially when I partied and mingled with the stars. Everything there is done over the top. Everyone caters to their every whim, need, and desire. So when I was with them, I felt a sense of entitlement, which can be very dangerous to someone who doesn't know how to handle pressure, fame, and success. Being around Lola, I sometimes felt that she was becoming consumed by the fame.

She would often say to us, "I'm going to be the first lesbian R&B singer. Y'all think I'm joking, but watch me. I'm going to come out and shock the world. All this prissy girly stuff they got me doing, it ain't me." The producers laughed half-heartedly, and didn't take her seriously.

As much as Lola wanted to be a trailblazer and open doors for other gay artists, she was still part of a machine. Lola had to do what the label told her to do. She was still at their mercy and on their dollar. In videos and on album covers, her look was softened with dramatic makeup, luxurious hair, and seductive clothing. It was like night and day seeing her transformation. In the public, Lola was the beautiful girl next door, but behind closed doors she would take off the girly clothes, gaudy makeup, and fluffy wigs. She liked to lounge in jeans and sweats. She preferred to be rough, edgy, and hard.

On another one of our excursions, Corey introduced me to Ms. Jamaica JaToi. Everyone in Los Angeles seemed to know of him except me.

Ms. Jamaica is one of Hollywood's top drag queens. He dresses and performs as a woman for a living and looks amazing. He is a tall, wiry, light-skinned man with flawless skin. His face is soft and delicate even without makeup, and his long, curly, jet-black hair is kept tied in a ponytail. Very feminine, his mannerisms are those of a woman. His hands with his long fingernails hang daintily in the air. His walk isn't hard like a man's but soft, as if he is gliding across the room.

He appeared in *Bad Boys II* and *Baby Boy* as the over-the-top gay hair stylist, but his most animated appearance was on BET's, *Oh Drama!* The hosts loved that he spoke candidly about his sexuality and the many down low married thugs and gang-banging men he often encountered. He was invited back by the show's producers to discuss a special episode on down low men.

I had my apprehensions about drag queens. My first introduction to them was the ones Aunt Lisa hung out with when I was a child. I didn't like being around them, and I certainly didn't understand a man's desire to dress like a woman. I couldn't imagine putting on a dress and makeup and acting like a woman. I had no desire to be a woman, or act like one; if I wanted to be with a woman, then I would get a real woman, not some man in a dress. It seemed more unnatural than my down low behavior.

Initially, I was nervous around Jamaica. I was angry with Corey for bringing me to his house. Corey had odd friends, but this took the cake. I was afraid to find out how he met Jamaica.

But Jamaica was a lively character, and his mouth never stopped running. After a while I forgot he was a drag queen. He felt it his duty to let me know all the ins and outs about the men of Los Angeles. He said to me, "Don't let these L.A. punks fool you. These thugs love dick just as much as you do. They ain't fooling anybody. Trust Ms. Jamaica, because I know."

And I took his word for it. Jamaica knew what he was talking about. I discovered that Jamaica loved men, and the men loved him, too. I even loved Jamaica. It was impossible not to; he was infectious. He always had groups of young hoods sitting around, getting high and eating tacos in his house. The sight of these men made me do a double take. These thugs had girls at home and rode with the hardest crews in their neighborhoods.

They laughed and smiled. Their hard edge was gone. There was no need to boast. They had no problem hugging Jamaica and giving him a kiss. They had no problem touching one another, either, and yet no one knew they liked to get down with men. That blew my mind. But all in all, they were cool brothers. They offered to show me around the city and take me to a few clubs. Their hospitality was genuine.

"If you Jamaica's people, then you our peoples too," they told me. These brothers were the epitome of what rappers rhymed about— hard-core thugs, life on the streets, drug dealers, with an abundance of women, and body counts. These men lived that life. They walked the walk and talked the talk.

But despite our different backgrounds, we had something in common—we all were down low brothers.

Everything was confirmed for me. These brothers looked and acted like I did for the public, but behind closed doors we were comfortable and free to be with one another. We all were of the same cloth. We had shared experiences as it related to our sexuality. We were together in knowing we could not be open about who we shared our beds with. We couldn't speak candidly about having feelings for another man.

Even as we chilled in the house listening to rap music, nodding our heads and rhyming the words, we knew we could never stand up and be who we truly were. None of us could. We were what rappers hated—faggots, booty bandits, homos. *But then, how could you make a rhyme dissing gays when it's something that you are?* I wondered about these rappers who shared my secret of being on the down low. I also pondered how *we* could recite their hate-filled lyrics knowing they were talking about us? We were burdened with the weight of hiding our secret, and none of us wanted to carry it.

18. WHERE THE PARTY AT?

THE SPOT WAS FULL of brothers—tall, short, dark, light, slim, husky, muscular—whatever piqued your interest it was there. The living room and dining room were packed. As we gradually made our way to the kitchen where the drinks were, I realized I didn't recognize anyone. It was unusual to not recognize anyone at a down low party. Because I mainly partied with film and television people, there was always a familiar face in the crowd. Corey traveled in a different circle than I. Many of the men he partied with were from the music industry, and most of them worked at night. In the studio for endless hours, they slept during the day and only socialized with one another. If they weren't in the studio then they were attending an album release party or a showcase. In the TV and film world, we worked during the day and attended film premieres and wrap parties in the evening. Our worlds rarely crossed paths.

Corey introduced me to a few brothers who were songwriters, singers, producers, and record label executives. They worked with some of the biggest names in the industry from Jay-Z, Tyrese, and R. Kelly to Toni Braxton, Whitney Houston, and Mariah Carey. I recognized them from their music and Hip Hop magazines I read.

While I was checking out the scene, a guy came over and talked with me, and we discussed the industry and what we did. Two guys I met were music producers and a third was a songwriter. They were trying to talk game, but I wasn't really feeling it. I was trying to figure out my environment and what was going on.

As it got later, the crowd grew smaller in size. I went to the bathroom and when I came out a crowd was gathered in the living room watching television. I walked over to see what was on. To my surprise everyone was watching a porn movie. "What the hell?!" I turned away. I was ready to go.

It brought back memories of when I was a teenager and my high school guidance counselor invited a few of my male classmates to his house. We would sit in his basement and watch porn movies and flip through his collection of porn magazines. I knew it was wrong, but I was hanging with the boys. I was in the "in" crowd.

I tried to turn away from the television but my eyes were glued to the images of the naked men. Their dark bodies filled my lustful, teenage mind. Watching their hard penises enter a woman turned me on. I was embarrassed to be around the other boys when I got an erection. Even though we all were transfixed on the television and having the same physical response, I thought they would find out I was more interested in watching the man than the woman.

Here I was, yet again, with a group of men watching a porn movie starring black men and women. I didn't want them to see me get aroused.

I went into the kitchen to see if Corey was there, but he wasn't. The guy whose house we were in came over to me. "You want something to drink?"

"Naw, I'm cool."

"You want to hit the blunt?" he asked as he pulled out a Phillies Blunt.

"Naw, I'm straight."

I went upstairs to look for Corey. It seemed like everyone was up there. Weed smoke was everywhere, and I saw a few brothers popping pills. The hallway was dimly lit so I had to readjust my eyes to find my way. I saw a group of men walking from room to room.

I heard some grunts coming from one of the bedrooms. As I got closer, the grunts grew louder and louder. I entered the bedroom, which was void of any furniture. The moonlight crept inside the window, providing enough light for me to see. In the middle of the room was a very attractive brother who was bent over with his pants at his ankles while another brother fucked him from behind. He wasn't taking gentle strokes, either, but pounding him while the guy on the receiving end was practically screaming from pain. There were three other men who were putting condoms on their dicks, waiting for their turn. One of the guys was the music producer I had talked with downstairs earlier. He was stroking his dick to full erection. The attractive producer getting fucked had been featured in Hip Hop magazines and produced music for rap's elite. I was stunned. Everyone looked on as if it was nothing. I tried to play it cool, but I was nervous. At first I couldn't move. My eyes wouldn't leave the erotic scene happening in real time right in front of me. Before my body could respond and get turned on, I walked out of the room, but ran into a tall, naked, chocolate-colored, big-dick brother.

I had heard of parties like this before, but I had never experienced one firsthand. A lot of down low men don't go to gay clubs and don't socialize within the gay community. They need a place where they can meet other brothers or have discreet sex without worries.

When I finally found Corey I was heated.

"What the fuck?" I asked. "Why didn't you tell me we were coming here?"

"Just chill," he said, pulling me to the side. "I knew you wouldn't come if I had told you the truth."

I looked around and saw other guys kissing and fondling one another. Men had their dicks out stroking themselves. He was right. These brothers were comfortable and had no inhibitions. Most of them looked like L.A. thugs. They had on their fitted caps, T-shirts, Dickies pants, sneakers, and Timberland boots.

The down low parties I had already attended were more subdued. The music industry didn't seem to have any inhibitions; it was like they were living out the music they created.

"Man, Corey, I didn't come here for this. I thought we were just coming to a party to hang out."

"It's all good. Just try to relax and enjoy it. You don't have to do anything."

"You damn skippy I ain't doing shit," I said. "As a matter of fact, I'm ready to bounce."

"Come on, T-man, don't bug out on me."

"I ain't bugging out. I just don't feel comfortable."

"That's cool. I understand. But I'm not ready to go. If you want to leave, you can. I can get a ride home." I couldn't believe it. But then again, I knew Corey partied hard.

The host of the party asked me to come into the kitchen. He noticed that I looked upset and offered me a drink. This time I accepted. I needed something to calm me down, and downed a glass of Bacardi. He kept pouring, and the more he poured, the more I drank. I was drinking it like water. I could no longer taste the alcohol.

I walked out of the kitchen pissed because I still hadn't caught a buzz. As I made my way to the front door, a fine brother came in. Goodness, he was sexy. His T-shirt revealed a tight body filled with tattoos. He had the prettiest brown eyes I'd ever seen and a glide in his step.

We looked at one another and nodded what's up. He smiled and I smiled back. I went outside to my car but couldn't get him out of my head, so I turned back.

He saw me when I came back in and walked over and introduced himself. "J.P." We shook hands but refused to let go. Our fingers intertwined, lingering long after the introductions.

Corey saw me and said, "I thought you were leaving." I smiled.

J.P. and I found a spot in one of the rooms. We stood against the wall, staring at each other. We were smitten.

"I was really about to leave until I saw you," I said, grinning.

"I'm glad you came back," he replied.

Damn, he is fine. What the hell is he doing in here? I asked myself.

Then he tried to kiss me, but I stopped him.

"Yo, I'm not here for that," I said, stepping back. "Besides, I don't think we should be showcasing for an audience." I pointed toward a group of men staring at us.

We left and talked by my car for what seemed like the entire night. As we sat on the hood of my car, more men arrived at the party, but I couldn't help staring into his golden brown eyes. He had the sexiest gaze. When he spoke, it was like his eyes were speaking their own language, and all I heard was sex. My heart was racing. My body was aching to get him home with me.

"You a sexy nigga," he said and smiled. "I love tall dudes, and you're good-looking, too."

"Aight. You ain't too bad yourself," I said. "Look, I'm really feeling you, but I ain't going back inside. You want to come to my spot?"

"Man, I wish I could but I can't. I generally work nights, but tonight I got off early. When I get off early, I party before getting home to my girl and three kids. It's already late, so I can't chance it. You live too far and I wouldn't make it home in time. I ain't trying to hear her mouth."

I was glad he only had a girlfriend. It was an in for me. I didn't want to cross the boundaries of being with a married man. I couldn't consciously be with a man who had made vows before God to love and honor his wife.

"Oh, aight. I feel you on that." I was disappointed. I really wanted him to come home with me.

We exchanged numbers, and a few days later he called. We hooked up for sex quite a number of times. We didn't get to hang out much, though, because of his family, and I was not going to Compton.

J.P. would leave work early and we would meet at the Bob's Big Boy restaurant on Wilshire Avenue near my house, sometimes at three or four in the morning.

After our late-night talks at the restaurant, we would go to my house and have sex, which was generally oral sex and mutual masturbation. I loved watching him walk around my house naked. His penis always seemed to stay semi-erect, as if he was waiting for the opportunity for me to touch him and get him started.

He seemed oblivious to his nakedness as sauntered into the kitchen to get us cold drinks, his tattooed body rippling with muscles. He was completely comfortable without any clothes on, and we'd end up talking for hours with our bodies exposed.

Over a period of four months, we got to know one another well, and I started to develop real feelings for him.

J.P. opened up and confided to me about his growing up in Compton. His father abandoned the family when he was a kid. He didn't want to end up like his father, and decided he wanted to be there for his kids when his girl got pregnant. He had been working for the city of Los Angeles for nearly ten years, and dabbled in music only because his boy was a producer. He always knew he liked guys, but didn't start to act on his feelings until recently.

"It's real cool talking with you," he said. "I never told anybody none of this. I can't talk to my boys because they wouldn't understand. I definitely can't say anything to my girl. It just stays bottled up in me."

I could tell he was frustrated. I was frustrated. It's hard to keep your sexuality a secret when society disapproves of you.

J.P. found a friend in me. He could open up and share his innermost struggles. I knew his desires because they were mine. I listened to him. I didn't judge him, and that's what all men, gay or straight, seek—for someone to listen and not judge us. To allow us to say what we have to say and get it off our chests.

When we hurt we want to be able to let down our guard and be vulnerable, but we can't. We're told to suck it up, to be strong, to be a man. There is no outlet for us to be emotional, and all those feelings—rage, anger, hurt, pain, bitterness, and disappointment—stay bottled up inside us.

Many times when I was confused and didn't know what to do, I simply wanted a hug. I just wanted to be in someone's arms to let me know it would be okay. Women support one another emotionally and physically. They comfort one another. Women can cry and embrace one another. However, we as men are not allowed to be emotional, let alone physical with one another. If we hug, kiss one another on the cheek, or show any type of physical comfort to a man, society makes us think it's something sexual, when in actuality it has nothing to do with sex. As men, we sometimes need to let go of the stress and anger we feel on a day-to-day basis. Some men are unable to manage their pain or hurt and resort to violence and abuse.

That's why J.P. would leave work early, lie in my bed as we caressed and kissed, and let me into his world. He didn't have to be anything but who he was with me. He, like so many down low men, only wanted the comfort of being with another human being sharing an emotional experience. He felt he had the weight of the world on his shoulders, and I helped relieve him of the load, if only for a few hours.

After four months the sex ended, however, because J.P. confessed that his girlfriend was actually his wife.

"J.P., why are you wearing a wedding ring? Are you married?" I asked one day. He usually never wore a ring, and it was the first time I'd noticed it. We were inside my apartment and he was taking off his clothes. I had just come from the kitchen and saw something shining on his hand. I was hoping he would tell me he wasn't married, but deep inside I knew the answer.

"Yeah . . . I'm married."

"Why didn't you tell me?"

"Because we're not technically married. We didn't have a wedding. She's been my girl since high school, so we say we're married because we've been together for so long."

He wasn't telling the truth. Why was he wearing a ring?

I was not comfortable having sex with a married man. He'd made a vow to love, honor, and cherish his wife. Morally or spiritually, I couldn't come between those vows. Although it happens a lot in the down low world, I do know men and women who will not cross the boundaries of marriage. It's about principles and their own moral character.

However, it was okay to sleep with men who had girlfriends. There was no commitment on his behalf to be faithful to her. He hadn't taken an oath. If he wanted to leave her, he could. It made sense to me then. I justified it with my own twisted way of thinking, and many down low men think the same way. Technically, as long as the man is not married, he's available.

Once I discovered he was married, I knew J.P. and I would never be serious. I desired a serious relationship. Hanging with Marcus and Gary made me think it was possible, and I wanted what they had. I wanted someone to call my own.

J.P. didn't think he was doing anything wrong. I did. "What do we have to lose?" he asked me. He said that he wasn't sleeping with other men and that I knew where he was at night.

"At least you don't have to worry about me being with somebody else. I ain't fucking no other woman, and you're the only man I'm with," J.P. said.

As much as I tried to convince him that he was cheating on his wife, and that it was something I didn't want to be a part of, he was still willing to live the lie. I couldn't. It said a lot about his character. If he'd lie, cheat, and steal from someone he loved, he'd do it to me.

19. WHO CAN I RUN TO?

MY FRIEND EDWIN, who I met while I was working for Keenen, had a lead for a job. He was working as an assistant to Minnie, a producer/talent manager.

Minnie was working with a top rapper, "Craig," who was part of a successful rap group that changed the dynamics of Hip Hop with their philosophical rhymes over hard-core beats. Craig garnered attention because of his rugged good looks that made him a standout in the group. Though the group never disbanded and all the members produced solo albums and were respected in their own rights, Craig's solo venture propelled him into chart-topping success.

I had previously worked with Minnie on a television show where she served as a producer. She was a thorough sister—very elegant, poised, and a Hollywood player. She was able to make her entrée into the entertainment industry using her powerful wit and knowledge. Not one to mince words, Minnie was direct and stern with her directives. She was straight business on the set.

I liked her and she garnered my respect because I knew how the entertainment business could be, especially for a black woman. Although it was rare to see black men in power, it was even rarer to see a woman of color making things happen. It was not common to see a sister producing a film or television project.

Minnie managed to carve a little niche for herself as a power player.

She was able to get Craig a lead in a movie that she was involved in.

Despite Craig's being married, he and Minnie struck up a sexual relationship, a no-no when conducting business. Never, ever jeopardize your business relationship by sleeping with your client. It can get really ugly and salty once emotions and feelings are involved.

Minnie decided to play that game with Craig. He traveled from his home in New York to Los Angeles frequently. During the filming, it was undeniable they were in a sexual relationship. She would go above and beyond making sure he was well taken care of on set. She catered to Craig, and he let her. He knew he could get anything he wanted now that they were sleeping together.

The odd differences between them, though, were obvious. Minnie was poised and confident and she held a respected position at an entertainment company. Craig was a weed-smoking, high-energy rapper. He also had a family and his devotion was first and foremost to them.

Minnie developed deep, strong feelings for Craig, but she had suspicions about him. Minnie's womanly instincts kicked in and she felt there was something that was just not right. She couldn't quite put her finger on it, but something was causing her to question his manhood. There had been some grumbling about the rapper's sordid past, about him being bisexual. She asked my friend Edwin if he could help her out.

I never would have suspected the rapper of being bisexual or gay, but I knew a good friend of his was gay. I'd partied and seen him with a number of my down low friends on many occasions.

Instead of letting it go, Minnie wanted to know for sure if her instincts were accurate. She called Edwin and encouraged him to pursue a position on the film. Edwin was a sexy, young, gay guy and he had no qualms about people knowing about his sexuality. Minnie befriended him because he was very talented as a researcher and associate producer, but mainly because he had slept with a number of Hollywood celebrities.

Minnie hoped that if he got the job on the film, Edwin would pursue Craig to see if he would bite. She wanted Edwin to really put on the charm and seduce her man.

I knew it would be difficult for Edwin to pull it off for a number of reasons. Going by my instincts, I could tell that the rapper was probably only interested in guys similar to his down low style, rugged thug types, who probably smoked a lot of weed, who were heavily into Hip Hop, and had a girl on the side. Edwin didn't fit into any of these categories. He was too soft and obviously feminine.

Edwin went for the job, but didn't get it. Minnie did get an answer of sorts. She didn't have any concrete proof, but she followed her instincts and stopped sleeping with the rapper. Both their personal and business relationship dissolved shortly thereafter, but he made a few more critically acclaimed rap albums and landed a few guest-starring roles on various television dramas.

Edwin connected me to one of his boys. He hooked me up with a job working on *Russell Simmons' Def Comedy Jam*. They were taping in Los Angeles for a week, and I was a talent assistant. I didn't mind the more menial position because I knew it would mean more opportunities to meet other blacks in the business. And I would get to see the show for free.

I had a blast working on *Def Comedy Jam* with famed director Stan Latham, the father of beloved actress Sanaa Latham. The auditorium was packed with people. Comedians from all across the country were in town to tape segments for the show; it was a family reunion for them. Those who had not seen each other in months or years were reunited and greeted each other with big laughs and warm hugs. During the rehearsals, the comedians who were observing and waiting for their spot would be in the audience telling jokes and poking fun at one another. There was never a dull moment. They really made it a fun environment.

Part of my job was getting them ready for rehearsals. Joe Clair, Sommore, and Jamie Foxx were especially nice and kept me laughing.

Sommore, however, was the one I clung to the most. She had a warm spirit that made her easy to approach. She reminded me of the sexy and attractive distant cousin you didn't know you had who lived way down south. She has the most beautiful glowing skin and an amazing body. Goodness! Sommore's low cleavage showcased some of the juiciest breasts, her jeans fit like a glove, and she smelled like fresh flowers. She didn't have a diva attitude, and with a permanent smile on her radiant face, she always seemed to be having a good time. She was the party, but she also said what was on her mind.

While we were backstage watching the comedians check in and go to their dressing rooms, Sommore would comment on each one. "I can't stand her, she think she's all that." But when the comedienne got closer, Sommore was friendly. "Hey, girl. It's been so long. What you been up to?" Her facial expressions were priceless. The way her eyebrow would rise and her lips would curl, she'd have all of us rolling around in laughter.

There was one fine brother from Chicago. My goodness he was fine. When he came through the door, I was like *Sweet Jesus!* Even Sommore did a double take. We all stood there in silence staring at him. Then Sommore just blurted out, "Damn, he is fine. Baby, my clitoris just jumped." She said what was on her mind and pretty much what the rest of us were thinking too.

Sommore made her way over to him and introduced herself. Within a few minutes, she came back to the group with all the details on him, and let us all know she was going to have him that night. I didn't doubt for a minute that she wouldn't.

Many times I would have to go to the dressing rooms and inform the comedians they were needed for rehearsals. Walking into many of their dressing rooms, I saw quite a bit more than I probably should have. Often the men would be changing clothes and felt very comfortable walking around in their underwear.

A now-popular comic on the comedy circuit, "Ian" travels from city to city performing his raunchy, sarcastic stand-up, and sells out the venues whenever he performs. He's been widely hailed as one of the premier black comics to hit the circuit.

Ian asked me to help him find some new underwear as his naked, chocolate-colored body rushed feverishly around the room. He definitely was not penis shy. I don't think he even noticed he was naked.

"Where the fuck is my bag?" he said out loud to no one in particular. I just stood there watching him go from one end of the room to the other. I didn't want to bump into him or for my hands to accidentally touch something they shouldn't have. He finally found his duffel bag and put on another outfit.

He was trying to change quickly because he was in the middle of rehearsal. He had to change clothes because the stage lights were reflecting through his white jogging suit and the audience would have been able to see everything.

I'm sure the situation would have probably been different if I were flamboyantly gay. He wouldn't have been too comfortable disrobing in front of me if he suspected anything. But when you look and act like a regular brother, you can pass for straight in any environment.

Being on the down low or down low gay creates the illusion you are straight. It's not that we are any different from any other heterosexual man. We want the best out of life—good homes, a quality education, the ability to earn money, and to have love. The only difference between heterosexual men and down low men is that we like sleeping with the same sex. But we are ostracized and made to feel different. To avoid being ridiculed or becoming victims of hate crimes, it's imperative that we make everyone believe we are just like them. We are straight men, living regular lives.

When I finished working on the show, I got a call from one my fraternity brothers, Dirk. He was on the down low, but didn't work in entertainment. He was coming to town from Tennessee and wanted to hang out when he arrived.

I had not seen Dirk in years. He was always busy with work, church, the fraternity, and his girlfriend. When he told me he was coming to Los Angeles alone, I knew he wanted to party and to meet some of my contacts.

When Dirk got to the city, he was ready to start partying. He was like a kid in a candy store. He told me he was itching to hook up with a guy because it had been a while. His girl lived with him and he couldn't really get out too often.

I understood his situation. He often expressed to me how he couldn't let anyone know about his sexuality. He lived in the south where they hated gays. "Man, I'm in the Bible Belt," he'd say. "But although they hate gays down here, there is still a large down low community."

The down low men in the south have to be more discreet. Their circles are even more close-knit than in any other part of the country. They wouldn't dare be seen publicly with a gay person, let alone be seen in a gay club. Dirk often told me about the down low parties he attended in Tennessee. "Man, it's usually church brothers, fraternity men, and businessmen." In the darkness of the night, they would sneak off to someone's house and draw the blinds. "The brothers down there are real freaks. They love sucking dick and getting fucked," Dirk told me.

I called up my friend, Corey, to ask if he knew of any parties happening over the weekend. He told me a prominent music producer he knew was giving a party. Corey was not going because he had to go to the studio, but he provided me with the address and said it wouldn't be a problem to get in. He said he would call his boy to let him know we were coming. I asked him if it was going to be a "jump off" party, and he told me it would probably turn into one.

I was very private about my life already, so for me to be at a jump off party was not in my character. These parties are often cover ups for regular get-togethers. They are invite-only and after a few hours of socializing, drinking, and drugs, they become sex parties. The men then convene in a secluded part of the house and participate in an orgy.

Certain down low brothers look down on these events. I traveled in a circle of brothers who would have severed their friendship with me if they'd found out I attended these parties. They considered jump offs crude and tasteless places for engaging in sex publicly and not places for real down low men. One of our biggest fears is to be spotted at one of these events and our business getting out in the streets. My friends prided themselves on making their gatherings more social places for down low men to meet. By attending a jump off party, you risked being found out because sometimes a gay brother would be invited to the event and down low men do not want anyone, especially gay men and women, to find out about their sexuality. Down low men feel gay men are always trying to spy on them and find out their secret so they can talk about them later. And if you engage in open sex, it gives gay men concrete evidence. But opposed to these jump offs, a social event like the regular down low parties with groups of men could be seen as socializing or networking.

We often separated ourselves from openly gay brothers, or those who were suspect. They didn't have anything to lose. Everyone knew they were gay. They were always on the hunt to out down low brothers. They made it their mission to find out who might be hiding because it made them feel like they were in the know and that they had something in common with the down low brother. Once they uncovered the secret, they didn't mind sharing this information with anyone who would listen, especially women.

I let Dirk know I was uncomfortable going to jump off parties since they were not my style. "Come on, Terrance. Now you a saint all of a sudden? You've done your dirt, let me have some fun." Dirk got me. He was right. I had had my share of dirt. There were many skeletons in my closet. But I still had some standards.

"You know I don't get out here too often, and when was the last time we hung out? You're not going to leave me hanging out here trying to find my way around are you? And you know it's going to be some fine-ass brothers up in there. You know you're curious," Dirk jibbed.

Of course I was curious. Of course I knew some fine brothers would be there. But the more I kept telling him I was not interested, the more he pushed. I offered to give him the address and directions to the party. I even offered to drop him off and pick him up. But he insisted I join him.

"Look, Dirk. We're going, but I ain't staying long," I finally said. "And we need to stop by the liquor store. I want to be good and fucked up before I walk in there." I needed to be relaxed and not too uptight in that environment.

When we arrived, the party was jumping. A fleet of BMWs, Mercedeses, Acuras, and SUVs were lined up along the driveway and street. A strong odor of weed hit us as we passed a few cars with black-tinted windows. Some men were turning up bottles in brown paper bags, sucking out the last few remnants of liquor. Ahead of us, I could see a group of men bopping as they walked through the door in their sagging jeans, sneakers, and fresh haircuts. It was a nice big house with a gated entrance that sat in the hills of Sherman Oaks.

The guy at the door asked us our names. I stepped back—was he serious?—but the big, black, buffed man didn't smile or flinch. I was ready to leave, but Dirk was drunk and antsy.

When we walked in, there were men parked from one end of the house to the other. The tri-level house was beautiful. The main level of the house was immaculately clean with white furniture and glass table tops. The room glistened from the moonlight that pierced the window. Two bedrooms and a bathroom were adjacent to the living room. The sitting room was complete with black leather furniture and musical equipment. A glass sliding door led to the backyard and a beautiful swimming pool.

The sound system in the house was amazing. The Bose speakers made everything vibrate.

Dirk and I made our way through the house and finally outside to the pool. A lot of brothers were sitting around it. I recognized a few of the guys from the last party I'd been to with Corey, and we nodded what up to each other. I wanted to check out the rest of the house before I got into a conversation with anyone.

We went back inside to the den area where the drinks and food were and got something to drink. I needed another one. The liquor we had drunk on the way did nothing for me. My nervousness and anxiety prevented me from getting high. Dirk, on the other hand, was quite intoxicated and was already flirting with some of the men.

I kept looking at my watch. Time stood still. Every time I looked at it only a minute or two had passed. I knew it was going to be a long night. I needed to come up with a way to get out of there before anything happened. But before I could come up with a fully devised plan, Dirk was off and missing. I turned around and he was gone.

At first I damn near panicked. *Where the hell did he run off to?* I thought. I didn't like being in environments alone where I didn't know anyone. It made me very uncomfortable. I looked around the room, but I didn't see him. There were too many men in the room. I walked around looking for him, damn near knocking some brothers over.

I then looked in the kitchen and saw a familiar face. At first I didn't believe who I was seeing. I stopped and stared at the lean, dark-skinned brother with the shiny, bald head. His perfectly trimmed goatee gave him a youthful appearance as I watched him laughing and rummaging through the refrigerator.

He was the music producer on one of the shows on which I'd worked, but I never suspected him of being gay or down low. We spoke on the set, but we never got into each other's personal lives.

I walked toward "Lenny," but before I could reach him, he rushed through the crowd.

"What the hell are you doing in my house?" He laughed.

"This is you? Hell, naw!" I laughed. We both were in shock.

"Man, I give this party every year around this time. It's just a little something-something to get the brothers together for a little release."

"I feel you on that. But I didn't even know you got down with guys," I said.

"Shit. I didn't suspect you, either. If I would have known I would have given you an invite. When Corey gave me your name I knew it sounded familiar.

"You want something to drink?" Lenny asked as we walked to the kitchen.

"Sure, I can use something else."

After we got our drinks, Lenny took me on a tour of the house. It was difficult navigating through the crowd, so most of the time he just stood and pointed toward something, explaining to me what it was.

Lenny had lots of plaques and awards throughout the house. I discovered that he was an accomplished musician, producer, and songwriter. He was also part of one of the most influential musical disco groups during the 1970s. What I found most interesting was that he'd joined the band while he was only a teenager. Their music is often heard today in clubs, homes, and movies. One of their songs is known as the best-selling single on Warner Records. An up-and-coming Luther Vandross even blessed their albums with his vocal ability. One of the first rap groups in Hip Hop sampled one of the band's hit singles, and the rap song became an international hit. The song is considered to be responsible for launching the rap/Hip Hop musical format. Lenny eventually branched out and wrote and produced music for a host of renowned R&B superstars like Whitney Houston, Patti LaBelle, and Chaka Khan. He even released a few of his own solo albums.

Lenny then took me to the bottom level of the house. There were a few attractive guys in the bedroom changing into swim trunks. In the background, playing on the television was a porn movie. It brought back memories once again.

Guys walked around the room butt naked with their perfectly sculpted asses and swinging dicks. It was a beautiful sight seeing these naked, well-toned bodies.

Another group of brothers were gathered in the guest bathroom smoking weed. I didn't think it was possible to fit more than four grown men in an average-size bathroom, but when weed is involved, brothers make room.

This level of the house was definitely the jump off area. Someone could have easily slipped down there, got their groove on, and slipped back into the party upstairs without being missed.

We went back to the main level and out to the pool area. The pool was still empty and most of the men were standing around or sitting by it with their drinks.

Lenny introduced me to a few of his friends. Many of them were musicians, producers, and songwriters as well. Some of these brothers were definitely my type—rugged, sexy, and eye-catching, everything to evoke in me a fanciful image of a wonderful, romp-filled evening of unending sex. I was surrounded by them. They were very masculine and if you had seen them on the streets or in the workplace, you would never suspect they liked men. A woman would have lost her mind in that house. I lost mine.

Lenny left me outside by the pool as he had to tend to more guests in the house. He told me to make sure to find him before I left because he wanted for us to exchange phone numbers.

I glanced around the pool area to see if Dirk was out there, but he wasn't. I went into the house to see if I could find him. As I surveyed the living room, brother's heads were bobbing to the rap beats that filtered through the air. Some nodded across the room at one another scoping one another out. I made my way to the bar, which seemed to be always replenished with bottles of vodka, Bacardi, gin, and champagne.

I finally went back to the part of the house I knew was probably the jump off area. I was extremely nervous, and my heart started to beat faster. It seemed like everyone was staring at me. My anxiety set in. I took a few deep breaths and forced myself to walk down the stairs.

I first looked in the bathroom to see if Dirk was smoking weed with the men in there. The room was very smoky. They had at least four or five blunts going at one time. Dirk was not in there.

I looked in the bedroom for him. The lights had dimmed, and there were men standing around watching the porno in the background. A few others were still walking around naked. Since no one was swimming, I wondered if people were really changing into swim trunks or using it as an excuse to get naked. I think my naïveté got the best of me. However, Dirk was not in this room either.

I went upstairs and got myself another drink. It seemed no matter where I turned men were gazing at each other. They were engrossed in conversations on the sofa, in the corners, anywhere they could find privacy. Each trying to find out if they were single and if they could exchange phone numbers to get together for a date.

I was mad as hell at Dirk. I wanted to kill him. It was totally out of character for him to walk off and not say anything. He was very responsible. Whenever he visited me in Los Angeles and he went out on a date with a guy, he would call to let me know his whereabouts. In Tennessee, he was very active with the local chapter of the fraternity. They depended on him to take care of a lot of their personal business.

I was proud of Dirk. He'd struggled through college, but managed to graduate and attend graduate school, earning his master's degree. He had recently had his home built and was driving a $50,000 car. He was someone who, if you needed anything, was there in a heartbeat. He didn't ask any questions. I was waiting for the day he would call to tell me that he and his girlfriend were getting married. They were a gorgeous couple and had many friends.

I did feel sorry for him at times. He would call me near tears, talking about his inner turmoil over his sexuality. He loved his girlfriend, but Dirk had known all his life that he liked men. He couldn't get enough of fulfilling his sexual urges. As much as he liked sex with his girl, he loved it just the same with men.

But Dirk's family in Tennessee was very religious and well connected in the community. He didn't want to bring any shame to them, so he hid his desires for men. He admired his father, who was a big businessman in the area. Dirk knew his father would be disappointed if he discovered his son was gay.

As I stood at the party fuming over Dirk's disappearing act, a thought entered my head. I knew that at any moment and as soon as everyone was comfortable and intoxicated, things were going to get freaky, especially downstairs. It was going to get filled quickly with more naked, hard bodies.

"You probably need to release some tension yourself." Lenny laughed. "You're all tense and pensive. You're too good-looking to have your face scrunched up like that."

"Man, I'm just worried about Dirk."

"All these fine-ass brothers and you worried about your boy?" Lenny grabbed me by the hand. "Come here. I want you to meet someone. He's been asking me about you."

Lenny led me over to "Ace," a chocolate dark-skinned brother with a short Caesar haircut. His tall, thin frame was draped with Hip Hop gear and a thick platinum chain. He smiled when Lenny handed me over to him.

As much as I didn't want to be there, meeting Ace turned out to be the best part of the night. I didn't think about Dirk because Ace kept me laughing with his jokes. He was very easy to talk with and loved the liquor. He made at least four trips to the bar. His tolerance level for straight vodka had me beat by a long shot. I could drink, but Ace was putting me under the table. We talked for a little while and exchanged numbers.

Ace would become one of my best bed partners, but the demands of him being in the studio, on the road, and maintaining his girl didn't give us much time to spend together. But we would talk endlessly on the phone. He would play his beats for me over the phone asking what I thought. He'd be excited like a kid at Christmas when he felt he created the perfect beat. "Yo, Terrance, you sleep?" he would ask, calling from the studio. It was usually three or four in the morning. Before I could reply, he would yell, "Listen to this. This shit is hot!" I think Ace appreciated the fact I would awake from my slumber and engage him for those moments. He was creating and he wanted me to be a part of his life.

After Ace and I exchanged numbers at the party and his alcohol was starting to take effect, Dirk resurfaced smiling from ear to ear like a Cheshire cat. He tried to hug me as if nothing happened, and before he could say anything I just cut him off. He knew he fucked up. His smile disappeared. He tried to lighten the mood, but I wasn't interested in what he wanted to reveal. Besides, I was afraid of hearing the details. I told him that I was ready to roll out of there.

We left the party, and I drove Dirk to his hotel. I think I may have driven through several red lights rushing to get him back. There was complete silence in the car. I didn't even bother to turn on the radio. I wanted him to experience my anger. I thought I was clear before we left to go to the party that I really didn't want to go. I was only going because of him. He knew I didn't like being alone in crowds, especially around people I didn't know. When we stopped to buy the liquor before going to the party, it was because I wanted to quiet my nerves. I wanted to be calm and not anxious. I couldn't understand Dirk's disregard for me.

He asked me to stop at a drive-through restaurant, and I just turned and looked at him. I pulled up to his hotel and pushed the automatic locks on the car to open. I was done partying for the weekend, especially with him. "Man, I'm sorry, Terrance," he said as he exited the car. "I'll call you tomorrow." We talked right before he left L.A., and it was the last time we ever spoke.

A few months passed, and Dirk was heavy on my mind. I had not heard from him since his visit so I called his office. When I asked the secretary for Dirk, she paused and didn't say anything for a good minute.

"Hello, I'm trying to reach Dirk Johnson," I said again.

"Please hold," she said and then transferred me to someone else's extension. This all felt odd, so I hung up and called back.

"Hello, I just called for Dirk Johnson and was transferred to the wrong extension."

"Please hold," she said again. Almost two minutes later a different woman came on the phone.

"Hi, are you looking for Dirk Johnson?"

"Yes. This is Terrance Dean, a good friend of his and one of his fraternity brothers. Who am I speaking with?"

"This is Shelia Brown, and I worked closely with Dirk."

Worked? What does she mean 'worked'? I thought to myself.

"Is Dirk still with the company or has he moved on?" I asked.

"I remember Dirk telling me about you. He spoke very highly of you."

I was stunned because I never heard of her and I wondered what he may have told her about me.

"You don't know, do you?" Sheila said.

"Know what?"

She sighed and took a deep breath. "Dirk died last month."

I was speechless. I couldn't believe my ears. I was blown away.

I finally regained my composure. "What? What do you mean died? I just saw him a few months ago. What happened?"

"Dirk swore me to secrecy about his illness. But because you are one of his good friends and he talked about you regularly, I will tell you.

Dirk died from the AIDS virus. He had been seeking treatment privately and didn't want anyone to know. Only a few people knew and I was one of them."

I sat there and cried. I couldn't believe it. Dirk didn't even tell me. I was mad and upset. I hated him for not telling me what was going on with him. I was mad at his family and friends because they caused him to hide his sexuality. It must have been hard for him to suffer through his illness alone.

"Would you like a copy of his obituary?" Sheila asked.

"Yes, please send it to me."

I got it in the mail a few days later. I held on to it because I hoped Dirk's spirit could feel that I loved him and that his silence had not been in vain.

After learning about Dirk's death, I became scared. The weekend he came to Los Angeles and the party we attended quickly flashed through my mind. I couldn't confirm if he'd had sex with anyone, I couldn't confirm if *anyone* had had sex, and I had pretty much blocked the evening from my mind. For Dirk's sake and anyone else's I hoped that if he'd had sex with someone, they used protection.

It also made me think about the men I had been with. Those intimate moments we shared. I thought about the many men who were on the down low and lived secret lives. I thought about my friends and how I hoped they would be honest enough to tell me if they had the HIV virus. I wondered if I would have hid it from my friends.

I called my down low friends and told them if they needed to talk with me about anything they should not hesitate or second-guess our friendship. I told them they did not have to hide, or be afraid of trusting me with anything. I let them know how much I loved them and I was always there for them.

Although I was afraid, I went to get an HIV test. I felt it was important to know my own health status. For so long I refused to think about HIV/AIDS. I did not want to think about the deadly disease. Just like everything else in my life, I blocked it out.

Thank God my results came back negative. Those two weeks of

waiting for my results were nerve-racking. I made a list of all the people I'd been with, which was the most frightening thing. After my doctor relayed the wonderful news to me, I faithfully got tested every six months.

Unfortunately, I also became a hypochondriac. I dramatized any small thing related to my health. If I got a cold, I thought it was HIV. If I got a bruise or scratch on my body, I thought it was HIV. It got to the point where I was driving myself crazy. After calling the HIV/AIDS hotline and visiting my doctor frequently, they convinced me that I was fine and overreacting. Now I make sure to get tested once a year.

At times like these, I hated the down low lifestyle. I didn't want to be associated with anything it represented. I started to resent the men and the lies they told. I despised them for the cheating and sneaking around. I had become one of them and I hated myself for allowing it to happen. I was dishonest. I lied to friends and loved ones. I kept my cover because I was afraid of being found out. I didn't want anyone to accuse me of something so vile and disgusting. I became all the things I heard many ministers, pastors, and church folks say. I was a faggot and I hated myself for being one.

Things started to change for me after I learned about Dirk. I looked at everything differently. I wanted and needed to find some sense of purpose for my life. I didn't want to be like my boy and die in vain. I didn't want to be alone in this world with no one to talk to. I wanted to be somebody. I wanted to be loved by somebody, anybody. I needed to feel it from something and someone tangible. I did what I knew to do, which was to turn to my faith. It had sustained me in times like these. I needed to learn to depend on it when times were also good. I needed to remember I didn't have to wait until some unforeseen tragedy to occur in order to turn to God.

Going through this experience hurt like hell. Dirk's death from AIDS wasn't my first or second time losing someone to the virus. But his dying brought back everything I tried desperately to escape.

20. MOMMA

IT WAS MY JUNIOR YEAR in college and time for winter break. I went home to try to enjoy my Christmas holiday. Unlike other students who would be celebrating with their families, I was dealing with my mother's illness. Watching her lose weight, constantly in pain, and barely able to walk was unbearable. My mother was doing what she could to put up the good fight, but she was losing, and AIDS was winning. It took hold of her body and refused to let go. Her once voluptuous body was thin and wiry. Her figure was gone and the clothes draped her body like a rag doll. Her face became sunken and sullen. The sight made me long and wish for the beautiful mother I once knew.

I frequently visited my mother at her apartment over the Christmas break and decided to stay with her for the final week. She needed assistance. I could tell she was in pain and didn't want me to see her in the condition she was in, but she needed someone to be with her. Other family members pitched in when necessary.

My mother and I talked a lot. It was the first time we sat down across from one another and held a conversation. It was refreshing to have her listen to me. It felt good to share all the things going on at school and in my life. It was also the first time I laughed with my mother.

My mother revealed to me that her youngest brother, Alex, was killed right after I was born. They were extremely close, and he kept a tight rein on my mother because of the attention she got from guys.

Alex was on his way to work one day, and while he was waiting for the bus a group of his friends pulled up in a car and offered him a ride to work. He hopped in the car with them.

Unfortunately, they didn't take him to work. They drove out of Detroit and ended up twenty minutes later in Ecorse, Michigan, joyriding. Then they were stopped by the police. Apparently the car was stolen. The police pulled all the guys out of the car and told them they had thirty seconds to run. As they attempted to flee, the officers shot and killed Alex.

My mother was devastated when he died. Her brother Alex was her everything. His death sent her into a dark depression from which she never recovered. Drugs and sex became her new confidante and fix.

As my stay with my mother came to an end, I packed my bags in preparation for my return to school. As I was leaving and walking out the door, my mother called to me. I stopped, turned, and for the first time, my mother gently said, "I love you."

For a split moment the words lingered in the air over my body waiting for me to let them land someplace in my heart. I had never heard those words before from her. Hearing them felt similar to when I had first gotten the Holy Ghost. It grips your body and fills you with so much emotion that your body goes into convulsions like an unexpected earthquake.

I looked at my mother and told her, "I love you, too." Then I walked out the door, crying uncontrollably because I knew it would be the last time I would see her alive.

On February 3, 1991, I got a call in my dorm room from Grandma Pearl, telling me that my mother had died. She was thirty-six years old. I cried the entire day and made arrangements to go home to be with my family. No one had prepared me for death, especially my mother's. Burying my mother was extremely painful. I knew I wouldn't see her again or hear her voice.

I would have given anything to spend a day, an hour, or five more minutes with her. Despite the prostitution and the drugs, she never stopped loving her children and I finally got to hear what I'd longed for all my life, to hear my mother tell me she loved me.

I stayed an extra week in Detroit after the funeral because I needed to grasp my mother's death. I wasn't sure if I could return to school. I didn't care about anything. I hated that this was happening to my family. I found solace once again in alcohol. I drank so much that week I think I was trying to die myself. I swallowed whole pints of liquor attempting to drown out my misery. I hated waking up in the morning because it was a reminder that my mother was still gone.

My sexuality didn't even matter to me. I had just lost my mother and the feeling overpowered anything I thought was of any significance. This was the woman who gave birth to me. I would never have the opportunity to hear her voice again. She wouldn't see me grow into a man and make something of myself.

I found myself, again, wondering, questioning, and trying to make sense of the confusion. When you're in the midst of madness and chaos, all you hear is noise. Nothing is comprehensible. Everything just sounds like mumbo jumbo. All I wanted was someone to comfort me and to let me know everything would be all right. To me, my life was all wrong.

But I got on my knees and prayed to God. I knew if I prayed and talked with God everything would work out just fine. It was then, for the first time, I heard a voice say, "Your mother wouldn't want you to stop. You must graduate and make her proud."

After all those years praying to hear God's voice, I finally heard it. Soft, gentle, and calm. The voice came and went. It was a wonderful feeling to know God does answer prayers. So, I returned to Fisk better and stronger.

I got an unexpected and nice surprise when both Vincent and Gerrod came to visit for homecoming. It was great being with friends who really knew me. It was also when Vincent discovered I was gay.

Gerrod and I had been arguing in their hotel room. It was something trivial, as were most of our disagreements. Gerrod then blurted
out, "But you're gay." When he said it there was a sharp pain in my
chest like I'd just been shot. My stomach turned over three times. My
body was numb. The room fell silent. I looked over at Vincent. There
was a blank expression on his face. Up until that moment I had never
discussed my sexuality with him. I was too afraid. He was someone I
looked up to and admired. I figured if Vincent knew, he wouldn't want
to be my friend anymore.

I asked Vincent if he was okay.

"Yeah, I'm fine," he responded.

"So, how do you feel about what Gerrod just said?"

"I mean . . . I guess . . . why didn't you tell me?"

"I don't know. I thought maybe you wouldn't want to be my friend."

"It doesn't really matter to me. You're still my boy. We're still cool."

It felt good to hear those words. I still had my two best friends and
frat brothers in my corner.

May 1992 couldn't get here fast enough. I was so ready to be out
of school and out of Nashville. Too many things were happening and
everything seemed to crumble around me. It was hard watching my
mother deteriorate from AIDS, but it was much more difficult seeing my baby brother Jevonte struggle. Watching a three-year-old baby
struggle with a deadly disease was overwhelming. He took a beating.
He could barely walk because his little body wasted away and his legs
were unable to carry his body. He was in and out of hospitals. Tubes
were connected to all parts of his body. Seeing him in constant pain
made me hate my life. I wondered why this was happening to my
family.

Jevonte had his up days and his down ones. I would pick him up
and tickle him just to see his little smile. Those moments would warm
anyone's heart with hope.

I hated the thought of receiving another call from home about
death. I couldn't take it. It wasn't fair. I hoped beyond all hope he would

live longer, but my mother's death prepared my family for Jevonte's. He died during my senior year.

Going home and being with family wasn't easy. I didn't want to be there under those circumstances. I would rather have been home celebrating his birthday or his recovery and defeat of the disease. Not to bury my own brother.

Although he lived a short time on earth, he made such a huge impact on everyone's life. Uncle Andrew and Aunt Catherine had cared for Jevonte and took it hard when he died. The entire family had grown to love him. While they were feeling an emotional loss, I was feeling both a loss and distance from my family. I no longer connected with them. Watching my mother and little brother die before me made me realize that I was in this world by myself. I couldn't depend on anyone. I only had myself. If I needed anything, materially or emotionally, my family were the last people I wanted to turn to. It was just me. I had to make something out of my life and I just simply blocked out any feelings toward them.

Just like when Mr. McGhee, Grandma Pearl's husband of nearly twenty years, the bane of my family's existence, died that same year. No one cared. None of us did.

When I came home that summer I didn't feel his presence. It was awfully quiet in the house. I spotted Grandma Pearl cleaning out his things from the closet. "Where's Mr. McGhee?" I asked.

"He died," she said casually as she stuffed his suits and shoes in a suitcase.

"Died?" I watched her go from the closet to the suitcase on the bed. "When did he die? Why didn't anyone tell me?"

"He died in his sleep a week ago. His family in Ohio came and took his body. They buried him there. I didn't want to bother you." She walked into the kitchen and grabbed her cup of coffee. I followed her. I wasn't sure if I should cry or be happy. I was emotionless, just like Grandma Pearl.

I didn't even know Mr. McGhee had family in Ohio. He never talked about having any brothers or sisters. I thought we were his family.

That weekend my entire family gathered at Grandma Pearl's house. It was the biggest celebration I had ever seen. Even people from the neighborhood stopped by. It was everything Mr. McGhee would have hated, people in the house, on the lawn, blasting loud music. It was his going away party, and he wasn't even there to experience it.

21. SO FINE

ONE DAY I happened to be over at Corey's house, and he was in a cheerful mood. He was preparing to go work out with some of his friends. They were going to the sand dunes to run. Almost everyone in Los Angeles ran the sand dunes. It was definitely a workout.

Corey's friends arrived—a smooth, chocolate brother with a body that rippled with muscles and a face molded to perfection. He was with a stunning, mocha-colored sister who had a radiant smile. Her tiny, well-toned body made her look as if she was a fitness trainer. I never met them at the house before, so I was puzzled.

Derek Luke and Sophia were married. Derek later become a huge star from his roles in *The Antwone Fisher Story, Biker Boyz, Friday Night Lights,* and *Glory Road.*

They were struggling actors at the time. They had not scored any roles, but they seemed perfectly content with their lives.

Derek asked me to join them at the sand dunes, but I knew I couldn't handle it.

"Naw, not this time. Maybe next time."

Derek and his wife looked as if they had been training at the sand dunes for years. Their bodies were amazing and well sculpted.

After they left I went home thinking about that fine man, Derek Luke. I needed to find out from Corey if he was someone he was trying to date and if he was a part of the down low circle.

I went by Corey's house the next day to find out about Derek.

"All right, what's up with your boy Derek? He is fine as hell." I gleamed.

"That is my boy. He's definitely straight. He and his wife are real cool people and happily married. They have opened my eyes to a lot of different things," Corey said as he dressed in slacks and a collared shirt. "He is fine as shit, though." He laughed.

"Where are you going dressed up like that?" I asked.

"To church with Derek and his wife."

I was surprised because Corey had never mentioned church. Also, it was a weekday. Something was going on.

Derek and his wife arrived at the house. They were smiling and happy, you could feel the love between them.

He invited me to join them for bible study.

"I had not planned on it. But I will definitely go next time."

"It's an open invitation. Whenever you want to come, me and Sophia would love for you to join us."

They went to church, and I drove home thinking about Corey. He was different. Something had a hold of him. I remembered that feeling. It's a sense of power, light, and energy when God is in your life. Nothing seems to trouble you.

Over the next few weeks, Corey changed dramatically. He was attending church services every Sunday. He was going to bible study on Wednesdays. He even joined the church and became a part of the choir.

Seeing his transformation was inspiring. Although Corey was still a party animal, he seemed to be outgrowing it. He began focusing on his career and God. Corey always talked about how Derek and his wife were so supportive of him. They encouraged and empowered him to be his best. Although he never told them about his sexuality, he suspected they knew.

I became so intrigued by it all I began to hang out with them. I wanted what they had. I wanted to be back in the conversation of enlightenment and inspiration. I needed God. I was growing further away from myself and into what I thought everyone wanted me to be. I knew what I wanted in a career, but not in relationships.

I didn't think I could ask for monogamy. How could I? It was impossible to have a monogamous relationship because as down low men we have girlfriends and wives but still sleep with men. Some down low men consider themselves monogamous if they only sleep with one man, even though they may be sleeping with several women. We are okay with our partners having sex with women, but not with another man. Being with another man—now, that's cheating and disrespectful. I should be the only man that you are with.

I sure as hell couldn't ask for honesty and truthfulness. How could I ask someone else for it when I couldn't even face my own truth? I lied and deceived my family and friends. All down low men do it. If I did it to those people, I would do it to another man, and I had. I found it hard to believe most things down low men told me. I'll never forget one down low brother I was sexing who told me, "My girl thinks I'm cheating on her with another woman. She's right about the cheating part, but she's not asking the right question." I learned a very valuable lesson from him. If you don't ask a man the right question, you'll never get the right answer.

Did I want love? I craved the experience Derek and his wife had. Marcus and Gary had it, Charles and J. P., too. They had someone they could lean on, someone they could say was their own. Charles was going to get married. He must have loved her. J. P. had been with his girl since high school. They had a foundation. They knew each other. Maybe love was what I needed, but how could I ask for it if I'd never known it? I didn't know how to explain to another person the way to love me. I didn't know how to love me. If a man liked me or thought I was cute, I slept with him. I figured he must have had feelings for me if he slept with me. To me, sex was love. It was my addiction, along with pain.

I prayed for an answer to know what to do next. I wanted to leave the down low life, but my body was calling for attention. My spirit was definitely willing, but the flesh was weak. I loved being touched by a man. I longed to lie with another hard body who knew how to satisfy my needs. The soft, gentle kisses all over my body. Licking and sucking the right spots. It felt great to be held in another man's arms, feeling protected, feeling wanted.

I committed myself to the church, reading books on spirituality. I was ready to be healed. That's what the ministers said when I went to church. I could be healed through the power of prayer. They said I couldn't serve two masters. I had to choose God or being gay. I couldn't please the flesh so I had to deny myself.

I hated that Charles, J. P., Dirk, and other down low men I knew didn't have to choose. They knew what they wanted. They were having it all, dick and pussy. I guess they never heard the ministers I did. I was always told I had to choose one or the other. I was willing to do it. I didn't want the burden of carrying my homosexuality any longer. The minister said when you get tired of carrying your cross, you can just hand it over to Jesus. I was sure he wouldn't want to carry my cross; it was vile and disgusting. I didn't want to be gay anymore. I knew if I prayed hard enough I could overcome it. I could be straight, a heterosexual male. I could be normal like everyone else. Then my family, friends, and community would love and accept me. I could stop all the lying.

I even heard about gospel singer and minister Donnie McClurkin who, after years of struggling with his sexuality, was delivered from his homosexual urges. He said it was by the power and grace of God. If he could do it, so could I.

It was time for me to be with myself, with no interruptions. I was willing to leave the down low lifestyle behind and everyone in it. No dating, no sex, and no more men.

I first stopped going to the down low functions. I didn't accept the invitations and I made excuses of being busy. I stopped hanging around the men I met. The only way I could do it was by alienating myself. I was weak for men. If I didn't put myself in those environments then I wouldn't have to worry about the temptation. I became a recluse. I didn't need a lot of friends. Sandy, Jimmy, Marcus, Kathy, and Corey were the only ones who mattered.

But rest assured, just when I told myself I was making a change, my past and everything in it showed up to test me. Two of my best sexual partners resurfaced.

Charles had not married his fiancée, and I don't think he'd ever planned to.

The other was Ace, who I met at the down low party with my boy Dirk. Ace was too sexy to resist. His sexual prowess made me weak. His stamina made our lovemaking sessions last hours. I nicknamed him "Snake" because his penis looked like a black mamba snake, dark, long, and wide. It was vicious. He was something dangerous when he got into his groove.

Ace could never seem to get away too long without his girl calling him every twenty minutes. She was quite the inquisitor. "Where are you? Who are you with? When are you coming home?"

He was a busy man, producing hits for artists, being in the studio for long hours, and traveling on the road. With her constant nagging and insecurities, he felt at home in my bed. It was a sanctuary from his world where he had to be strong. But with me he was soft, he let his guard down. I didn't inquire about whom he was working with, what album he was producing, or when he was coming back. When he came to my house his mind seemed to be free of the pressures to create a hit song and keeping his girl happy. That's why our sex was so intense. All the build up and all the frustrations were redirected into his sexual release.

Temptation is a motherfucker when you are weak. I was fresh on my journey to the new me and these two knuckleheads showed up. I did what any sensible, normal human being would have done. I had sex with both of them. I missed Charles's tenderness and his commitment to making sure I was pleasured. I missed Ace and his snake. He always made it feel like he was marking his territory. He wanted to make sure I desired no other man. I know I shouldn't have done it, but they were my last romps in the hay. It was my good-bye to it all. I had to go out with a bang.

22. EMOTIONAL ROLLER COASTER

COREY, MARCUS, DEREK LUKE, and West Angeles Church of God in Christ really helped on my search for self-identity. In my new environment, people had positive attitudes. Interacting with likeminded individuals was what I needed, but when you get an itch that won't go away, you are bound to scratch it. My itch was sex and scratching it felt good, really good.

All I did was replace one addiction with another. My addiction to work and sex was now replaced with going to church. That's how life works. I went from one drastic measure to another.

An ex–sex partner and accomplished actor friend, "Flip," had done the same thing. He worked constantly to keep his career and personal life separate, but it was taking its toll on him. He was conflicted. When I met him, he had just finished a television movie where he had a small bit part. He often got small roles on television and in films so he was able to make a comfortable living as an actor.

He and one of his boys came to a down low party at the Spot where I saw them. Flip and his boy Donnie, were in the kitchen. I was checking to see if they were a couple because I was interested in Donnie. A few minutes went by, and Flip approached me. He leaned in and whispered in my ear how he thought I was attractive and asked if I was at the party alone. I was sure he was about to tell me that Donnie wanted to meet me.

"I'm here with one of my boys." I smiled at Flip. He was a pretty boy. Light skin with curly hair and hazel-brown eyes. He gazed lustfully into my eyes, but I was feeling Donnie, who was much darker and looked more street with his Timberland boots and saggy jeans.

"You want to go over here so we can talk?" Flip asked. I had little time to make up my mind. I didn't want to blow him off and tell him that I wasn't interested in him, and that I wanted his boy, so we went to a corner of the house and chatted.

Flip and I ended up dating for a few months and I discovered that Donnie was his best friend. I enjoyed being with Flip, but I fantasized about Donnie. I think Donnie knew it because whenever Flip would leave us alone together, he and I would flirt endlessly. There was a sexual chemistry between us that was undeniable. We were both in heat and we wanted each other badly. I wasn't going to cross the boundary of sleeping with Flip's best friend, however. I couldn't bring myself to do that. But when our relationship ended, I was at Donnie's house the next day, lying his bed, engaging in a sexual release that both of us were so desperately waiting for.

Flip would often share biblical scriptures with me of how we were to be strong on our spiritual walk and not falter to the evils of homosexuality. I knew that conversation well because I grew up hearing it from the ministers in church. I didn't want to hear it from Flip because I was still struggling to figure out my life, and sleeping with him only complicated it. Then I couldn't take it anymore and neither could he. Flip married a high school sweetheart and moved from Los Angeles to the countryside of Virginia. He abandoned Hollywood and his thriving acting career. The temptations in Los Angeles were proving too much for him. He figured if he moved away from the big city, he would no longer be tempted. He could resist his desires for men and live happily ever after with his wife out in the middle of nowhere. He even cut off all communication with his down low friends. After they married, Flip and his wife had a baby, and he started teaching in Virginia. All was well in his world, but after being away for a little over a year, he resurfaced in Los Angeles. Flip was back in the Spot where he found himself resorting to what was familiar—sex with men.

I didn't transition subtly from my down low lifestyle, I made a very radical change. Now, for some people that will work, but for me it was a pattern in my life.

Some people never recognize the repetitive patterns in their lives. They keep making the same mistakes over and over again. The world of Hip Hop itself is addictive and is filled with addictive personalities. It's a breeding ground. It's a world filled with an abundance of drugs, sex, and people seeking more money, power, fame, and love. In it we all are looking for one or several of these to fill a void in our lives. When we burn out on one, we replace it with another. I'd personally had my fill of drugs, sex, money, and love. The power would come later.

In Hip Hop, many do not see their abuse of drugs, sex, or money as an addiction. It's a coping mechanism. It's a way of life. Many of us come from dysfunctional broken homes, but we learn to operate in our dysfunction as if everything is normal. We learn how to deal with the stresses and obstacles in our lives. Many of us are from single-parent homes where our mothers work to maintain the basic necessities such as providing a home, food, and clothes.

I witnessed my family and my friends' parents smoke, drink, fight, curse, and struggle with money. It was an everyday existence and a vicious cycle that is passed on from generation to generation. I was in the drama and a part of the mess. I didn't see what others did because I was attached to it, just like every man I met who told me of his sordid past. As a young child I didn't have the necessary skills to break out of it or know how to differentiate between the drama and normalcy.

I was around young, impressionable people who suddenly became superstars. They came from a dysfunctional family and community environment only to end up in another dysfunctional environment called show business.

The industry devoured them. They came into this industry filled with the ideas of who they thought they were, but the marketing, promotions, A&R (Artist and Repetoire) reps, and sales executives told them otherwise.

They were created into an image to sell to the buying public. They became the jewelry, clothes, and money. They were pulled in several directions and had to be everything to everyone. Everyone was in their head and ear.

Drugs, alcohol, and sex became their refuge. The drugs and alcohol numbed them to their reality. Sex was a way to have control or to find love. They went from one bed to the next, hoping each new partner would be the one. The connection would help them stop searching for something that they're missing within themselves. Maybe falling in love would fill the void.

That's why so many of us connected. We knew how the entertainment world operated. It's pretty on the outside but an ugly mess on the inside. Working in it and dealing with my sexuality had me falling into an abyss of emptiness. Being with the celebrities gave me something to feel good about. We all led destructive lives, especially those of us who were on the down low, but I was going to discover my salvation in church.

But the black church is extremely homophobic, and a discussion of gays turns into a gay-bashing session. What black gay man is going to stand up and say something during a sermon when the entire congregation is whooping and hollering, cheering on their minister? Most ministers spew hate and ignorance.

If we lose everything, what do we have? I'd rather have something than nothing. We can't be who we want to be. To be our true selves is a lie, so we live other people's truth so we can be free in a community that has been oppressed itself.

I wanted desperately to reject my desires for men. I didn't want to be with men and I was willing to do whatever I needed to to stop it.

I hated that I had desires and feelings for men. I hated that I thought about being in a relationship with a man. I constantly fought with my inner man. I refused to accept that part of me that wanted to be with a man, and if I didn't accept me, how could anyone else?

That's why sex meant so much to me. The men made me feel wanted. I was loved in the act of sex. I gave them a part of me and they gave me a part of them. Even when they let me in that small part of their world, I had something and it was better than nothing.

When I attended church to find the real me, I only became troubled and confused. My life was spiraling out of control, and I couldn't make sense of what was happening.

I kept attracting drama, lies, deceit, and mistrust. My solution was to change my situation with God, but I had not learned to change my mind as well. I denied to myself that my situation remained the same.

Unconsciously, I would seek out that which was comfortable and familiar—other down low men who were confused and in denial. Men who couldn't be trusted. Men who had sex with men with no emotional connection.

It was a security mechanism and since I was spiritually, emotionally, and mentally wounded, I couldn't effectively choose anything else to better my situation. As much as I thought I did, I was only running in circles.

Bishop Charles E. Blake is a powerful minister and truly a man of God, and I often found comfort in his teachings. Being among other fellow Christians was a wonderful and exhilarating feeling, but I knew their troubles were not mine. I needed a word, a song, just something to make me feel better about myself. But most of all, I wanted a cure. I wanted to be healed of my homosexual tendencies.

I often drove to the beach off the Pacific Coast Highway in the evenings. I would stare out at the ocean and think about the slaves who journeyed across the vast waters on slave ships and what it must have been like. Those who took their own lives to avoid being slaves. Those who fought and struggled in a new world. I was a slave to my own self. I beat myself up. I tortured me. I fought and struggled to be free.

I wished for a new life and a new start. Something needed to be different in my world. It wasn't like everyone else's I'd admired. People seemed to be happy like they hadn't a care in the world. They got up and went about their days carefree. Unlike them, I was constantly covering up the lies I told. I prayed that no one outed me to my friends or my family.

No matter what happened, nothing could change me or make me anything other than who I was. Accepting myself was something I couldn't do because that person wouldn't be right. And nobody wants to be wrong.

Some nights, I would sit in my apartment and just think about ending it all. My life was nothing anyway. There was no hope for me, and according to many pastors of the black church, as well as my own community, I was a vile person who deserved to be in hell because I was gay.

To rid myself of the entire problem, I once took a bottle of aspirin, popped off the top, and downed the bottle. I damn near choked to death from the pills as they lodged in my throat because I didn't chase them down with any liquids. It was such a futile attempt. I couldn't even die right. I laughed at myself because I thought of what they would say to my family when they discovered my body. "Well, he tried to kill himself by taking a bottle of aspirin, but the actual cause of death was from choking on the pills."

Strange twists occurred whenever I was out. I randomly met people who would just strike up a conversation with me. It was weird because it would be in the oddest places like the supermarket, gas station, or gym. Our conversations often began with them recommending a book to read.

I read the books and found solace in them. I devoured the writings and messages in *The Isis Papers: The Keys to the Colors* by Dr. Francis Cress Welsing, *From Superman to Man* by J.A. Rogers, and *Conversations with God* by Neale Donald Walsch.

But it was hearing Iyanla Vanzant in Long Beach that truly transformed me. She was speaking at a community college and I traveled to hear her words. I was already familiar with her work and teachings, but I had never seen her speak in person.

When I entered the college auditorium and saw the place filled with hundreds of women, I almost left. I felt out of place, like they were having a secret meeting about men that I shouldn't attend. But the organizers and women in attendance made me feel welcome.

I was mesmerized by Iyanla's message. She was engaging and personable. She made us feel like she was speaking directly to us and she was there just for us. I had never seen anyone command an audience the way she did. Everyone hung on to every word she said. She was it. Iyanla was the real deal. She had experienced pain and hurt that many of us were hoping to recover from. I found someone who indirectly helped me to stay on my journey and not give up because no matter what, I was a child of God.

After that evening I felt invincible. There was nothing and no one who could stop me from doing what I was destined to do. I spent a lot of time writing, meditating, and learning more about who I was. It felt good being by myself, no distractions, no emotional ties, and no drama.

23. ME, MYSELF, AND I

I ENJOYED THE TIME OFF I had from work. No alarm clocks to wake me up, no job to rush to, and no one bugging me about something.

Corey called one evening, and we decided to have a fun night out. Nothing serious or outrageous. I was sex free and feeling spiritually rejuvenated. I didn't see anything wrong with going out to have a drink and checking out the night life of Los Angeles.

A huge gay club on Olympic Boulevard, the Catch-22 was the hot spot of choice.

I did my usual schtick when I got in the club. I went to the bar, got a coke, found a spot in a dark corner, and stood there until a short, very light-skinned woman with fiery hair sashayed in front of me. I recognized the popular and legendary funk R&B songstress and had seen her before at the club, always with a drink in her hand and not shy about approaching women she found desirable.

She approached Lola once. They danced, but the celebrated vocalist wanted much more with Lola. It didn't take long before Lola's girlfriend, Roslyn, stepped up and made it known she was unavailable. Lola didn't hear the end of it, and neither did any of us. Roslyn ranted and raved about how the beloved R&B singer was a washed-up has-been and she knew Lola wanted her. The singer may have been older, but she definitely was not a has-been. Her voice has transcended generations to cross over into Hip Hop. She helped redefine the 70s and 80s with her funky sound. To remain current, she signed to a gangster rapper's label to reach a younger audience.

As I was posted up in the corner, boys would cruise by making eye contact and flirting endlessly. I knew the spill. It was always a dance with men. You stare endlessly at someone for the night until one of you decides to make a move. One of you will move subtly closer to the other, and you continue sizing each other up. You observe his friends and who he's with. The fewer people he's with, the more likely he's not known in the gay community. But it's better when no one speaks to him. That means he's probably a down low gay man and hasn't been to many gay clubs.

One such man caught me at the bar. I was having my drink refilled when he approached me.

"What's up?" he said.

"What up?" I looked at him, trying to see if I recognized him. I didn't. He was short, but definitely a cutie. Nice low-cut hair with waves, light-brown skin, beautiful brown eyes, and a sultry voice. He had a masculine swagger with a little thug in his style.

He offered me a drink.

I recognized the tone of his voice; he was from New York. He reminded me of my home away from home.

"I noticed you over in the corner," he said.

"Oh, so you're a stalker?"

We both laughed and the ice had been broken. He introduced himself as "Jason." We talked for the rest of the night at the bar. He was in town visiting some friends. As we flirted and made sexual innuendos to each other, I knew in my head I should walk away and leave well enough alone. But the man inside was awakening. My loins were hungry and needed to be fed.

Jason ended up at my apartment that evening. It was nonstop sex once we walked through the door. Clothes strewn throughout the apartment. We couldn't keep our hands off each other. His sexual appetite far exceeded mine. Passion and fervor overtook everything going on in the bed.

While lying there afterward, sweating and breathless, he said he had something to tell me. My heart skipped several beats. I hoped he was not going to tell me he had a disease. I prayed to God that the condom I wore hadn't broken from the intense friction that was the result of our passion. I braced myself.

"I don't know how to tell you this," Jason started. "I am a man of God."

I was like, okay, so am I. We are all men of God. But he gauged my answer and explained further.

"No, you see, I am a *man* of God. I am a minister."

I sat up in the bed. My mouth dropped open. My eyes grew. Then he continued.

"I'm one of several ministers at a church in Brooklyn and I am also married with a child."

I got out of the bed and stood before him naked. My erection and anything else that was aroused had all gone limp. My entire body had no feeling.

"I should have told you earlier, but I didn't want you to judge me."

"Oh, okay, so now you think I won't judge you after we just had sex?" I was pissed. I just knew that lightening was going to strike me down. I had just committed a mortal sin. I slept with a minister who was married with a child. What shitty and lousy luck. Just when I thought I was doing so well on my spiritual walk. I had been doing a lot of introspection and was feeling a little better about myself. And just when I decided to go to the club and have some fun, I meet a man of God, a minister, a pastor. This man represented all the men I heard in my past who told me that I was going straight to hell for my homosexual feelings. That I should rebuke those desires and be strong in the Lord. I felt like I'd had sex with my entire past, and with everything that I was running from, from being gay. He was a minister. Everything was staring me straight in the face. Well, actually, he was lying in my bed.

I told Jason he should leave, although, truth be told, neither one of us wanted it to end because the sex was off the chain. Jason continued to call during his stay in Los Angeles, but I didn't see him again. He made several attempts to keep in contact when he returned to New York, but it was over. I'd no desire to keep in contact with him. He also invited me to his church the next time I visited New York, but how could I feel comfortable sitting in the pews of the church with folks seeking salvation, while I knew he was seeking salvation in my bed?

My sexual itch was returning. Having the taste of another man's lips, scent, and body stirred up my desires. As the scripture states, "the spirit indeed is willing, but the flesh is weak." I was becoming malnourished. I needed another fix to compensate for the ill of sleeping with Jason. Maybe, just maybe it was my design and makeup to be a gay man.

If only I could accept myself and not worry about what others thought. Some things sound great in theory. It's a wonderful speech when you're giving it to others, but living it yourself is another story.

I got an unexpected call from my friend Kathy. She'd recently accepted a new position in New York with MTV in the Human Resources department and was leaving. Although I was happy for her, a part of me was sad. Kathy and I had developed a close bond and shared a lot with each other. I could call on her for advice and she could call on me. She had become someone I could depend on and we looked out for each other. Whenever either of us was going through something, we knew we had each other's back. We spent a lot of time together, and I felt like she was abandoning me. But that feeling only lasted a short time, because once she was settled in New York, Kathy called and told me she had the perfect position for me there and made me an offer I couldn't refuse.

The thought of returning to New York was exhilarating. I had lived there before, and it was where I first gained entrée into the down low life. I was returning to the place I dreamed about as a child. New York was it for me.

It brought back a lot of memories for me. Memories from long ago. As I sat in my apartment contemplating Kathy's offer, I knew I was ready to devour Hip Hop and contribute my part to it. I reminisced about the day when I first arrived in the city and was hooked. I was young, fresh, and innocent. It was where I first got my cherry busted, when someone bit into my apple. And once you've been bitten, you're never the same—I know I haven't been.

DISC
THREE

24. SHAKE YOUR THANG

THE FIRST TIME I went to New York, it was January 1993. I landed an internship in CNN's New York bureau. I asked a college friend, Henry, if I could stay at his house. He convinced his mom to let me stay with him and his sister, Trina. Little did I know that I was going to be living in the Queensbridge projects in Long Island City.

As much as I'd heard about Queensbridge in Hip Hop, I quickly learned that it isn't a city or a borough but one of the largest housing projects in New York City. It was the place where Tragedy, Nas, Havoc of Mobb Deep, Cormega, and Lakey Da Kidd all grew up.

Walking through Queensbridge with all those fine, young, and hood brothers was a beautiful sight. I had to be careful. No slipping and staring at men. They couldn't even think I was gay.

Although I was familiar with the hood from living in Detroit, there was something different about Queensbridge men. They were filled with lots of bravado and machismo. New Yorkers don't like to be stared at. Not unless you got beef and you're looking for it. You don't strike up conversation with someone just for the hell of it.

The men in Queensbridge hung out on corners, in front of buildings, and on the benches. They knew one another because they were from generations of project residents. As the new guy, I drew stares and questions—where was I from and where was I living? Thank God for Henry and his friend Lena, who helped in my transition.

Lena became a friend of mine. She, too, lived in the Queensbridge projects, and she and Henry helped me navigate the city—where to go, how to get there, and where not to go.

I had to find a means of income and a place of my own right away. Although I sold my car, $2,500 would go quickly in New York City. My living situation was temporary, so I once again had to make things happen in short order.

My first month in New York was going great. My internship was demanding, but I loved every minute of it. I learned how to get around on the great New York subway system. I began exploring parts of the city to acclimate myself to my new home.

Henry's mom, Phyllis, was a short, feisty woman. She had a lot of spirit and kept a tight rein on her children. When I came in from my internship, she would make small talk with me. She was extremely pleasant. She would often tell me to not get caught up in the streets. "You are doing great things. Be careful because New York can be dangerous," she would say.

One evening we sat down and talked about my dreams and aspirations. It felt good to share my hopes for the future with an adult. After that discussion, I came home cheerful and excited, but something had changed. Phyllis had a lot on her mind. Henry left for military officer's school in Oklahoma and would be gone for a year. Phyllis's youngest son, Dale, was recently locked up on Riker's Island. He was facing some serious time for criminal assault and gun charges.

I didn't want to be a burden, so I made it a point to stay out of her way and hung out in the city. Phyllis's mood began to change. She snapped at her daughter and became short with me. When she wasn't in the kitchen cooking, she was in her room with the door closed. Trina and I were walking on eggshells around the house.

One evening Phyllis announced she wanted me out.

I was completely thrown for a loop.

"You didn't hear me. I want you out of here tonight, right now." She didn't give an explanation, she just wanted me gone.

I didn't know what to do. What did I do wrong? I never disrespected her. I never ate her food. I cleaned and I was never there.

I gathered her instincts had kicked in and she discovered I was gay. I retraced everything I said and did. I didn't act differently or say anything to anyone about my sexuality. I couldn't put my finger on it. How did she know?

I felt abandoned. I was young, and it reminded me of when my mother left me. I still yearned for a motherly connection. I thought all mothers loved their children. I was Henry's frat brother, one of his best friends. How could she do this to me? I had nowhere else to go.

Trina begged her mother for me to stay, but it was too late. Phyllis wanted me out of her house.

I met Lena in front of the building, and she took me up to her house. Lena called her friend Valerie who said I could come stay with her in Harlem, at the St. Nicholas Houses.

Valerie's apartment was huge and had two bedrooms. She had two teenage daughters who didn't live with her, so she let me stay in the other bedroom, although her daughters would occasionally stay the night. They were very nice, but I didn't bother to ask why she didn't have custody of them. I was only a tenant. Besides, I grew up in the same situation.

Whenever a mother didn't have custody of her children, I attributed it to her being on drugs and unable to care for them. She was probably trying to clean up her life and she sent the children to live with their grandparents. What other reason was there for a mother not to be raising her own children? Valerie seemed like she had it together, but so did my mother. People on drugs are good at fooling people and convincing them to believe otherwise.

I had to get a job quickly. I was living in the projects, with barely any money to buy food with. Talk about hitting rock bottom. I felt like I was licking the bottom and that God had forgotten all about me. Moving from one project to the next used up more money than I imagined. I was grateful I was in Manhattan and closer to my internship, but I was stressed out. Living in someone else's house again, I was afraid Valerie would put me out too. I hated living the way I did. I was unsure of my future, which seemed to be in the hands of someone else. One day things were going great, and the next I was out on the streets.

To save money on train fare, I learned I could walk from CNN on Thirty-fourth Street uptown to 127th Street to the St. Nick projects. I used the money to buy hot dogs, hamburgers, and other fast food items. My money was dwindling so any extracurricular activities were out of the question.

The first few days I walked home, I was pooped out from the trek. My feet ached and my legs were sore. After a few weeks, though, my body grew accustomed to the pounding. I walked along Central Park and just daydreamed about making it in New York. I was determined to be somebody.

I couldn't believe how no one understood why this was so important to me. I found something that made me happy. I enjoyed waking up each day and going to work, even though I was not making any money and was starving most days. I didn't think I could rely on others. I couldn't call up my family and ask for help. I was in New York, alone. Talking with my family became unbearable. I just didn't have the energy anymore.

My family was not supportive. They begged and pleaded for me to come home, but it wasn't like I could go to any of their houses and stay. No one offered their house or for me to stay as long as I wanted. There was no offer to help me get on my feet. Aunt Lisa told me that they didn't want me too far away from home, especially not in New York because she'd heard how bad New York was. She didn't want anything to happen to me where the family couldn't get to me.

I didn't take her seriously. My family didn't seem to care about me growing up. Where were they when I was struggling in college and hungry? Where were they when I needed adult supervision? Where were they when I needed love? Grandma Pearl was the only person who took care of me.

She was the only adult who told me I could make it, who encouraged me to leave Detroit. So I couldn't understand why my aunts wanted me to come home. It wasn't like they had a job waiting for me or could offer any advice on what to do. I raised myself. What could they have possibly told me? It didn't make sense to me.

Working in the entertainment industry had become my new life. The industry was my family, though I didn't rely on anyone but myself. This industry was filled with many people who were ready to be my friends. It would have been great to have my family or someone to depend on. But my experience thus far had led me to believe that I couldn't depend on anyone but myself. From growing up without a mother, struggling through college with barely any money, to moving to New York City and getting kicked out of my first residence, I had no one but myself. I had no companionship or any shoulder to cry on. I had to suck it up and keep it moving. Other than sex, I found I loved working in entertainment more than anything, and it helped to replace the love I never received when I was young.

As much as I explained to Aunt Lisa about my passion to work in entertainment, she couldn't understand it. She couldn't understand why anyone would work for free, and live so far away from home. I got tired of explaining myself.

And like that, I stopped speaking to my family and friends for a long time. I stopped calling them. I didn't want to hear their comments about my dreams. I already felt bad and didn't need anyone else adding injury to my pity party. There was truly no love lost in not speaking with them.

One day after I came home from CNN, I stripped off all my clothes and I prayed to God.

"God, I need you, now more than ever. I need you to come into my life. Direct me, guide me, lead me. I love you, God, and I only want to serve you. I only want to do what's right in your eyes. Please, open the doors for me. You said if I ask anything in your name, it will be given to me. I need a miracle right now and only you can deliver it. Please, dear God, I know you did not bring me this far to leave me. Oh, God, I need you to show up in my life right now. I feel like I can't do this any longer."

The next day a black female producer at CNN asked me to come into her office.

"Terrance, what is it that you want to do in television?" she asked me.

I told her I wanted to be a producer. I was good at researching, coming up with great topics, and that I loved how the whole process of television worked.

She told me about a friend of hers, Rachel, who was in Arizona working on a film with Bill Duke called, *Waiting to Exhale,* and she put us in touch with each other.

Rachel told me about the Mayor's Office of Film, Theatre and Broadcasting and how I should go there and get a tech list. On this list was every film and television production company that was shooting in New York.

I made fifty copies of my résumé and started walking. I hit up every production company located in Manhattan. I either walked or took the train. I started from Lower Manhattan and worked my way up to Midtown Manhattan. There were at least twenty production companies and I personally stopped by each and every one of them.

I patiently waited for the phone to ring. Out of fifty résumés, one was bound to hit. And sure enough, a few days later I got a call to be a production assistant at the world famous Apollo Theater for their amateur night.

Working at the Apollo was a great way for me to break into the industry. Just as with New York itself, there's a saying at the Apollo that if you can make it there, you can make it anywhere. I knew I was going to make it. This was my entrée into the entertainment business. This was my step onto the ladder of success. I had to outshine the other production assistants, who were just as determined as I was. We all were running through the theater doing various jobs. I made sure to keep myself busy. No standing around talking. No horseplaying. No getting personal with anyone—no one could discover my secret. I had yet to meet another gay man in the business.

There was a plethora of black men working there. It was unusual seeing that many black men working together, and I finally found a place where I saw people who looked liked me.

There is nothing like working at the Apollo. I was a part of history, and everyone treated me with the utmost respect. I met Ray Chew and The Crew, the infamous KiKi Shepard, the Sandman, and a host of musical talent, like Lauryn Hill. At the time she had just finished *Sister Act 2* and was attending Columbia University. I was so impressed by her laid-back attitude. When she wasn't rehearsing, we would sit in the auditorium talking.

After a few weeks, I got a phone call from Kami, a secretary, who offered me a position as an intern on the movie *North*.

I was a little disappointed that it was not a paid internship. The Apollo was paying me, and I didn't want to go backward. I needed to make money. I didn't want to go back to eating Snickers and potato chips every day. I liked having my own money and the ability to go without rationing the few dollars I had. But I thought about Kami's offer for a moment and then accepted the job. It would be the smartest move I made in my budding career.

I arrived at the production office for *North* the following week to begin work. They loved me, and Kami introduced me to everyone in the office. All white women. No males. No blacks. I was it. I wasn't shocked, but I definitely noticed.

I noticed how blacks mainly worked on black productions, and how rare it was to see a black person on a major white production. Unfortunately, the black productions were few and far between, but there were always white movies being made. In order to work consistently in this business, I quickly learned that I had to make friends with the whites. They had the jobs. They were connected in the business, and when it was time for a production to start hiring, they called those people they were familiar with. People who looked like them.

I had to get into that crowd. I needed to be a part of their circle to maintain work.

The women in the production office were friendly, and I was glad. I didn't want to be around a bunch of catty or bitter women. It could have made my experience unpleasant. They asked basic questions about what brought me to New York, but it didn't get any more personal than that. I was cool with it. I didn't want any conversations about my personal life. The less they knew, the better our working relationship would be.

I don't know if it's a cultural thing or not, but white people tend to ask a lot of questions. They like to know what you did over the weekend. If you are dating. Where you are from and who your family members are. Blacks on the other hand know to stay out of your business. We do not ask a lot of questions about someone's personal life. I know I don't. Unless someone in the office was willing to share with me about their personal relationships, I just listened. I didn't repeat any information and I didn't get involved in gossip. I stayed clear of any office chit-chat. Besides, I didn't want to share any information with anyone and become the topic of discussion. The less they knew, the less likely my sexuality would come up.

The first couple of weeks were very fun. I had to do a few errands in the city, and true to their word, I was fed three meals a day. At the end of each week, I got tokens for the subway.

But I got smart real fast. I would do my errands on foot and pocket the tokens. This way, I could use the extra tokens to hang out and get around on the weekends. Besides, the exercise was good.

I loved working on *North*. Not only did I learn a lot, I also got to experience what a production with *real* money had the power to do. When we ordered meals, they were not from run-of-the-mill joints but from real nice restaurants. The first couple of days I was shy, but when they kept encouraging me to order anything I wanted, you best believe I upped the ante. I was finally eating full meals again. It felt good not to have to worry about where my next meal was coming from. We also had a craft service table set up right outside the production office door where we could get any snack our hearts desired. I couldn't stop going to the table. I would snack just for the hell of it, which really spoiled me, and I would sometimes sneak food home in my bag.

However, I still needed to make money. Realizing my pockets were not going to get fat interning, I got a sales job at the Gap.

It was there that I met Georgia. She was one of the most beautiful, dark-skinned sisters I had ever laid eyes on. She was a short, thick young lady with a banging body. She had the whitest teeth and a smile that would melt your heart. My gosh, I was a schoolboy around her.

Georgia was a manager and did some visual displays for the store. Her responsibilities included dressing the windows and the mannequins on the floor. I thought that was a dope job, especially for a young sister to be doing.

I often caught glimpses of her looking at me while I was folding them damn Gap jeans. We flirted with each other, and I got up the nerve to ask her out. I don't know what I was thinking, but I certainly knew she made parts of my body respond like men I was attracted to did.

I loved women and men equally, but I spent more time fantasizing about men. On the production sets, I did not make many social friends because I was so focused on my career and made sure no one suspected anything about my sexuality. I only saw them as networking opportunities. Helping me to get from one point to another. They were business associates, and I kept them at arm's length. When I was at work, I blocked out my desires for men. I was in a professional environment and didn't look at men in a sensual manner. I didn't think of sex as often. I suppressed my desires.

Georgia and I went out on several dates. Man, she was so easy to talk to and fun to hang out with. Most times, we went to dinner and then a movie. I would walk her to the train station where we would kiss until her train arrived. She lived in Jamaica, Queens, with her parents. To go all the way out to her house, spend the night, and try to get back in the morning for work was like traveling to another state entirely. It's a haul to go from Jamaica, Queens, to Harlem. It could take an hour by train, and then I had to take a gypsy cab or bus to her house.

On some nights, when I knew Valerie wasn't going to be home, I would invite Georgia up to my spot. A real sex machine, Georgia taught me things I never imagined could be done. Thank goodness for stamina. I love freaky people, especially someone who's uninhibited sexually.

I would soon discover not only was Georgia a freak, but so was her cousin.

25. NEXT LIFETIME

ONE EVENING, Georgia and I were eating at Dallas BBQ when I met Georgia's cousin, Richie, who was out with his girlfriend and noticed us in the restaurant.

Richie was eye-catching. He was a little shorter than me and had a body that was screaming he was physically fit. His black, fitted T-shirt spread across his broad chest and his biceps looked like small melons. There was no denying he was Georgia's cousin. They both had the same small nose. I swear I tried not to stare at him, but his dark coal-like eyes danced when he spoke. He had rich, smooth, dark skin and curly hair. He was sexy, and I wanted to know what he was like in bed.

"So you're the man my cousin been talking about," Richie's deep voice slid from his perfectly massive lips.

"Boy, shut up." Georgia blushed.

"Oh, for real? I thought she would have been bragging about her other man," I joked. She jabbed me with her elbow.

"Well, it's good to finally meet you." *And it is certainly good to meet you, too, Richie,* I thought. He smiled and I noticed the dimples in his cheeks. He would be my fantasy later when I was home alone.

That night ended with us leaving Richie and his girl smooching at BBQ's.

One evening Richie came by the Gap to visit Georgia. He often stopped by to see her and use her employee discount, and he and I would have some casual conversation. I would steal glances at him while he shopped through the store. He would ask my advice about jeans as he held them up to his waist. I enjoyed watching him go back and forth to the dressing room trying on different pants and shirts.

This particular evening, Georgia had the night off, so I hooked Richie up with some clothes on my employee discount.

Appreciative of my generosity, Richie offered me a ride home after I got off work at nine that evening.

"Yo, man, you mind if I come up and use your bathroom? I got to take a leak," Richie asked.

"No problem." I wasn't sure if Valerie was home or not. I generally didn't see her at night. She spent a lot of time at her boyfriend's house.

I pointed out the bathroom to Richie, who didn't close the door behind him while he was pissing. I didn't think too much of it; most men are comfortable with the bathroom door being open while they piss.

"This is a nice spot," Richie said when he came out.

"I'm just here temporarily."

Richie got comfortable, took off his leather bomber jacket, and sat on the sofa.

"You want something to drink?" I asked.

"You got some Hennessey?"

"Naw."

"Beer?"

"Naw, just some Kool-Aid."

Richie laughed. "Give me some of that."

When I walked back into the living room with the glass of Kool-Aid, Richie was standing by the window.

"Here you go." I handed him the glass.

"Thanks, man."

The vibe in the room was different. I couldn't put my finger on it, but something was definitely different.

"Sup with you and my cousin?" Richie asked.

"What you mean?"

"Are y'all serious?"

"She's cool. We have a good time," I said trying to figure out where he was going with the questions.

"Aight." Richie reached into his pants pocket.

"You smoke?" Richie asked pulling out a blunt.

"Yeah."

Before I knew it, we had smoked three blunts. I was high. No, I was floating around the apartment. I smoked a lot when I was in college, but only did it periodically after I graduated. It was a habit I had seen many of my friends spend their money on, and at the time I couldn't afford to support a drinking habit as well as weed habit.

I was sitting on the sofa next to Richie listening to Hot 97, and my body was buoyant. I was feeling good.

Without any provocation, I felt Richie's soft, tender lips on mine.

It was wrong. I knew it was wrong. And every time we lay in bed, naked, I felt the guilt. I was sexing my girl's cousin. The same bed I had sex with Georgia was the same bed where I stroked and ejaculated with her cousin Richie.

Richie justified his actions. "As long as we ain't fucking, then we cool. We ain't cheating. We just sucking and jacking each other off."

Cheating was cheating to me. No matter what was going on. We were sexing each other and giving each other unmentionable pleasure.

"As long as I'm not with another girl, I'm not cheating," Richie would say. That's how it goes in the down low life.

As down low men we feel it's okay to lay with another man and enjoy mutual masturbation. Even if a man is sucking my dick, I am the receiver, so I am not doing anything wrong. I am not the giver. I have not placed my mouth on another man's dick. We don't see anything wrong with that. Nothing about these acts makes us gay. There is no penetration involved so no one has to assume any type of role as the top or bottom.

Also, as long as I am not fucking a man like I would a woman, then I am not cheating. Once a man places his dick inside another man, then cheating has occurred. I am doing to a man what I would to a woman.

I am treating the man like I would my girl. He is on the bottom and I am on top, however I am not gay. The man who is receiving is gay.

I ended my relationships with Georgia and Richie because the guilt I was feeling was too much. The lying, deception, and sneaking around were catching up to me. Breaking up with Georgia was hard. She didn't take it too well. I told her that I needed to move home to be with my family. I lied, but I had to end it. But ending it with Richie was even more difficult. His touches made my body shiver, and feeling his body next to mine was like a hand in a glove.

26. MR. BIG STUFF

I HAD AN UNEXPECTED SURPRISE on the movie *North* when I was promoted from intern to production assistant. I was making money once again. It felt good to have cash in my pockets.

After a few months, I happened to be reading a magazine and learned Spike Lee was gearing up to shoot his next film, *Crooklyn*, starring Alfre Woodard, Delroy Lindo, and Isaiah Washington.

Knowing Spike Lee would be filming in the city made me excited. I had to get on that film. It didn't matter in what capacity. I just had to work with one of the most prolific and controversial black filmmakers of my time.

It just so happened that the assistant office coordinator, Jennifer, had worked with Spike on *Malcolm X*. She was good friends with Karen, the office coordinator on *Crooklyn*. When Jennifer heard of my excitement and eagerness to work with Spike, she put in a phone call. The following week I started working as a paid production office assistant on the film.

Working with Spike opened my eyes to working with an all-black film crew. It felt good to be on the set around people of color working in various positions from the producers to the assistants.

While working on the set with Spike, I suspected some of the brothers of being on the down low, but I wasn't sure. If I tried too hard to find out, I was taking a chance of being caught myself and I didn't want to risk the odds of outing myself.

Even the men who worked in wardrobe and hair and makeup were masculine. Oftentimes those positions were for the more flamboyant types—men who were openly gay and have no problem with anyone knowing who they sleep with. But working with Spike and on other black productions, I noticed these men put on their urban clothes and acted just as normal and regular as any other man, giving no indication about their sexual desires.

Whenever I was on set, the men seemed to be tossing their testosterone around. Everyone was trying to be more manly than the other, boasting about the women they had and how much pussy they were getting. I knew it was best to keep up my straight image. The men working with Spike seemed like they didn't particularly care for homosexual men. I just kept my mouth closed and did my work.

Part of my job was to deliver Spike's mail to the set and run little errands for him. I tried to make small talk with him, but he had a quiet demeanor. And though small in stature, he was filled with creativity and energy and his presence commanded attention.

I remember the incident that broke the ice between Spike and me. It was in the early stages of the production, and we had not started shooting yet. I was in the production office making copies of the script to send out to the actors. Spike came in and was talking with Karen. He noticed a hickey on my neck, which I had gotten the previous evening.

"What's that?" Spike asked, pointing at my neck.

"What's what?" I looked at him, perplexed. I had forgotten about the hickey.

"The red mark on your neck."

Then it hit me like a ton of bricks. I remembered the hickey.

"Oh, that mark." I smiled.

"Yeah, *that* mark."

I came up with a lame explanation of how a mosquito bit me on the neck. Spike laughed and told me to "be very careful of those mosquitoes."

Another incident occurred when we were walking down DeKalb Avenue to the offices of his production company, 40 Acres & a Mule, which were located inside an old firehouse Spike had bought. In order to get inside the gate you had to be buzzed in. Just before we hit the buzzer a woman came out from nowhere and was all up in Spike's face. She was going on and on about what a great filmmaker he was and how she was writing a script. She wanted him to read her script. Spike got this all the time. People were always coming up to him with their story ideas.

Spike kept peering over at me giving me the *do something* look. I started chuckling to myself. I found it amusing.

We finally made it inside the gate, leaving the woman standing outside still trying to sell her pitch. Spike appeased her, and she finally walked away hopeful that her big idea would make it to the silver screen. Spike then turned to me and said, "Why didn't you stop her? She could have done something to me."

I looked at Spike and replied, "Well, she didn't, and besides I am not your bodyguard." He shook his head and fell out laughing.

My entire time working on *Crooklyn* was filled with great moments like these, as well as lots of learning and making new friends. The crew was exceptionally nice and many of them are friends to this day. It's amazing to work on Spike Lee's films. You not only gain a world of experience, but you become part of the Spike family.

One of the family members, Lucy, was moving to Los Angeles to pursue her acting career. She threw a going-away party at her home in Brooklyn. There were many actors, crew members, and a host of her friends at this party. Since I was relatively new, everyone questioned who I was, where I was from, and how was it working for Spike?

A man named "Desi" and I struck up a conversation and instantly hit it off. Desi had worked with Spike in the past and was now a producer who had put together several major projects and was working with a hot actress on her new series. There was something both he and I picked up about each other. We were different. We were of the same cloth. We were "family" inside the Spike family.

Desi was cool. He knew everyone and everyone knew him, yet his B-Boy look and demeanor distracted everyone from his sexual preferences. He sported a bald head with scruffy facial hair. He had a thuggish look and appeal to him.

Desi had invited me to hang out with him at his home in Brooklyn and meet some of his other friends. These men were just like him—street with a hint of business savvy. I called it corporate thug. They talked the talk and walked the walk. They were savvy, smart, and had a Hip Hop swagger. We all were educated, but we loved to dress in urban gear. It was chic and fashionable. I loved that they all looked like me. I finally found a place among men where I felt comfortable. These men made me feel right at home. Many of us worked in the entertainment industry. We all were just starting in our careers.

One evening a few days later, the crew—myself, Desi, "Gus," "Steve," and "Eddie"—hooked up at Desi's house. We were a small clique of men who, on the outside, were just regular young guys having fun. In public, no one would have guessed we were gay. We just didn't fit the stereotype. I think that is one of the reasons we bonded so well together.

For me, I found a kinship with these men, because for so long I searched to find men who looked and acted like I did. The images we generally see of gay men are flamboyant, over-the-top, finger snapping, switching men who I could not identify with. Whenever I worked with flamboyant gay men on a project, I stayed far and clear away. I didn't want to get close or socialize with them. It was automatic guilt by association. I was looking to grow in my career and I had not seen any of these men in a powerful position. I was just a regular, all-around man with no interest in fashion, decorating, dressing up as a woman, doing hair, soap operas, Patti LaBelle, Chaka Khan, or Whitney Houston. No disrespect to these legendary women, but I loved Hip Hop.

So meeting my crew gave me some sanity. We all understood what it was like to hide your sexuality and struggle with it on a daily basis. We knew we had to wear the mask in the workplace. But I don't think they suffered as much as I did. I came to New York from Detroit because I was running from my family and a life of destruction, chaos, and mayhem. I was hoping I would find in New York someone who could understand me. I hoped New York would give me the answers and direction I needed to lead the life of a full heterosexual man.

My crew didn't understand when I skipped out early when we went to the gay club, it was overwhelming to me. I would have anxiety attacks, and still do. My heart races, palms get sweaty, mouth becomes dry, and I feel heavy and can't walk. Something about being around a lot of gay men in one place scares the hell out of me. I feel like I'm being ogled and sized up. Growing up, I heard so many negative things about gay men, that they're bad people and like to prey on men. When I am around gay men I anticipate this is how they will be.

It took a lot for me to go into a gay club or party. Even now when I go, I stand in one spot and do not move. I find a corner and stay there the entire time. I will usually only stay for an hour or two. My crew knew the drill with me. If they didn't see me, they knew I'd gone home.

Going to a straight club was a completely different experience. I felt comfortable. I socialized with people, struck up conversations with women, and danced. I didn't feel any pretension or need to impress anyone. The environment was filled with everyone having a good time.

When I started hanging out with my crew, "Gus" was singing from the very moment I met him. The boy was bad. Even though I had not heard of Gus, I knew of him through his songs on the radio. He was a songwriter and had written major hits for many artists including En Vogue, SWV, and Changing Faces.

Gus was a fly guy. He dressed trendy, with the latest sneakers and designer jeans. He put on his Timberlands and baggy jeans, but he wasn't a street thug. He always had a smile on his face. His clear skin, dark eyes, bushy eyebrows, and short, wavy hair did not give way to a thug image. He was just too pretty.

Me, Desi, and Gus hung out a lot. If we weren't together it was because we were working.

One morning, I turned on my television and I wasn't prepared for what I saw on BET. Nothing could have pulled me out of the trance I fell into. I was transfixed, lying in my bed, staring at the screen, with my mouth wide open for damn near five minutes.

I was in shock. No, paralyzed. I just stared at the television and watched my boy Gus parade in his video with a host of celebrity cameos, mean mugging the camera.

My friend Gus was pimping and profiling like he was the last gangster in the world.

I blinked to focus on the picture in front of me. My eyes had to have been deceiving me, but they weren't. It was Gus. Damn, he looked good. Hell, I never saw him flossing with that much jewelry, let alone mean mugging anyone.

I was even surprised by all the top rappers and singers in the video. Sure, he was in the game. He was a songwriter and had written quite a few hits. Other singers sang his songs on the radio. His melodic words were heard throughout the world. But here he was. This time he was singing his own words. He was the star in the video. Gus was now the celebrity.

Gus secured a recording contract with a major label. I was shocked when I discovered the news. It wasn't that he couldn't sing. I just wondered how he would keep his sleeping with men a secret. He knew it was a big gamble if the record company discovered he was a homosexual. They wouldn't have touched him with a ten-foot pole. It would be hard to sell his image as a ladies man if everyone knew he liked sleeping with men.

There was one R&B duo who had a smash single over the airwaves. Both the male and female were sexy and attractive. They were discovered and produced by one of Hip Hop's premier East Coast producers. Their groovy style made them a viable entity in the industry. The record label was behind them and helped to get them into every media outlet possible.

Then rumors started circulating in the industry that the male singer, "Zach," was gay. All of us in the down low clique were well aware he was part of our family.

My friend, who was a publicist at the record label, and the executives decided to make the R&B team an intimate couple. They would spin the story to the press that the duo was having a torrid love affair.

They were lovers and the chemistry we saw in their videos was that of love.

It worked. The media loved it. The fans ate it up.

The record label had a retreat in the Caribbean. They brought their staff as well as the R&B duo. Then a disaster happened. A male employee was caught in the room with Zach. This was not good. The media would soon discover what happened. The phones began to ring throughout the down low brothers in the industry. We all were calling one another. We watched to see what would happen.

The employee was immediately sent home and then fired. The label executives met with Zach, and they created an elaborate plan. The story became the male employee trying to seduce the singer. Zach was trying to get him out of his room as the employee made several advances. But it was too late. The record label knew Zach was a homosexual. Instead of putting more money into publicity for a cover-up, they dropped the duo and their careers were over.

A record company is in business to make money, not lose it. When you make them money, they will love and support you. If you are gay, forget about it. Hip Hop is all about heterosexual men making music for the streets. They need that appeal in order to sell records.

Record labels plot and plan the convenient dinners, supposed dates, and club appearances with the right woman on a celebrity's arm. Especially if an artist is single and there are speculative rumors about his sexuality. Having him linked to a beautiful woman helps his image as a playboy. It isn't a coincidence when photographers just happen to be at a certain restaurant, club, or store when a celebrity and their date show up.

Publicists and marketing and product managers go to great lengths to mastermind their artist's photos being plastered in gossip magazines. They send e-mails to other publicists searching for other relatively well-known celebrities who are single and can be used as an escort for a red carpet appearance. They find dates to soirees, events, and parties. The publicists call media outlets to notify them that their artist is attending an event with so-and-so. Once the publicist has photos of them with their beautiful dates, the pictures get sent to magazines and newspapers. When the fans see their favorite artist with a gorgeous woman at an event, all speculations about their sexuality are thrown out the window.

One R&B singer, "Quinn," had a velvet melodic voice and broke out with a sensual single in the late 90s. His self-titled debut album produced two top Billboard hits.

At the beginning of Quinn's career, a down low friend introduced us. His debonair style became his signature look, a well-groomed man with a flair for fashion.

He was a cool brother, and whenever I saw him we were always cordial. I once ran into Quinn at an after-party as he jumped out of the limousine with his publicist and manager. As soon as he exited the limo, the photographers were snapping away. At that moment he looked extremely nervous. He fidgeted with his coat jacket and put his head down, rushing inside the venue.

Once inside, we shared a laugh about him being bum-rushed by the paparazzi. I wondered why Quinn continued going to events with his manager instead of a woman since his popularity in music had sky-rocketed.

A good friend who worked at Quinn's record label called to tell me the R&B singer was getting married.

"What?" I practically yelled. "I thought he was dating his manager?"

"Yeah, he was, but now he's getting married. Can you believe it?"

Sure enough. It was in all the magazines. Quinn was getting married.

Rumors had been floating around about his sexuality. He wasn't the most manly of men and after being in his presence most people were left with the impression that he was gay. We in the industry knew. To keep his cover, my friend at the record label had to set him up on dates and make sure he was seen at events with beautiful celebrity women.

"He's really getting married," my friend would often call to tell me. He was still in shock, as were most of us.

"This is really tripping me out," I said. "Maybe she knows."

"Everybody knows. How can anyone not know?" he said. "But I got to do my job. I ain't got time to be in all these kids' business. I'm getting my check at the end of the day."

Once Quinn was married, it helped his career because he produced a few more albums for the record label. The very song that made him a success became his own fairy tale.

It's all part of the image and illusion. Record labels have double duty in protecting the secret of their homosexual clients. Everyone working in the industry knows about their sexuality, yet, no one says a thing. It's never discussed. When they do interviews, they dodge the questions about their sexuality. It's all a part of the media training.

Record labels spend lots of money putting their artists through media training on how to handle the press. They are taught what to say during interviews. They learn how to turn a question around to work in their behalf.

Gus was now a part of this machine. He belonged to the record label. His image, lifestyle, and anything resembling something of his true self had to be disguised. He was from Brooklyn, where life is hard and the streets are mean. Gus fought his way out of poverty and possibly a life of crime.

He'd had a normal childhood, but in the media he was raised by his hard-working mother who fought to keep him from drugs and gangs. She wanted him to have a better life. She sacrificed her own to give him a good life.

He didn't have a girlfriend, but in the media he was a player. Gus was a ladies man and they played up his cute boyish looks with couture clothes, jewelry, and homoerotic photos showing off his chest and abs. He was now a sex symbol.

Yet, all in all, behind closed doors with friends, he was one of us. He liked men and nothing could change that. He was a gay man. No one could know about his secret desires.

"Let's go out and see who's at the club," Gus would say. "I need a cute boy tonight."

"You're not afraid someone will recognize you?" I asked.

"I'll just pull my hat over my face. They won't know it's me."

Gus would get the boys. He stopped after a while because he didn't want to risk someone going to the record label and telling them about him. It's a gamble, but if a person sleeps with a celebrity, they usually won't say anything afterward. They know they have to keep the secret, especially with down low men. And a down low man is already leading a life of secrets so he won't say anything. He will not jeopardize outing himself. He has just as much to lose as the celebrity.

Hip Hop is a male-dominated culture with lots of machismo, testosterone, and ego. The more hetero a person is, the more accepted he is.

It is a world dominated by money, power, thugs, wannabe thugs, so-called gangsters, bling-bling, and video vixens. It is an environment filled with hard-core young men overcoming a life of struggle and obstacles to make it to the top as the ultimate hustler.

Just like the iconic movie *Scarface,* nearly every man thinks he can dominate and take over the world. A few have—Jay-Z, LL Cool J, Sean Combs, and Russell Simmons to name a few.

However, when Hip Hop is mentioned what doesn't come to mind is gay men. Yet it is an unspoken but known fact that deep within the confines of Hip Hop there is a prominent gay subculture. A world that industry insiders are keenly aware of but choose to ignore. It's a culture fueled by the testosterone of men striving to be on top and in control who have a "by any means necessary" bravado. These men will do whatever it takes to get what they want in Hip Hop. Rob, steal, lie, cheat, kill, have sex with another man. Hiding is a reality at nearly every level of Hip Hop.

So when rappers rhyme about killing the faggot, or treating a man like a bitch, or calling one another faggot-ass niggas, it's an insult to a man's ego. It's a threat to his masculinity. No man wants to be seen as soft, a punk, or a sissy.

As young boys, we've been taught at an early age to not display our emotions or feelings because only faggots and gays are in touch with their inner feelings. We're forced to suppress anything remotely effeminate. It's false information like this that starts the tougher than tough, "I'm a hard-core gangster thug," and "I ain't gonna be no faggot" mentality in young men.

In Hip Hop, being macho and masculine is the image. Nothing about a man can appear soft. Men in Hip Hop don't socialize with homosexuals. To them, they are better than gays. They are men and gays are not.

The same can also be found in ethnic communities. White is better than black. Black is better than Asian. Asian is better than Hispanic. And so on and so on. We find it necessary to make other ethnic communities feel inferior and less than.

So imagine being a black man in America, where we're already made to feel less than or inadequate. The justice and social systems rarely work in our favor. Sure, many of us are in corporate America, but many of us are not in decision-making, power positions.

As people of color, we have created one of the most powerful and influential phenomenons, Hip Hop. It's a global phenomenon that affects the lives of people throughout the world. No matter where you go, to any ghetto, city, neighborhood, or community, young people are affected by Hip Hop. I've seen firsthand how young people emulate the rappers in the videos with the stance, dress, and material possessions. They have on the platinum chains, diamond-encrusted watches, luxury vehicles with rims, and profile on the corners holding their crotches.

Even in the most foreign countries, young people know the lyrics to the songs better than most Americans, yet they can't even speak English.

As significant an impact as we have made on the world, we've allowed Corporate America to come in and practically strip Hip Hop away from us, leaving us feeling powerless, vulnerable, and emasculated. One group oppressing another. Which is why it's called the entertainment business.

All the young men involved in this business have is their ego, pride, street credibility, and manhood. You can take their material things, but they will not have those other things compromised or threatened. If a group of people is oppressed, they generally take their anger, frustration, hatred, and oppression out on another group of people, and in Hip Hop, it just so happens to be the gay community and women who get the brunt of it.

When the rappers rap about the hatred they have of homosexuals, I know it's because many of them are struggling with their own issues of sexuality. They hate what they are and in turn spew their hatred toward men who are reflections of themselves.

To see Gus bopping and leaning in the video made me understand that no matter what or who you are behind closed doors in the bedroom, you cannot let the world see that real you.

I immediately picked up the phone and called Gus. He laughed when I told him I was watching him on television.

"How do I look?"

"You look good. Why didn't you tell me you were doing a video?"

"It all happened so fast. They really wanted to push this single out."

"So you have an album coming out? When . . . who . . . what label are you signed with?" I was stumbling all over my words.

Gus filled me in on all the details of his album.

We talked for a few more minutes about his career. I was proud of him. He accomplished a lot for a young kid out of Brooklyn. It inspired me. Listening to him made me feel invincible. I knew I could do this thing called entertainment. I also understood that it was no place for an openly gay man. Gus had it all on the outside, but he struggled on the inside to fit into society's view of a man. "I wish I wasn't gay, but I can't help it," he would say. "I'm not going to say anything or admit anything to anyone."

When all of us arrived at Desi's spot, we all started clowning Gus. You see, Gus was the most flamboyant one in the group. You would never guess it by looking at him in his videos, but with us he was always making us laugh with his antics.

We were all happy and proud of Gus, but we knew we had to be extra careful when we were out in public. We couldn't let any slip-ups happen. No saying anything that would bring suspicion to us. We all knew we had to protect not only ourselves but Gus, the artist, the celebrity.

We all were hiding in Hip Hop.

27. HEAVEN

THROUGH GUS I HAD ACCESS to other celebrities and recording artists who were pursuing their dreams. I met men from famous groups
like Intro. I swear that damn near every male group during this time
had at least one gay member. It was crazy hearing their songs on the
radio and seeing their videos on television. They were gyrating, grinding, and singing to women when I knew they were thinking about the
men in their life or in the audience.

I'd met many of the entertainers through my acquaintances they
were dating or at gay clubs like the Sound Factory Bar. The Sound Factory Bar was the hot spot for young gay boys. It was a Hip Hop heaven.
Everyone dressed in their latest sneakers, Timberland boots, baggy
jeans, oversized T-shirts, and fitted hats. We all were swaying to the
beat, bopping and waving our hands in the air.

I saw quite a few celebrities sneaking in and hiding downstairs in
the dark corners, trying to avoid being seen. I met a very attractive
R&B singer from a hit-making quartet who became a bed partner for
the evening. The group struggled for years, singing on the streets, when
a record executive walking by heard them and signed them to a recording contract. Their career shot through the roof.

"Sterling" was in the club trying to be inconspicuous. We made eye
contact, and when he introduced himself, the smooth, melodic singer
gave me a fake name, Winston. But I knew who he was. His group was

one of the popular acts at the time. Their music was all over the radio. I smirked and told him his secret was safe and that he didn't have to worry about me saying anything. We left the club and had the most sensual evening.

I came across a stand-up comedian, "Isaac," who's had several hit television comedy shows. His off-beat humor and candor made him a sensation. He's become one of the all-time favorite comedians in America, especially known for his character parodies in his comedy.

Isaac had a sexy smile with bedroom eyes. Seeing him in the club really threw me because I never had any suspicions about him. When we made eye contact, I just figured he was in the club doing research for a movie role. Isaac had done several movies and in a few of them he portrayed gay characters. But in that eye contact there was a familiar look. My heart raced, and I felt awkward like I was being cruised and picked up. He smiled and I smiled. He walked off, but before he headed out of the room, he turned back again. I wasn't sure what to do. I just stood there in a trance. I shrugged it off, until I met him again years later.

Isaac didn't remember me from that night at the club, but the look was still there. His eyes gazed into mine as if he was looking into my soul. I felt awkward again. I liked the way his hands felt when we shook hands, and he even smelled nice. I didn't know what to say to let him know I wanted him. I didn't want to let this opportunity slip by again. His friends came and swooped him away. He gave me that same smile as he looked back. Damn, I missed out again.

Another R&B singer, "Omar," from a four-member male group out of New Jersey, was seriously dating a friend of mine. Every time I went to my friend's house, the singer was laid up in his bed. Omar was chilling like it was nothing. He walked around with no shirt on, revealing his bare chest, and his small frame that matched his baby face. He had no qualms about us knowing his secret, but he also knew we were down low. He trusted us.

Omar would sing the group's hit songs around us. He even sang songs from their upcoming album and asked our opinions of them.

It bugged me out being around him because on stage and in the videos he had a different persona. Women screamed for him. His image was that of a macho man, but then I would see him hugged up and smooching with my friend.

Many times I came across a short and thick, up-and-coming hard-core rapper, "Nyce," who was being pegged as the next best thing to hit rap. The skillfully lyrical rapper's music hit the streets hard. Nyce had been featured as a guest artist on a few other rap albums, as well as mixtapes. His name was everywhere at the time. He and his boys would roll through the club deep, and he would post up in a corner like a superstar while everyone looked on in awe.

It was audacious of Nyce to be in a gay club, but no one could say anything because it would be outing ourselves. Every time I saw him, he had an "I dare you to say something" look on his face. His boys surrounded him like they were his bodyguards. How could we tell anyone we saw Nyce in a gay club without explaining why we were also there?

The rapper wore an over-sized hoodie, baggie jeans, and a skull cap. His chubby cheeks always seemed like they were ready to spit a few rap verses. He would send his boys over to pick up whichever guy he was interested in for the night. "Yo, sup?" his crony would say. "My boy wants to meet you. You do know———."

Of course everyone knew him. The question was if you wanted to go home with him.

28. WHENEVER, WHEREVER, WHATEVER

WHEN *CROOKLYN* WRAPPED, I needed to get another gig. The players of the game were changing and I needed to align myself with those who could help me land another production job. In film and television, most production jobs last three, maybe four months. Then you either have to have something else already lined up or start the search for work on another film. You're always on the lookout for your next paycheck.

I was fortunate in that I saved most of my money. Since I didn't have to pay for meals and I didn't have too much of a social life, my checks went directly into the bank.

While I was searching for my next job, I got a call from my cousin Alfreda in Detroit. It was strange for me to receive a call from her because I had not spoken with anyone from my family with the exception of my grandmother in months.

"Hey, cousin," Alfreda began. "There is something very important you need to know."

"What's up?" I asked. My heart was racing.

"It's about your brother George." I was scared. *What could it be now?*

He was the third child born to my mother. He and I were much closer than I was to my other siblings. And like most brothers, we disagreed with each other and fought, but loved each other in spite of any disagreements. He was my everything. I went out of my way to do anything for him. I gave him all my clothes and shoes when I outgrew them. I gave him money when he needed it. Whatever George wanted he got. I spoiled him.

George was in the hospital. My cousin wouldn't tell me why. She just gave me the number and told me to call him. When I dialed the number, anxiety rushed through my body, and there was an awful feeling in my stomach. I wasn't ready for what my brother told me.

"George, what's going on? What are you doing in the hospital?"

He paused. His breathing was heavy.

"I have AIDS." George's voice stuttered.

My brother was in the hospital fighting for his life.

When George told me he had AIDS, I felt like all the life had left my body. I couldn't speak—I didn't know what to say to him. I cried silently holding the phone. Listening to him speak in a raspy harsh voice made the tears stream down my face. He was only nineteen years old.

My brother was being taken away from me. Just like my mother and baby brother Jevonte, I was losing another family member to AIDS. I screamed in my head, *Why God? Why are you doing this to me?*

"How did this happen?" I cried into the phone. "How long have you had it?"

George mustered his strength and explained everything to me.

"When I was in the group home I was molested. One of the male attendants molested me and some other boys." He had run away from the group home when he was thirteen and fourteen years old and vowed never to go back. Now I knew why.

As he was speaking to me, I became filled with hatred for the attendant at the group home, and for my mother for splitting us up. I was furious with my family for not saving us. Everyone related to me was dying. There was nothing anyone could say to me to make me feel better about life. What I thought I had worked so hard to get away from came crashing down on me in that moment. *Fuck the world and everyone in it,* I thought.

I told my brother I was coming home to see him. He wanted to come back to New York with me. "Of course you can come back with me," I told him.

Two days later, October 24, 1994, in the midst of my planning to go home, Alfreda called to let me know that my brother had died. Only a few weeks before his twentieth birthday.

George was gone. He didn't wait until I got there. Why didn't he wait? He left me just like my mother and Jevonte.

But death doesn't wait for anyone. I just hoped I could have seen my brother and spent some time with him before he left, before he took his last breath.

Again, I had to go home to bury another family member. Again, I had to deal with the pain I'd left in Detroit. It was no longer the city I knew growing up. It had become a place of desolation. While I was there, I should have had my own funeral. I would have buried my sexuality and the abandonment I felt from my mother. But I didn't. I just bottled it all up inside me.

Seeing my brother in the casket took the life out of me. I wanted to be in there with him. I was just learning how to cope with my mother and Jevonte's deaths. Now I had to go through it all over again, and it was too much.

I cried so hard trying to understand. Why didn't he fight? My brother was a fighter. He would take on anybody. He wasn't afraid to get down and dirty. I remember when he came home hysterical one day. A teenager who was a troublemaker in our neighborhood had pushed him. We rushed to the corner where the guy was standing, and George just starting swinging. I coldcocked the guy, and he went sailing to the ground. George wouldn't stop punching and kicking him until my cousins and I pulled him away.

George wouldn't back down from anyone. No matter who it was. He stood his ground. I couldn't understand why he gave up and left this earth. He could have fought. He should have.

When I returned to New York, I felt defeated. Life was flipping around and I was caught in it. Nothing seemed to matter to me anymore. I didn't bother to pray or try to find a spiritual answer. What good was it to continue praying when damn near every member of my family was dying? It was obvious to me that God wasn't listening or hearing my cries. Maybe I was a degenerate. Maybe this was punishment for my being gay.

DISC
FOUR

29. NEW YORK, NEW YORK— BIG CITY OF DREAMS

KATHY'S OFFER WAS A JOB at MTV as a production coordinator in their special events department.

When she called me the first time to tell me about the job, I was not interested. I was still getting adjusted to the lifestyle in Los Angeles. I wanted to do more work out there and build my résumé. I had only been there for a little over a year and wasn't ready to leave the great weather, the beaches, and my newfound friends.

Two months passed, and Kathy called a second time. "Look, there are a lot of people who want this job. You better bring your ass to New York." And just like that, I packed my bags, got out of my lease, and headed back to New York City.

When I arrived in New York, it was summertime. Being back East was like slipping into a pair of comfortable jeans. They just fit right.

Hip Hop's finest filtered the airwaves and became the backdrop to the city when I arrived. The city's theme music was that of the Notorious B.I.G., Lil' Kim, Method Man, Mary J. Blige, and Fat Joe. There was a big party in the city, and everyone was having a good time. It was definitely a great time to be in the Hip Hop industry, especially in New York City.

It was great being back. The hustle and bustle. My old friends. My old life. Damn, not exactly what I needed, but old friends and old habits are hard to break.

MTV, my, my, my. A blessing and a curse. It afforded me a lot, especially working in special events, where I was yet again the only black person in the department.

We did all the after-parties for the big award shows like the Video Music Awards, Movie Awards, Nickelodeon, and VH1 Fashion Awards. I traveled frequently for work, something I loved.

Working for MTV had its privileges and advantages. Whenever we were in a particular city for an awards show, series, or event, the businesses pulled out the red carpet for us. It was amazing to see how people fawned over me just because I worked for MTV.

Many times we got VIP passes to clubs just so the club could say that MTV people were there. I remember when I was in Las Vegas for our annual Sports & Music Festival. We were staying at the Hard Rock Hotel. Man, we had the free admission and our names were on VIP lists at the clubs. The drinks flowed freely. Owners of the clubs and their staff smiled and shook our hands. They just wanted to be around us because they hoped that we would use their club for a future event or party.

I remember the House of Blues wanted to host an MTV night at their club. They wanted to have some of the celebrities we had performing at our event to make an appearance at their place. They wanted us there badly. Even the MTV guy they had approached was trying to sell the idea to our executives. In the end, it worked out, and many of the artists performed at the House of Blues.

But it didn't stop there. Restaurants, bars, and hotels also handed out perks. It blew my mind. I never abused the opportunities, but when they offered I never said no, either. Working at MTV definitely opened many doors.

Working in special events, I was able to party and socialize at these functions with some of the hottest celebrities like Jay-Z, Christina Aguilera, Sean "Diddy" Combs, Will Smith, Snoop Dogg, and Lil' Kim. These parties were the "it" places to be seen, and I was there. Couple this with free-flowing liquor and food and you have a bad mix, especially for free-spirited men and women eager and willing to do anything to get in this business.

I came across many young ladies in dressing rooms, flaunting their breasts and drinking shots of liquor, hoping it would be their moment. They were doing anything to catch the attention of celebrities, hoping they'd get an opportunity to sing a few bars or spit a few rhymes—their one shot at fame.

Some women used their beauty and body as their marketing tools. We hired additional production assistants to work with us on our events. The young women showed up for the job interview looking very professional, but once they came to work on show day, they had on short shorts, miniskirts, high heels, and revealing tops. Their makeup was impeccable.

"How do you expect to get any work done dressed like that?" I asked.

"Oh, I thought I would be working the green room or doing something light."

We just sent them home.

Then there were the many young men handing their CDs to an artist or his manager while explaining their desire to get put on and willingness to do anything to make it happen. They tried to maneuver their way into the artist's entourage by letting him know they knew where and how to get the best weed in town—something many artists won't pass up. They were happy to befriend a local who knew where to get the best weed.

"Yo, can my boy get a credential to get in?" an artist would ask.

"It's really tight. We can only give you your allotted amount."

"Yeah, but he needs to get in. He is dropping something off for me."

"Can someone from your entourage meet him outside?"

But with the persistence from the artist and complaints to the producers, we let his boys in. It was obvious they were not really his boys. They were trying to get in the industry and they brought with them their demos and weed for the artist.

"Make sure to check out my joint. The shit is hot," they would say as they handed the artist their CD.

There are also many heterosexual men who play dangerous games with gay men in the business. These straight men are well aware that many men in the business are homosexual. In some circles it's no secret. They know how to flirt just enough to get what they want. Some men will toy around and lead gay men on. It's all a part of their plan to get from point A to point B.

A good friend of mine, "Kyle," is an accomplished songwriter. He's been lauded by the entertainment industry with numerous awards for his lyrical and producing abilities, working with everyone from Brandy and Whitney Houston to Marc Anthony. He was approached by a gorgeous entertainment lawyer who was managing a new R&B group.

The lawyer called Kyle and invited him out to lunch and dinner meetings. He told Kyle how much of a fan he was of his music and how he admired him.

Kyle called me because he wasn't certain if the man was a down low brother or a straight man trying to get close to him for a hookup.

"He is fine," Kyle said. "But I'm not sure if he's coming on to me or not."

"Why don't you just ask him?" I said.

"You know I can't do that. I'll just play it out and see what happens."

Sure enough, the lawyer's only interest was getting Kyle to help him make contacts in the music business. Once he got what he wanted, he stopped calling Kyle as often and didn't invite him out any longer. He remained cordial and made excuses why they couldn't hook up.

"Nick," a very attractive, straight actor/model, is a good friend of mine and has an abundance of gay friends. When I first met him, he and his beautiful wife had recently moved to New York in order to pursue their modeling and acting careers. Unfortunately, they divorced shortly thereafter, and Nick became a sexual beast, slaying many women.

It was easy to get caught up in him because of his seemingly adorable naïveté. I was even smitten with him. His charming smile and inviting eyes made him easy to be with. He loves being out in the public meeting new people. He has to. His looks and personality are his profession. He has to sell himself and he does a good job of it. Nick is extremely intelligent, earned his bachelor's and masters degrees, and has traveled the world becoming an expert on art, culture, and design. He's cohosted several cable television programs.

Most of the men I know who have come in contact with him always fall for his good looks and outgoing attitude. Nick flirts just enough to get what he needs. He will hug, hangout, and maintain contact with gay men. Nick has no problem being around them because he realizes that in order to get work he has to be friends with gay men. We have the connections and resources.

In entertainment, it's all about getting what you want from whoever you can. This is a business, and if you don't know the rules you will get used. Just like Q-Tip so eloquently stated in the hit song "Check the Rhyme" by A Tribe Called Quest: "Industry rule number 4,080, record company people are shady."

My life was filled with entertainment-related parties—movie premieres, clothing line launches, album release parties, networking events, or an executive's birthday party. And at each of these soirees, I met and partied with many down low brothers who worked in the industry.

"Terrance, let me introduce you to someone," a friend would say.

It was either "John," or "Mark," or "Ray" and he was a manager, director, or VP with Def Jam, Arista Records, Elektra Records, Columbia Records, or Sony Music.

We would exchange business cards and then make plans to get together for a lunch meeting or drinks.

As soon as I met one brother, I was being introduced to another. The party began to seem more like a down low convention. From the moment I walked through the door, over to the bar, on the dance floor, and to the VIP section, there was always a brother to meet.

They'd be mingling in the crowd, bragging about their next new project or the new marketing gimmick they were about to launch. Everybody was somebody. They all had titles.

My world was expanding. I was crossing over into the music

industry. I was surprised to discover there were a lot of brothers on the low.

I'd had my suspicions about some, but about others I'd had no idea. I met many of these men through my contacts. Once you're a part of the circle it doesn't take long before you are being introduced and invited to various events.

My phone would ring in my office with an invitation for a record release party. I started receiving e-mails about music showcases.

"Hey, Terrance. You want to come to my artist's party tonight?" an executive asked.

"Sure."

"All right. I'll put your name on the list."

And like that I was in. I had my entrée into the exclusive world. Once I started showing up for the parties and being a familiar face to the men in that world, they opened up. They kept inviting me into the fold.

"Terrance, you should come with us to brunch this weekend. A group of us get together once a month to hook up and hang out."

"Okay. I'll be there."

When I went to my first brunch in SoHo, I was amazed to see several handsome men sitting around the table. All of them were in the business in some capacity—working at record labels, Hip Hop magazines, managing artists. I never would have assumed anything about them. They had on their sneakers, velour sweat suits, designer jeans, and fitted caps. They looked like they were the artists themselves.

I became a member of one exclusive group. While at a music conference, I received an invitation from a fellow executive. He handed me a white, sealed envelope and whispered in my ear that the password was "brunch."

The contents of the envelope contained an invitation with directions to a private party.

When I arrived at the secluded location and rang the buzzer as instructed, I was asked for the password.

"Brunch," I said into the intercom.

The door was unlocked and I took the elevator to the top floor of the building where a sea of black faces greeted me.

Men who I never would have suspected to be in a place like that were mingling in this clandestine world. There were no airs, no judgments, and no pretensions there. It was filled with solidarity.

There were men everywhere. I walked through the room shaking hands and being greeted by new faces. There were a lot of music executives, but also successful businessmen, and a cable television host. When I looked at "Simpson," I grinned. His award-winning smile and charming personality were in full effect. It seemed like he was on television as he spoke with the men at the party.

What I noticed in particular were the number of men with wedding bands on. It is something I learned to look for after my incident with J. P. I made a mental note that such men were off-limits. I didn't want to be in that predicament again.

Now that I was back in New York and working at MTV, things seemed to come together. I had new connections, new resources, and a new network with brothers who were directors of their departments, vice presidents, and gatekeepers of an artist's career. The fate of an artist was in the hands of these brothers who navigated and calculated their moves. They got the artists promotional and marketing sponsorships.

I began to see how gay men were in all capacities of the entertainment game. If an artist needed to start their own clothing line, we were in the mix. If they wanted to get in television and films, we made it happen. If a singer needed songs, we wrote them. If an artist needed beats, we produced them. If an artist needed a publishing deal, we made it happen.

My boy "Raymond" was recruited by a sports star who started his own record label. The ball player wanted to break into the Hip Hop game and capitalize on rap. Raymond had worked at several labels and was a hustler. He was everywhere. You name it, he was in the mix. The ball player made Raymond president of his record label, and he was able to sign a lot of good acts. But he let me know that no one, not even the athlete, would ever know of his down low status. "They don't know, and I'm going to keep it that way," he told me. "I'm trying to go to the top and make this label a force to be reckoned with."

Raymond isn't the only one creating and in charge of an artist's career. There are other powerful gay men who are responsible for the artist's image in the media. If an entertainer needs a magazine cover, press coverage, or an article written, we have it. Whenever there is a photo shoot, there is one of us styling it. Whenever a director is needed to shoot a video, we are there.

It's no accident that black gay men created the Hip Hop drag which many Americans have embraced. These stylists are able to re-create and emulate the fashion-forward styles from Paris, Milan, and Fifth Avenue, and bring them to the streets of New York, Atlanta, D.C., Detroit, Chicago, Los Angeles, and Philadelphia. Most people in the hood didn't know anything about high fashion until a black gay man put it on a rapper.

When a rapper would show up on a video set, he would bring his own wardrobe. A stylist would go through his clothes to see what they could use. Most of the times there was nothing. The stylist is always looking to create a new trend and a new look. They are out in the streets constantly looking for creative ideas. The whole world is fodder for them. When big names like Diddy, Biggie, Lil' Kim, and Mary J. Blige were dressed in Versace, Coogi, Gucci, and Louis Vuitton and rhyming about them in their songs, the couture market opened up. Stylists had turned chic into ghetto chic. People in the hood wanted to look like their favorite artists.

Then male stylists wanted to buck their image, because it was always assumed that if a man is a stylist he is gay. In order to cover up their sexuality, they began dressing in urban street attire—big hoodies, white T-shirts, baggy jeans, and fitted hats. When hard-core rap came along, they didn't have to reach too far for creative ideas. They knew what the streets wore and they put it on the artists.

Now everyone was dressing in drag like a gay man.

Despite being the invisible force helping one of our own get ahead, regardless of his sexual preference, we are the ones ridiculed and the brunt of the jokes. And in spite of the love affair many gay men have with Hip Hop, the other members of the culture do not love us back. But at the end of the day they must remember that we create the style and image of the artists. We help them navigate the media, what to say and how to say it. If an artist fucks over a gay man he fucks over his own career, because we ultimately help in shaping Hip Hop.

A lot of times when there was an MTV event, I would make sure my down low friends had passes to attend. They scratched my back and I scratched theirs. Whatever CD I wanted, I just had to make a phone call. If I needed concert tickets, I just sent a quick e-mail. If I needed some new gear, it was only a call away. There was nothing we wouldn't do for one another. If anyone needed anything we knew we could call one another and utilize the resources in our down low circle.

One of my colleagues, "Ennis," worked for Clive Davis. Clive is the music industry. He helped launch the careers of Whitney Houston, Aretha Franklin, Monica, and TLC. He was president of Arista Records up until the late '90s. After Arista closed, he created J Records, and his music magic continued with artists like Alicia Keys and Luther Vandross.

When it was time for Clive's Grammy party in Los Angeles, Ennis's office was flooded with calls and requests to be put on the exclusive party A-list. I loved talking with Ennis because he knew he had power and he wasn't afraid to let anyone know it. On many occasions Ennis was helpful to me in offering advice and sharing his resources in the business. Through him I made new introductions to brothers in the music industry as well as outside.

I didn't see this world any differently than the fraternities in college where men helped one another and used their power to make things happen. One of the recruiting techniques used by fraternities is telling potential members that once you're a part of the organization you are part of a huge network of men with connections. I often called upon my frat brothers for assistance and resources. We all did. If any one of us needed a hookup, a reference, or a job, we helped each other.

But one thing is for certain about fraternities—the discrimination against gays is universal. When I was pledging, they made it known that they did not want any punks or sissies as part of the organization. There was no place for faggots in the fraternity.

So, as down low men, the networking and camaraderie we were doing was all about looking out for and helping one another navigate a system that is intolerant of our lifestyle.

There were two prominent publicists I befriended who had the daunting task of media training for their fresh new artists, who were very green about the media. Or they were constantly doing damage control with the seasoned artists who disregarded their pleas to show more discretion.

Their jobs were 24-7. They constantly were guarding their artists' images and, at the same time, protecting their own. The publicists knew the game and how the media worked. They knew the importance of perception. Yet, too many artists have to learn the hard way, and it's none too pretty once they're being scrutinized in the public.

On several occasions when I made trips to their offices, I'd listen to them go back and forth with their artists. Explaining to them why they needed to be at an industry event, why it was important to show up on time for an interview, why they needed to be seen with a woman or man, and why they couldn't speak their mind to the press if they had not been trained on the savvy and manipulative ways a journalist can get information.

One such artist learned the hard way how to keep his indiscretions discreet.

"Drake" was a member of one of the most popular R&B groups. They had several number one Billboard hits, and the young girls loved them because the adorable, sexy front singer, Drake, had a flamboyant stage presence. He was very eccentric in his style, defying most conventional looks in his appearance. Drake didn't hold back when he performed either—dancing, spinning, gyrating, stripping off his shirt, and showing his muscular frame. He loved the attention. Drake branched out on his own as a solo artist and had a huge hit single which garnered him more success. This led to a few acting roles in major motion pictures.

The record label arranged for the R&B group to meet with one of the most revered publicists in the business, who just so happened to be a colleague of mine. They wanted him to assist with the publicity for their next album.

"Chile', I walked into that meeting and I knew who the diva was." He laughed.

"It's a new girl group coming out?" I asked.

"Girl group?" He looked at me. "Honey, it was a girl all right. I told them that Ms. Thing is fierce, and they better watch him because he is going to cause the most trouble."

"What did they say when you called him a diva?"

"What could they say? That's why they called me."

I fell out laughing.

My friend tried everything to steer the attention away from the colorful artist's lifestyle. They tried to link Drake to a sexy pop star, but the diva attitude had already gone to his head and damage control was too little too late. Drake's sexuality was smeared across the media. Even other artists starting calling him gay.

Later, when I met the superstar group at MTV, it was confirmed. It was definitely obvious the lead singer was trying to hide his little secret.

I soon learned that the music industry world was more alluring than television and film. They had hustlers, ballers, pimps, players, and gangsters. Partying with them was a rite of passage. It was a privilege to be in the same space and location as these masculine men who made Hip Hop so sexy and hetero.

The perfect place to find men like these was at any industry record release party, an executive's birthday, or a Diddy party. Without a doubt everyone and their momma tried to get into Sean's parties. They are legendary.

Just as MTV parties had free-flowing liquor and food, Sean Combs' parties were like roller coaster rides with grandiose, over-the-top theatrics. When you walked through the door your body started moving. The music filtered into your body and you couldn't help but start jigging. The dance floor was packed with everyone waving their hands in the air. You no longer cared about sweating out your new designer outfit. Girls danced with girls. Half-naked girls were in cages. The bar constantly crowded with people getting their drink on. It was nothing but pure fun filled with high exhilaration throughout the night. No attitudes, no pretenses, and no drama. Just pure fun. Everybody just letting loose.

And we were all there, straight, gay, and bisexual. You had to leave your inhibitions at the door. And many times I exchanged glances and phone numbers with many men, because Sean's parties attracted some fine brothers. I don't know where they came from, but they were there. I enjoyed myself thoroughly, especially when a down low brother made introductions.

Attending an executive's birthday party was almost as grand but with fewer theatrics. These parties are great because they are low-key and exclusive. They are invite-only and you definitely have to know the executive or socialize in the same circles. The parties are more like social gatherings for the who's who. We give endearing hugs and air kisses. Everyone drinks in moderation and no one gets too drunk. You are in the presence of the elite of the industry, and you don't want them to see you acting out.

My first invitation came by way of "Brandon," an extremely handsome, impeccably dressed, high-level record executive. He has his own private stylist who caters to him when he attends award shows and special events. Brandon is responsible for creating many Hip Hop superstars' careers. Under his tutelage many rappers and singers have been able to turn their dreams into reality. He has also helped many aspiring songwriters establish publishing deals. Brandon was recognized for his accomplishments with many recording awards.

Brandon's invite-only annual function was complete with bodyguards checking the list for names, making sure the party remained exclusive in its all-male atmosphere.

His parties were always at a different location each year, and I looked forward to seeing many of the down low brothers I didn't get to see often. We all were there. Even some new brothers who had just come into the industry. This was their introduction to the crew.

It was nothing to see brothers dancing with brothers, grooving to the Hip Hop sounds. This was our party, our time to be free and uninhibited. We could openly check each other out, make conversation, and exchange numbers.

The record release parties, however, were my least favorite. They were all about egos and profiling, more for appearance purposes. It wasn't uncommon to be at a record release party and see Mary J. Blige, Fat Joe, Eve, Foxy Brown, Jadakiss, Nas, Ashanti, Busta Rhymes, and Funkmaster Flex. Being at these parties became a staple of my nightlife diet.

Once I attended one, they all became very much the same, with generally the same people I saw every week. Everyone standing around with drinks in hand, checking their BlackBerrys, talking on their cell phones, and waiting for the artist to arrive.

Most people attending these functions were music executives, the artist's entourage, and those who desired to be in the music industry. Then there were those who stood outside, hoping to get in just so they could say they were there.

Many of the men there I knew were hiding. Some had secrets swirling about them. Yet they were up in the club overcompensating with the hardest swagger and meanest mug, bottle popping, and manhandling the pretty, available girls. Some were celebrities, others were executives, and speculations were rife about their sexuality. People wanted to know. I knew about some for sure. I'd seen them at parties or gay clubs, or I knew members of their crew.

One record mogul, "Malcolm," who has diversified his success in music, business, clothing, and politics, and who always has a stunning woman on his arm, had his boy toy up in VIP with him.

Unbeknownst to his date and the many other women sashaying in the area, Malcolm's lover sat across the table, smiling, sipping his champagne. He was enjoying the fruits of his success just as much as his girlfriend was. The mogul and his lover had their system down to a science.

Many down low artists have their lovers in their entourage. We blend in well with everyone. We're inconspicuous and we know how to play our position. Only those who are supposed to know are in on the secret. We never display any signs of public affection. We may make eye contact and share a smile, but nothing further. We befriend the girlfriend. It's best to make her feel comfortable and not threatened by our presence. To her, the two of us are the best of friends. I am his boy.

It was crazy because we would clown the gay men in the room, pointing and joking about them behind their backs. All of us standing around in a group with our glasses of Barcardi and Hennessey trying to act gangster. We were dressed in our thug apparel, giving the illusion we were street thugs. We nodded what up to other men in the club and cozied up to the women to give the impression we had game and the women loved us.

"Man, look at that faggot-ass nigga. Don't let him up in here. Tell him it's full," some of the down low brothers would say. They didn't want to be seen in public with men who were obviously gay or whose sexuality was suspect. But behind closed doors they were the best of friends. When they needed something, it was all chummy-chummy.

When I heard those derogatory words they stung me. The blows from the words knocked the wind out of me. But my down low brothers and I would laugh so we wouldn't bring attention to ourselves. We didn't want anyone to think we were like those guys we were poking fun at. Yet, I knew I shouldn't have laughed. I should have stood up and said it was wrong because I was one of them.

We were all imitating the rappers who spit those words out and are forever immortalized on their CDs. Homophobia at its finest from some of the most revered men in Hip Hop like DMX, Eminem, Busta Rhymes, and 50 Cent.

Many of us wanted to stand up and say something, but the thought of being outed in the industry and losing our jobs kept us silent. We were tolerant when we should have been intolerant.

At one time, I approached my friend "Andre," who was a major publicist at one of the foremost record labels. He worked with some of the top names in the business like Janet, Blu Cantrell, and D'Angelo.

"Let me ask you a question," I said to him. "How do you feel when you are working with artists who are blatantly homophobic? How does it make you feel when you hear them say words like 'faggot' or 'homo'?"

"Yeah, it does bother me," he said. "I hate it when I go into the studio and hear them saying those words. But I can't be in the studio with every rapper or singer trying to tell them how to do their music. It's not my job to monitor every artist. At the end of the day I still have a job to do and I know every two weeks I'm going to get a paycheck."

And his sentiments were across the board with most of the down low men in the business. Sure they didn't like hearing those words, but they had a job to do and they didn't want to run the risk of losing their steady income.

I knew my faults, so how could I point out someone else's when I refused to address my own? Especially in a world where celebrities are put on pedestals. Everyone caters to their every whim. They are a part of something that many try desperately to break into every day.

It's no secret the entertainment industry is a hard nut to crack, so of course those of us who worked in it were seen as gods. We were on the inside, and people loved us—not only because of who we were but also because of what people thought we could do for them.

As big as MTV was, there were only a few down low brothers I knew of who were on the inside. I was in special events, and there were two who were high-powered executives for the company. The three of us were tight and close-knit. There was a fourth, but he was so low-key, it almost came as a surprise when he later revealed to me his down low status.

One of the key players for the network and I would meet in his closed office and fill each other in on the down low brothers in the business and those who were potentially hiding at MTV.

Outside the office we were cordial to one another, but behind those doors we were the best of friends. We shared networking resources and personal stories. I learned, for instance, that on several occasions he would instruct one of his sex partners from Elektra Records not to wear any underwear when he stopped by his office after work hours.

My two new good friends got me acclimated quickly to the workings of MTV. They schooled me on who's who and what hands to shake. If I wanted to move up I had to network and meet those in charge.

It's necessary in this business to network. People move up the ladder quickly and if you're a nice, cool, and smart person who works hard, others will take you with them while they are climbing the ladder. But, again, the most important lesson to learn is never let your secret out. No one can know about your sexuality.

One woman in Hip Hop became the pivotal spokesperson in thrusting our secret lifestyle into the public light. Wendy Williams, the Queen of Radio, was a radio personality on Hot 97, New York's preeminent Hip Hop station.

Wendy was a firecracker. Someone in the industry was filling her in on celebrities' exploits. They were divulging the behind-closed-doors antics of Hip Hop's most revered men. Wendy went to town, giving her listening audience an earful with revelations of homosexual behavior in the confines of Hip Hop. She even went so far as to let us know that there was an actual gay rapper. This was a delectable tidbit that fed the insatiable appetites of inquiring minds.

The streets were buzzing. People everywhere were talking about the gay rapper in Hip Hop. Everyone wondered who he could be. People began making lists. Various names were thrown into the mix. No artist in Hip Hop was safe from the gossip.

It was mind-boggling listening to her discuss insider secrets, which many of my down low brothers and I already knew. We all tuned in to hear who her next victim would be. We all secretly prayed it was none of us or anyone we were sleeping with.

Some of her ideas of who was playing for the other team were far-fetched. But many times I wondered who might have slipped up and got caught. As close-knit and closed-mouthed as we were, it seemed impossible that anyone could discover our underground network. But like everyone else in the city, I found myself tuning in and listening for the latest details. Damn, if Wendy wasn't on point in some accusations, and, damn, if she was far off on others.

The no-holds-barred radio shock jock was now the holder of the keys to a locked closet and knew how to hit us. She went for the low blow and got Hip Hop in the gut. It was a devastating blow, and the people in Hip Hop have yet to recover.

For a long time, down low men have lived discreetly and out of the spotlight. But now our dark, closeted lives were being exposed. Many of us figured we were safe from a public outing. Who would dare say anything?

At that time, no man would come forward and reveal he was having a sexual relationship with another man. Not in the public light and especially not in the media for public consumption.

But the shit hit the fan with the constant, speculative stories about Diddy. The battle between Diddy and Wendy was nonstop. The accusations about his lifestyle caused a big media fight between the two. Ultimately, it ended with Diddy winning. Wendy was fired from Hot 97 and landed in Philadelphia with Power 99. After a few years, she returned to New York's WBLS 107.5, stronger, wiser, and ferocious.

The story was titillating and insatiable, but the media, as always, was on to the next hot, new thing. Newspapers and magazines are in business to make money, and if your high-powered name or dramatic antics help them sell their product, you can best believe you will be on every cover or inside each issue.

I became an avid reader of some of the industry's magazines like *VIBE, XXL,* and *The Source.* I was reading *The Source*'s 30 Powerful People in Entertainment issue and came across the name and picture of someone who worked at MTV in a very high-profile position. I figured it would be great to meet the brother and find out more about what he did for the company.

I did a name search in the company's database and got "Cecil's" e-mail address. I shot him an e-mail letting him know I read about him in *The Source* and that I hoped to set up an informational meeting with him to find out more about his role.

Cecil immediately responded and was impressed by my assertiveness. He mentioned I could set up a meeting with his assistant for later that week.

On the day of the meeting I was prepared. I had my notes and questions to ask. I was a little nervous, but it all subsided when I got in his office. Cecil was extremely personable. He wasn't pretentious like I'd thought he would be. Yet, there was something I couldn't quite put my finger on. The nervousness was gone, but an uneasiness crept in. I had experienced it before when I was in the company of a man who I felt was trying to read me. But I didn't want to draw conclusions and assume that Cecil was gay.

By the end of the meeting we were laughing and talking about other things unrelated to entertainment.

The next day I e-mailed my thanks to Cecil for his time. A few days later I got an e-mail back. He thanked me for stopping by and asked when we could get together again. I pondered it because I wasn't sure how to respond. Keeping things on a superficial level, we continued the e-mail correspondence.

I ran into Cecil a few times in the building, but it was always awkward. In his last e-mail message to me, he was blatant about what he wanted. He asked what type of guys I was into. I thought long about it. Should I answer and take him up on the offer, or not respond and keep things professional? I let it go.

A few months later I learned he was leaving MTV for a more lucrative opportunity.

30. IF THAT'S YOUR BOYFRIEND, HE WASN'T LAST NIGHT

THE MTV VIDEO MUSIC AWARDS were approaching. They were being held in Los Angeles, so I had to go back to the West Coast for a month to work the show.

When I got to Los Angeles, I hooked up with my boy Corey to get caught up on what I'd missed since leaving the city. Man, you leave for a few months and things change so quickly. Corey was back to his old tricks. He was still cool with Derek Luke and his wife and attended church services, but the lure of the clubs and the down low lifestyle had him struggling. As a friend once said to me, "Dick is addictive."

I did my usual rounds of hitting up familiar spots. I stopped by Club 7969 to see what new celebrity lesbians were making appearances at the club. But this particular night was different. There were no men parked outside waiting for the ladies. These women entering the club were transvestites. Men who dressed as and lived the lifestyle of a woman.

It was a Monday night. Transvestite/Transgender night.

Men rushed from their cars, hoping no one would see them entering. My curiosity got the best of me and I hustled in as if I was undercover myself. Once again, my nerves were on edge. I had that queasy feeling I always got when I entered a club filled with gay men.

My body was going through too much. My stomach was turning

flips, and I felt as if I was about to vomit. My heart was pounding, and I was sure I was going to pass out right there. I leaned against the wall for support. I needed something to hold on to.

My mouth was dry and I desperately needed some water. I made my way to the bar and ordered a few bottles of water. After gulping down the first bottle, I glanced around the club hoping to spot a familiar face.

Everywhere I turned, there were heads bedecked with blond, black, and brunette wigs. Their flawless faces were skillfully and delicately made up with Mac and Revlon. These men would give any woman a run for her money with their miniskirts, tight pants, and bustier tops spilling out their cleavage.

I slowly canvassed the room. The men I had seen rushing from their cars earlier were now quite comfortable here. They ranged from street thugs to businessmen and the transvestites reveled in and adored them.

And then there was one. A fine thoroughbred of a man. So many of us had fantasized about "Braxton" when his muscular, toned body had graced the television screen on his hit show. After leaving the show, he became a sensation working in theaters across the country.

The New York–bred actor smiled as a transvestite stroked his dark, chocolate face and I knew I could probably push up on him.

I waited patiently for the transvestite to leave so I could make my move and approach him. I'd say something nice and smooth to get his attention. Something to let him know his secret was okay with me. We were alike. We both liked men. Then, he and I would end up at his place going at each other like two long-time, passionate lovers. I would devour his entire chocolate body, leaving no morsels, no crumbs. I would swallow him whole. That was my plan. Maybe he would be like his character on TV—a bad ass who didn't take shit from anybody.

I loved Braxton's show for having him bare his burly chest. It drew the fans in. His deep voice poured from his mouth. I could only imagine what his big, beautiful lips felt like. They had to be soft.

But as I was lost in my fantasy, the transvestite won. She had him baited and hooked and scored the prize. No less than twenty minutes after smooching in the dark corner they disappeared out of the club and into the night, probably to her place.

My friend Edwin, the transvestite I'd met when I worked on Keenen's show, explained to me that men like Braxton don't consider themselves gay. They're not interested in sleeping with a man, regardless of how hard-core and masculine he may be. They're looking for men who give the illusion they are women. They rationalize that the sex is not with a man. They see a woman.

Edwin knew firsthand. He was one of them. When he wasn't working behind the scenes producing a show, he would put on a dress and play the part of a woman. His exotic boyish looks were soft. He was often mistaken for a woman even out of drag. But once the clothes and makeup were on, he was a woman. He no longer identified with being a man. Nothing about him was a man. "Lillian" was one of his alter egos, and he chose the name because he knew it would attract "Bailey." A star his entire life, Bailey rose to fame quickly from his roles in blockbuster films. He married and had several children but divorced and began traversing through Hollywood with single, beautiful women.

Edwin began a business that solicited men who had fantasies about transvestites, and business boomed. His phone never stopped ringing, not until he got the call from Bailey looking for Lillian. The A-list award-winning actor phoned and asked Lillian to come outside. He was circling the block and didn't want to be seen. Once he saw Edwin, that was all she wrote. Bailey laid out several one-hundred-dollar bills on the front seat of the car, and Edwin had accomplished his goal. Bailey was known in the underground world of transvestites. They knew his desires, and Edwin became one of his newest fixes.

Once I visited the video set of "Mario," one of the biggest rappers to hit the scene. His rough persona and lengthy criminal past caused many women, and some men, to lust for him.

My boy worked for the label and they were in Los Angeles shooting Mario's next single. While we waited for them to set up the scene for the next shot, Mario and his entourage were in his trailer drinking and smoking weed. The acrid smell of the weed reached well beyond the doors of the trailer and onto the streets, and I was sure that the policeman who was directing traffic away from the location would get a good whiff, rush inside, and arrest them.

By the time the well-built rapper and his entourage emerged from his trailer, I knew my friend would have trouble keeping him on the set. The chart-topping, platinum-selling rapper ranted and raved about being tired of waiting and announced he was going to get something to eat with his crew. "I'll be back!" Mario barked. "I ain't sitting up here all day waiting on you motherfuckers to get your shit together."

He strolled past me with a smirk on his ashy face, letting me know he was running things. As I looked at the young women surrounding him, I observed that they were not real women, they were transvestites. They definitely could pass for real women, though. They had the features, mannerisms, and dress of women, but I, like most gay men, can spot a transvestite. It's in the subtle things like the walk, the over-dramatized makeup, the larger hands and feet, and the muscular build of the body.

I asked my friend, "Does Mario know those women are not women?"

"Please. Yes, he knows. They've been with him since he got in town."

I smiled back at the rapper. He may have thought he was fooling everyone with his gregarious brood of women, but I knew better and I left it alone. Mario was the same man who was named by MTV as one of the greatest rappers of all time and lambasted gay men in his lyrics. He had one number one album after another. He often called out other rappers for being soft, feminine, and gay, and yet he found comfort in the arms of a transvestite.

After I left the club, I called Edwin. Seeing all those transvestites brought him to mind. When I reached him, he was out on Santa Monica Boulevard walking the streets. I should have known.

When I pulled up and got his attention, we barely got in a good conversation. When a transvestite is out working the streets, they are not into attracting attention unless it's from a paying customer, which I wasn't.

Not more than fifteen minutes into the conversation, Edwin spotted "Wallace," a young, popular comedian driving by in an orange Hummer.

"Chile', I got to go," Edwin said. "I'm going to get that."

"Be careful," I yelled at him as he adjusted his skirt and wig, hightailing it up Santa Monica Boulevard.

I waited to see how it would play out. I was certain the chubby comedian wouldn't turn around. I'd seen Wallace a few times at church, and he was well liked by the young girls. But his juvenile antics were becoming old as he turned into a man. Wallace later was featured with an all-star cast of improvisational actors on network television. The show has launched the careers of some of the most widely acclaimed comedic actors of our time.

The orange Hummer slowly turned and approached Edwin whose long, stockinged legs sashayed up to the car. After a few minutes of conversation, Edwin hopped into the passenger seat, and they sped off.

I found it interesting that some actors will dress up and play women on television and on the big screen, and yet offscreen they search out men in dresses for their sexual pleasures.

Later that week, I made a stop at Corey's house. We were chilling when a fine brother pulled up in a BMW. I peeped him as he stepped out with a cream-colored, velour jogging suit and crisp white Nike sneakers. He was six feet tall, with beautiful dark eyes, and thuggish. He was definitely my flavor. Corey introduced me to his boy "Derby." He and Corey were going to hang out. They invited me along, so I more than obliged. This brother was a cutie, and I was going to find out who he was. We went to dinner at a Mexican restaurant and then to a local bar.

Derby and I hit it off well—too well. I was not planning on meeting anyone, especially anyone from Los Angeles. I was there on business, working. But Derby and I got into a serious relationship.

Derby was an executive with BET. On weekends when I wasn't working, he made my time in Los Angeles fun. Derby was well liked and he introduced me to his friends. But it was his disposition that drew me to him. He was always in chill mode; nothing seemed to faze him or ruffle his feathers. Even when we spoke while he was under pressure at work, he didn't let anything get to him. "It's all good," he would say. "It will all work out."

I was floored when I first went to his apartment. He had so many clothes that they were bursting out of the closet. From sweat suits to designer jeans and T-shirts, all the way down to his expansive collection of Timberland boots. He even had damn near every color of Nike sneakers imaginable. I thought I loved urban gear, but Derby had me beat.

When we weren't together, we'd spend hours on the phone talking about everything. I couldn't believe that I found someone who I had so much in common with. We both worked in television and loved going to the movies. He was laid back and calm. He and I were not club heads and we didn't enjoy being around crowds of gay men. We were down low and we liked being low-key.

The time seemed to go by too damn fast. I hated making my preparations to go back to New York because the most difficult thing was leaving Derby behind. I didn't want to do it, but I had to. Los Angeles was a closed chapter for me. I needed to move on and continue my life in New York. Derby and I decided to have a long-distance relationship. We vowed to visit each other once a month and we wound up talking on the phone several times throughout the day.

BET often brought Derby to New York for work. It was perfect. I took him around the city to places like SoHo and Times Square. I introduced him to my network of down low brothers on the East Coast. Everyone was happy and excited for me. They helped me celebrate my first real relationship.

Derby was back on the West Coast, and my birthday was approaching. I was bummed out because he let me know he wouldn't be able to make it into town to celebrate with me.

It just so happened that my birthday was right around the time the Video Music Awards were being presented at Lincoln Center, so work kept me busy and I didn't focus too much on trying to have a big, elaborate party. I could enjoy the show and celebrate with my friends at the after-party later that night.

I was coming from backstage during rehearsals, when the production secretary said that someone was looking for me. I was frustrated because I had been running around the entire day making sure most of the talent and crew who flew in were picked up from the airport and taken to their hotels safely. I was sure it was someone who had gotten left at the airport or somebody coming to complain about their hotel. I rushed to the back of the theater, and standing in his gray, velour sweat suit and gray and white Nikes, was Derby. He was standing there with a huge grin on his face and a birthday cake in his hands. I couldn't have been happier. As excited as I was and as much as I wanted to kiss him right there, we gave each other a hug and some dap. I would have to show him my appreciation later that evening when we were alone.

Derby was full of surprises, and I liked that. He enjoyed the finer things, and didn't spare any expense when it came to us being together. I was glad I had Derby, very glad.

Everything was working according to plan. For the next year we were doing it. We were making it happen. But I noticed some things in Derby I hadn't seen before. His behavior and mood changed frequently. He often stayed out late. I wasn't in Los Angeles to witness firsthand any other changes, but the ones I became aware of set off a red flag for me.

The next time Derby came to visit, I discovered his drug use. It seemed like everyone in Los Angeles used some type of "candy"— alcohol, ecstasy, cocaine, marijuana. At parties I attended there were always plenty of drugs flowing through the room.

When I first got to Los Angeles, my parole officer warned me about attending parties and getting caught up in drugs. I thought it was weird that this was the first thing she mentioned to me.

Derby tried to explain to me that he didn't have a habit. He didn't use cocaine every day, only on the weekends.

I just looked at him. I didn't know what to say or do. They say the first sign of someone who's an addict is denial, and Derby was definitely in denial.

I ignored it and kept telling myself that I was happy in the relationship. But I knew that if someone had to choose between you and drugs, you'll always lose out.

Then in January, I was invited to a small, low-key party on the Upper West Side in Manhattan. There were just a few industry folks and one up-and-coming rapper. I couldn't help but notice him because he was definitely my type—a tattooed shorty and very confident. I purposely tried to ignore him.

The rapper came onto the balcony where I was standing. Out of the corner of my eye, I noticed him staring at me. I made a few glances toward him and he flashed a smile at me.

He finally walked over and introduced himself, saying his name was Trouble. I told him I wasn't looking for any. I know when someone tells you who they are, you have to believe them—however when I looked at him, he was beautiful. Just beautiful. But he'd told me he was trouble.

He laughed at me and recanted, telling me his rap name, "Fresh." We shook hands. His were massive and hard like he worked with them all his life. I didn't want to look in his eyes because I knew my body would win out. His touch alone proved to be too much. It sent chills through my body. *I am not going to be a sucker for this. Be strong. Be strong. Be strong,* I kept saying to myself.

Fresh made light conversation with me. He then went in and out of the house, returning to the balcony, each time getting closer to me. He'd purposely brush against me. I knew what was up. I played the game with him. I should have moved. I didn't want to respond the way I did, but something inside of me liked the attention.

We talked a little more, and Fresh was now making an imprint on my mind. I took him in mentally and physically. Everything about him was in my senses, and I knew I needed to take a cold shower when I got home.

I was happy when my ride said he was ready to go. I could just leave and not have to worry about doing something I wasn't supposed to be doing. I was in a long-distance relationship. I was to avoid men like Fresh. I was to be monogamous. But being around Fresh was making everything extremely difficult.

"Yo, can I get your number?" Fresh asked.

"Naw, I'm cool."

"Oh, word? It's like that."

I chuckled, but it seemed to turn him on even more. He followed my friend and me out of the apartment, onto the street, and to our car. He was persistent. Something in Fresh's demeanor, in his inability to take no for an answer, turned me on. I told him to give me his number and I would call him.

Foolishly I didn't toss the number like I should have. I went home with it, and it sat on my dresser for days. I debated and pondered over the number. Derby was in Los Angeles. We had not seen each other and I was feeling horny. I called Derby but he was busy traveling with some talent from one of BET's shows. We couldn't really talk. I missed him and needed the physical touch.

I broke down and finally called the rapper. He invited me to meet with him and his boys in SoHo for some drinks. Damn, he looked better than I remembered. A fresh haircut, his dazzling smile, and his inviting eyes.

After a few drinks and a long conversation, I discovered some cool things about Fresh. He had a deal with a major record label and said he planned on being huge.

The more I got to know about him, the more I liked him. Although he came across as pompous and arrogant, he was really a cool brother.

After a few more rounds of alcohol, we ended up back at my place. I knew this was a big mistake and I knew I would regret it in the morning but I convinced myself I could live with it. Fresh was about to give me some serious head and I couldn't pass it up.

Now every time I hear his songs on the radio I smile and think of how he likes being dominated in bed.

I never told Derby about the rapper, but things between us were getting strained anyway. The long distance was too much. My friends on the West Coast told me his drug use had increased. When we spoke on the phone, he all but confirmed his late-night binges. I could tell that he didn't want to admit it to me, but he had no choice. Drugs had become a mainstay in his life. He told me he didn't want to hurt me, and we agreed it would be better if we just ended it.

With the relationship over I jumped back into my work and frequented more social parties for down low men. Work was my refuge when things got rough for me. It was my escape. I never wanted to focus my energy on things that went wrong. I tried to avoid them at all costs. My career was my shoulder to lean on and talk to. I didn't cry because I didn't have any tears to cry. I would never let myself get to that point. I just forced all that energy into my work and pushed myself to not feel anything.

Being around emotionless down low men helped me to feel better about myself. It is a world where your feelings don't matter. You can't let them get in the way. You don't want to let another man see you vulnerable. It's a sign of weakness and many men will prey on it. I had been preyed on many times for showing and expressing my feelings for a man. I kept giving my power away to them. As much as I wanted to believe in those relationships and make them work, they were doomed from the beginning. We were all living a lie. We were lying to ourselves, families, and friends. No relationship can last if it is based on lies.

31. MONEY, POWER, AND RESPECT

A GROUP OF US were at dinner one evening discussing the state of the music industry, where it was going, and who the next trailblazers were who would take it to another level. We wanted to be powerful forces within the industry. We decided to call ourselves, "The Blow-Up Kids."

We all decided we were going to be the next big players in the industry. In order to get our names out there we decided to put together music showcases.

Our first showcase was held at Tramps nightclub in Manhattan. We were able to get Rah Digga to perform, and Busta Rhymes came out to support her. At the time, she was a force to be reckoned with. The hype around her had the streets buzzing. Rah Digga was a great performer and she let the audience know it. She didn't hold anything back. She let loose on the stage. And she brought the house down. The night was memorable with Rah Digga's energy, Busta in the crowd, and us, The Blow-Up Kids.

The next showcase was held at S.O.B.'s on Houston Street. At this event, we had *Parle*, an R&B group from the Ruff Ryders record label. Many executives from other labels were there, but there was an especially large crew from the Ruff Ryders camp.

When it came time for the group *Parle* to perform, the girls in the crowd screamed for the young men. One of the reasons the crowd was excited was because the group represented Ruff Ryders, the hottest label at the time, boasting artists like Eve, DMX, and Jadakiss on their roster.

During *Parle's* performance of their last song, the microphones went dead. Everyone got upset, and the group and members of the Ruff Ryders crew started screaming at the sound man. But as much as he tried, he never got the microphones to work again. People started accusing the club's management of sabotaging the group. We tried to keep everyone calm, but unfortunately, with all the insults swirling, a fight started next to the stage by the exit door. A gang of men were throwing fists, chairs, and liquor bottles. People started running frantically toward the front door. Security guards rushed over to break it up, but by this time the fight had spilled out onto the street. During the scuffle, a security guard was stabbed and rushed to the hospital.

We were stunned by the incident. We couldn't believe that everything we had worked so hard for had suddenly gone down the drain. The last thing you want as a reputation is your name associated with a club fight and someone getting stabbed.

Before the fight, however, I'd met a singer from another four-member, popular R&B group who was in attendance at S.O.B.'s. They had a song on the radio and a video in rotation on BET. "Maximo," an attractive man with a very muscular body, was the shortest member of the group. He wore baggy jeans, a T-shirt, and a do-rag. I immediately knew who he was. I was busy with another conversation when he approached me. He was very laid back, but his approach was all too familiar.

"Hey, what up, Terrance?" he said as we shook hands. "I'm not sure if you know me . . ."

"Of course I know you," I said, smiling. "I like your group's music."

"Thanks, man." He smiled. "Listen, I would love to have my group that I'm producing perform at one of your showcases. I'm going to the studio right now. I can get you some music to listen to if you're interested."

"No problem. I'm sure we can make something happen," I said, and we exchanged phone numbers.

I called Maximo a few days later and caught him just as he was leaving the studio. He suggested we meet up outside the studio and from there we would go to his apartment in Brooklyn.

It was a nice little spot near Prospect Park. I could tell he spent a little money on his place with the nice leather furniture and expensive electronics. I've found that most men like to spend their money on electronic toys.

"Check this out," Maximo said as he popped in a CD. I wasn't interested at all in his music, I just wanted to sex the hell out of him. I just wanted to throw him on the bed and rip his clothes off.

"This is my group I'm talking about," he said, turning up the stereo. A harmonic sound filtered from the speakers. "It's three of them. I don't know if I'm going to get a fourth member. What do you think?"

"It depends. You're in a group and there are four of you. I don't think it matters."

"But it looks good with four. Three is an odd number."

"They sound hot," I said. "They definitely can sing."

"That's what's up. You think they can be in one of your showcases?"

"I don't think it will be a problem."

"Aight, cool. I really appreciate it, Terrance. You smoke?" he asked, pulling out a small baggie full of weed and a Phillies Blunt.

"Not often."

"This some good shit. Brooklyn homegrown herbs." He laughed. He twisted and tugged at the marijuana leaves crumbling them into small bits to pour them inside the blunt.

He was right. The Brooklyn herb had my head spinning. I forgot all about the CD we were listening to. I heard Maximo talking about the industry and how nobody knows he fucks around with men. He thought it was comical that he was able to fool everyone.

"So what's up with you and my boy Adam?" he asked, pulling a long drag on the blunt and passing it to me.

How the hell does he know about Adam? I wondered. Adam was someone I had known for a few years. We met at a party and hooked up a few times, but we remained friends. He later went to work for Arista Records.

"What you know about me and Adam?" I asked.

"Nothing. I know you both are cool with each other." But I knew better. Maximo probably heard about Adam and me. That's why he approached me.

After smoking a couple of blunts, we finally made it to his bedroom. It was dimly lit and the weed had taken its effect. I was horny. I didn't want to waste any more time talking. It was time to do what we both really wanted to do.

He stripped off his T-shirt and pants. I got a good glimpse of him from behind as his jeans hit the floor, and he had one of the fattest asses I had ever seen. Perfectly round. His black Calvin Klein briefs hugged his cheeks. I immediately became erect. Maximo walked over to me and grabbed my crotch. He tugged at the zipper of my jeans until I was free and in his hands. He pulled me toward him and he lay on the bed. He lifted his pelvis in the air and pulled his underwear to his ankles. He kicked them off, he opened his legs, and he invited me to climb on top of him.

Maximo was vicious. I like an aggressive man in bed. He pulled no punches in letting me know what he liked. He turned on his stomach, letting me get a good view of his hard, round ass. I rolled on top of him and our bodies danced, rocking back and forth.

After we panted and sweated through our heat-intense sex session, Maximo later told me the other members of the group were not aware of his sexuality. He'd been keeping it from them. He didn't want to jeopardize either his or their careers.

We never went any place together. We only met up late nights at his place for sex. He was always in the studio with the group or in the gym. He had an amazing body with a huge chest and arms, but I swear he worked his ass muscles just the same.

Maximo was constantly singing every time we were together. He was into his music, so I knew our time together would be short-lived. Very much like his career. Although I was enjoying the time we shared, the group went on tour and the sex stopped, along with our communication.

It really didn't matter too much to me, though. I was used to it. Men on the down low come and go. It's part of the program. It's not like we're looking for a committed relationship, we can't have one—not with another man. It's too complicated, especially when you're a high-profile celebrity, or if you have a wife or girlfriend. Casual sex or a jump-off is about the best you can get.

When I was with Ace, Fresh, or Maximo, I knew how far it was going to go. There could be nothing more than sex and companionship. We were only fulfilling each other's sexual needs.

In a down low relationship with a celebrity, you have to know your position. They have their image to maintain. They are in the public eye and have a lot more to lose. For me it was like being a thief in the night. I came when the girlfriend or wife was not home. My man and I did what we had to do, and then I left.

Ace had become a top producer. He was now working with top names. He always came to my house, but on a few occasions when his girl was out of town, we were in his bed. They lived together, so it was difficult for him to bring anyone to the house. She was nosy and all in his business. She checked his cell phone and BlackBerry. She went through his pants pockets looking for any evidence he might be cheating on her.

Ace loved it when I came over. We would order some food, chill, and watch movies. The two of us would then climb into bed and devour each other. I'd make sure to take every bit of evidence that might show that I was ever there. I didn't want his girlfriend showing up at my house confronting me or calling me to ask how I knew Ace.

With Fresh it was different. He and his girlfriend didn't live together, though she was always at his place. Whenever he got her out of the house, he made me wait at least fifteen minutes before entering. He didn't want to run the risk of her returning because she'd forgotten something and discover us in the bedroom with him on his knees in front of me.

But just as quickly as I was there, I was out. I didn't spend the night. That was out of the question. We talked periodically, checking in on each other, but there were no everyday or long periods of conversation.

Other men would call me nonstop. They wanted to stop by as they were leaving the studio or a party. Sometimes it was just to find out if I was available later in the week or on the weekend. We would run into each other at the same events. We'd nod, give each other dap, and a little conversation. It was all good. But with Ace, Fresh, and Maximo, it was different.

I couldn't sit at home waiting and hoping that one day one of them would leave their girl. The reality is that no celebrity will risk losing his career and his livelihood to come out and say that he's in a loving relationship with another man. To say that they are together would be death to their careers, especially for black men. To date there has not been one black man in any area of entertainment who has come forth and admitted to being openly gay. That is a heavy burden to carry. To do so means being constantly scrutinized and judged. You stand a chance of losing your friends. No one will want to associate with you, at least not in public.

But also trying to have a relationship with someone outside of the entertainment world is challenging. As much as we may try, it takes a very special person to be involved with someone in this industry. We have long nights, commitments to parties, tons of socializing and networking, and a world full of egos. Everyone thinks they're important, better than you, and that their shit definitely doesn't stink.

I tried to be with guys who had nine-to-five jobs. Regular brothers who were just as discreet about their lives as I was. But it was challenging trying to explain why I had to cancel on hooking up. I got tired of talking about my job and explaining how I knew many of the men I did.

No matter how much of an attempt I made at being forthright and honest, I realized that dealing with down low men meant nothing but a life of suspicion.

I was still struggling with my sexuality, and it was killing me. I learned to be deceptive and manipulative. I lied to close friends and family members. Trying to maintain the façade was driving me crazy.

Whenever I went to an album release party, movie premiere, or some social event, it always felt like a down low soiree. I would stand around, laughing with my down low friends about our secrets. I would give brotherly daps and head nods acknowledging those I knew who were down low. We dared not give ourselves away to anyone. We knew who we were, but we partied and played along. Sometimes I would sit with them, stealing a moment or two for conversation or asking about an unknown face in the crowd and if my down low friend thought he was part of the family or some eager, young buck trying to get in the game of Hip Hop.

The exchange of numbers would go on throughout the night. People would introduce me and they would make it a point to mention my working at MTV. This always drew the men in. They became more interested, and I could see the gleam in their eyes, that anxious and hungry look. They were eager. They wanted more information. I was doing what many of them fantasized about, and they wanted to be a part of it. They wanted to hang with the celebrities, go to the big shows, and attend the parties. The men somehow felt they were missing out on something.

At one point I stopped telling people what I did. It just led to inquiries of who I knew, who I worked with, and how I had a great job. Sure, it was great, but I wasn't in it because of that. I loved what I did for a living. But many people are starstruck and want to work in the business to either get next to the stars or to become a star themselves. I was as close to meeting a celebrity as many of them would ever get, so they were eager to befriend me, especially men. In my head I would think, *This is too easy. It's like taking candy from a baby.*

If they were willing to play the game, I was willing to let them be a part. I had so many men approach me about hooking them up, or helping them get introduced to the right person. People are desperate to be a part of Hip Hop and are willing to do whatever it takes to get in. I would get demo tapes, videos, résumés, and headshots of people seeking to break into the game. I got random e-mails from people I never met asking advice on what they should do to get their video played on MTV or their music heard at a record label.

As much as I may have told them I couldn't do anything for them, they refused to take no for an answer, and I have to admit that I love persistence. A persistent man and I are a bad mix.

This game of Hip Hop is too enticing and appealing for anyone to turn it down. In the videos, artists are parading their many women, clothes, jewelry, cars, and big homes. They're in magazines, on television, and on the radio, talking about their lavish life and traveling abroad. They get perks like free clothing, VIP treatment at parties, front row seats at fashion shows, music concerts, and other events. It's very seductive and alluring. Hip Hop will coerce you and it will grant your wildest dreams. Every person who has seen and experienced her has been caught in her embrace. She's tantalizing, titillating, and enticing. Her beauty is mesmerizing. The language is symphonic and will lure you in. You will become so enthralled with her that your entire life will become hers. I was hers, and people tried to get to her through me.

After being in special events for nearly a year, I moved over to MTV's production management as a production coordinator. In this department, I worked directly with the producers and on all the award shows. So instead of doing the after-parties, I was working on the actual shows.

In my new role and new position, I started working longer hours and traveling more. Even though I enjoyed being on the road meeting new people and becoming cozy with some brothers in different cities, hos in different area codes, the demand of working large productions such as the Video Music Awards and the Movie Awards was taking its toll. Among other things, I had to deal with celebrity egos, which in itself is a full-time job.

One day, I was rushing to get to work when something came over me. After I stepped off the train, something seemed to take over my body. I felt heavy and loaded. Although I was walking fast, I felt like I was walking in slow motion. Suddenly, I was overwhelmed. My head started spinning and I just started crying on Forty-third Street and Eighth Avenue. I was having a nervous breakdown.

While walking, I heard a quiet voice say to me, "Are you tired of hiding?"

I made it to work but I was drained. I needed someone to talk to but there was no one I could pick up the phone and call. I sat there and asked God for some guidance. I needed a change in my life.

I was still dealing with anger and hurt toward my family. I felt abandoned and lost. I had no connection with them. They were not a part of my life. My aunts promised they would call, but I never heard from them. Even when they said they were going to visit me, they never showed. In each of the states I lived in, no one from my family ever came to see how I was doing, where I was living, and if I was okay. I hated that my family was so distant from my life. I missed home terribly. I missed family functions. I missed intimacy with my family.

I learned of pregnancies after a child was born. Many of the kids would never know who I was because we had no connection. When a few of my cousins got married, I found out about it months later. I didn't get any invitations in the mail or over the phone. I was the outsider.

My family had moved on without me, and I hated it.

I also needed to deal with my sexuality. I was scared to go home and be asked about why I wasn't married, or where was my girlfriend. I didn't want my family to know I liked men. As much as I resisted facing my sexual desires, it was everywhere. I was going to down low parties and events. My sex life was out of control. I needed to stop being promiscuous and focus on what I wanted out of my life. I needed to stop being afraid of who I was, but every time I thought I had it under control I was completely wrong.

32. THIS IS WHY I'M HOT

A SPARK OF LIGHT hit me, an idea to gather all my friends in the entertainment industry together for an in-depth discussion on how to deal with pressure and stress.

I wanted to find out if other black men in the entertainment industry were dealing with family and work issues. I wanted to know if they dealt with them and if so, how. I decided I was going to get all the men I knew together, both straight and gay, because I needed some answers.

I was completely overwhelmed. At times, I didn't want to wake up in the morning. Nothing seemed to motivate me any longer. I'd lost my desire to be assertive and aggressive at work. I'd become numb to sex partners. I totally blacked out of my life and was walking through it with my eyes closed.

I called "Hakim," a down low friend from MTV, because I needed someone to talk to. "I think I have a sexual addiction," I told him.

"Why do you say that?" he asked.

"I'm having sex with dudes damn near every day."

"Different guys or the same guy?"

"What does it matter? It's not like I'm horny or anything. I'm having sex just to be doing it." By this time I no longer identified with being bisexual or down low. I knew I was gay.

"How are you meeting them?"

"How else?" I said. He knew about the down low parties I attended.

It only took one meeting and I found myself being introduced to his boy and his boy's boy.

"You should speak with someone. Maybe get some professional help."

"I can do this on my own. I know exactly what to do."

I sent out an e-mail and made some fliers. It just so happened Sterling was hosting a viewing party for the Grammy's in a hotel suite that night. He invited all the industry executives to this party. Many of the assistants and directors from the record labels were going to be there.

The place was crowded. People throughout the room were networking, laughing, and getting ready for the awards. Sterling had the event catered, which wasn't out of the ordinary for him. He was always a top-notch brother. He knew how to entertain and draw a crowd.

I walked through the room and did my hellos to those I knew. They in turn introduced me to others who had come as their guests. Sterling gave everyone a ballot with all the nominees on it. He was going to give a prize to the person who came closest to getting the most correct winners.

It was a big night for the Grammy's. Destiny's Child was nominated, along with Eminem.

After the show ended, Sterling let me make an announcement. He got everyone's attention and told them I had an important announcement. I was a little nervous because I wasn't sure how people were going to respond to my idea. But once I made the announcement, all the men in the room asked for a flier. They agreed it was about time someone got the black men together for a dialogue. I was floored. I couldn't believe these men were interested in being a part of a serious discussion.

The first meeting was in a conference room at MTV. There were twenty men who came. At the end of the meeting they all asked when the next meeting would be held.

And just like that, Men's Empowerment, Inc. was born. The meetings took place the last Wednesday of each month. Over the next few months, the number of men continued to grow. We eventually outgrew the conference room at MTV when it became standing room only. We needed to move to a larger venue, and one of the men in the group offered to let me use a larger conference room at Sony Music.

I started receiving phone calls and e-mails from men who were not necessarily in the entertainment industry, but who wanted to take part in the dialogue and the meeting of black men.

The next thing I knew, Men's Empowerment was the new, hot, industry gathering in the city. It was not my goal or desire to make Men's Empowerment the new "it" thing, it just happened that way. I do feel, however, that at the time, many black men were seeking some type of connection. We all needed something to belong to and a place where we wouldn't be judged.

I honestly don't think I would have been able to pull Men's Empowerment off if I had been an out gay man. As I've mentioned, a lot of black men do not want to be linked or have any association with gay men. If they knew a gay man was running a group, most would never join or would leave as soon as they discovered the truth about the leader.

I invited men who were successful in their careers to come and share their stories with the group. Some of these men included Emil Wilbekin, former editor in chief of *VIBE* magazine; Kevin Liles, executive vice president of Warner Music Group; Stacy Spikes, CEO of Urbanworld Film Festival; Gordon Chambers, Grammy-winning songwriter/singer; Derrick Thompson, former senior vice president of Urban Music at BMG; Lloyd Boston, author/style expert; Kevin Powell, author/activist; and Omar Tyree, author.

Oddly enough, I brought in a few down low brothers as guest speakers for the group. I purposely did it because I wanted to show how powerful we were in the entertainment industry, as well as how instrumental we were in helping to make Hip Hop what it was. Although the men who came to listen never knew the difference, secretly, I found pleasure in knowing I was helping to empower other black men and I was a gay man doing it.

By bringing in these heavy hitters from the entertainment world, my popularity rose. People recognized me, and newspaper, magazine, and television interviews followed. They wanted to know the story behind Men's Empowerment. They wanted to know about the man who was able to bring black men together in order to heal and empower their lives. With this new popularity, I knew I couldn't reveal my sexuality, I knew I would lose all credibility. No one would want to be part of an organization started by a gay man.

Even the guest speakers were impressed. They volunteered their time to come and talk about the ups and downs of being in entertainment. They stressed the importance of networking, mentorship, and staying on top of your game. These messages were what I needed all people who were interested in a career in this business to hear.

Emil Wilbekin said he was the best of friends with many artists who would stop by his offices or have dinner with him like old friends.

But whenever he saw them out in public with their boys or at some other event, they would run from him like the plague. They didn't acknowledge him in public. They acted like they didn't know him, and it disturbed him. It was only because he was publicly a gay man.

I, too, had been guilty of avoiding openly gay men in public. I would walk the other way or pretend like I didn't see them. Even in the workplace, I prayed I wouldn't run into someone I knew who was openly gay. I chatted in private, never in public, with them. I socialized with them at parties, but never for longer than five minutes. I only said hello and asked what they were up to and kept it moving. I didn't want to be found guilty by association. I was afraid that I would be outed if someone saw me interacting with them.

It was fine to socialize behind closed doors, but to be openly gay was another story. We all knew that there were many gay people in Hip Hop, but we didn't discuss it. It remained behind the scenes. Most heterosexual and down low men just made sure to stay clear of gay men.

"Allen," a record executive, came and spoke to the group. We became friends instantly. We both were struggling with our sexuality and we shared many of our war stories from being in the business. Allen was a veteran, had more experience in the game, and already had several notches on his belt for working with everyone from Beyoncé to Whitney Houston. He was a celebrated industry vet and had numerous awards for his talents.

Hanging with Allen afforded me another entrée into the music scene circles and other down low circles. Allen was often invited to functions throughout the city because he was a legend in the business. He would invite me to come along and I was always happy to accept.

I also loved attending Allen's own extravagant parties. Everyone and their momma wanted to attend his parties! They were grand beyond grand.

There was a profusion of gorgeous black men, and many of them on the down low. My gosh, there wasn't any type of man you couldn't find at his parties.

Even though it was unspoken, we all knew we were there to party among like-minded individuals. We all shared the same secret. There was a slew of fellow entertainment executives, songwriters, and producers, along with a few R&B singers. And they really let their hair down. Hell, we all did. There was no pretentiousness or walls we had to hide behind.

Allen knew the repercussions of coming out in the business. He had seen a lot of industry people come and go. It was through his firsthand experience of working with the record labels and artists that Allen learned that in order to keep working and getting gigs he had to keep his mouth closed.

"Sure, I would love to come out, but I know I wouldn't work again," he often told me. "The industry is just not ready for an openly gay man."

We could tell one another anything. We talked nearly every day about the industry and the toll it was taking on him. Allen was a major player, but he still had to hustle and network like every other person. He often confided in me that although he was a seasoned and accomplished songwriter he still struggled.

Allen would tell me how A&R reps, and his own publishing company, constantly told him he needed to write hits. Even though he got placements on many albums, they wanted number one songs and hit singles.

When I needed someone to listen to me, Allen was there. He would encourage me and let me know how important and intelligent I was. He pushed me harder than anyone I had known.

Allen recommended that I do a seminar called Landmark Education, which opened my eyes and mind. My entire life changed after I completed the intense workshop. Everything I struggled with, even things I didn't know I was holding on to, were let go, such as the resentment toward my family.

Only at work did I ever feel any value or self-worth. My relationships with men were superficial. As much as some men wanted to have something more with me, I didn't want anything more with them. I only pretended to be in love. I was in love with the idea of being in love. I knew love wasn't for me, but I made men feel like I did love them. Even when I knew they put me second or third in their life. I made them feel more important than me.

My relationship with my mother was the basis for all my relationships in my life, and I always felt that people would come and go as she had. There was no need to get close to anyone. I didn't feel obligated to open up and share with them. They wouldn't stick around. If they did get close, I shut them off. I felt like they were imposing on my life or trying to pry into my private world.

Sex became a coping mechanism. I found myself only engaging in sex because I was lonely. I hated being alone some nights. It was easy for me to pick up the phone and call someone. Usually, I didn't want to be doing it and just went through the motions. Sex only proved to me that I was liked and that men found me attractive. It was my value system; sex made me feel worthy.

After Landmark Education, I learned to put things in the past. Because I was harboring a lot of anger and bitterness, I could actually see and hear all of the negative things I told myself. I took off the glasses of pain, hurt, and anger. I let go of my own self-defeating tape recorder that told me I was a victim and that my family was responsible for the mess of a life I had.

The self-help work I did based on the books I read was only the tip of the iceberg. I learned how to create an entire new life full of limitless possibilities.

With this newfound energy there was nothing I couldn't do. Everything Allen told me was true. I was not only intelligent but I was worthy. I was valuable and God did have a purpose for my life. Although I had long been on the path to my purpose, for the first time I could actually see what it was.

I let go of those old behaviors and gave myself a fresh start. This time I had the proper tools to do it. I understood the drama I kept creating and attracting in my life. I realized that I was not an anomaly. Everyone has drama. I had just refused to acknowledge mine until now when I reflected on my life. I tried to blame everyone else for the drama in my life, but I was responsible for it. I couldn't blame anyone else; I had to take ownership of my life.

I called my aunts Lisa and Priscilla and we really talked for the first time. I asked them what had happened with my mother. I wanted to hear their side of the story. Aunt Lisa explained to me that the family did step in to try and help my mother. They put her in rehab when they discovered the drug abuse. Each time she relapsed, they waited patiently until she was ready and put her back in rehab. When my mother was diagnosed with AIDS, my aunts made sure she went to her doctor appointments, took her medication, and had someone with her at all times. Everything she explained was new to me. I had been so busy being angry at them that I hadn't seen their intervention.

I asked Aunt Lisa about my siblings and me being separated. I asked her why no one wanted us. Again, she explained that the problem was that everyone wanted us. I was at Grandma Pearl's, and the family knew I was taken care of. George was with Grandma Pearl, but when he started acting out, the school intervened and the court system placed him in the group home. The family went to court and fought to get him out, but George didn't like living with any of our relatives. Our neighbor Mrs. Hughes was the only person he listened to.

My baby brother Jevonte was with Uncle Andrew and my sister was with my cousin Donna. Aunt Lisa said that she had wanted to take us in, but the family agreed on who was going where. This was something I never knew. The thoughts of abandonment and unworthiness I felt were only because of what I thought I saw. Although I was living it, I didn't have real firsthand knowledge.

Aunt Lisa went on to tell me how much she loved me. She was extremely proud of me and was glad that I'd left Detroit and made something of myself. Aunt Lisa and Aunt Priscilla both said that as a young boy I was mature for my age and I didn't seem like I needed any help. According to them I had it all together, I was strong.

I hated that all these years had gone by and that I had blamed them for everything. I'd missed out on important family events. I'd completely avoided the birthdays, holidays, and reunions. I shut them out of my life. Grandma Pearl was the only person I remained in contact with and I begged her not to tell them how I was doing.

I told my aunts how much they meant to me and how much I loved them, and man, it felt good to communicate with them. Aunt Priscilla and I talked for hours about everything. I filled her in on my working in the entertainment industry in Los Angeles and then moving to New York to work with MTV. She was impressed with my determination to work in a very difficult field. After our conversation we prayed together on the phone. It brought back so many memories of being a young boy and waking up and going to church with her and her children.

I got the most amazing surprise when Aunt Priscilla and her daughter Tiffany took a bus trip to New York. They came with some church members on a two-day shopping spree. I met them in Chinatown and spent the day shopping with them. I couldn't stop smiling when I saw my aunt. We hugged and I didn't want to let go. For the first time in my life since I left Detroit, a family member actually came to visit me. I felt like I mattered. I felt worthy. I felt loved.

I met everybody on that bus, and Aunt Priscilla bragged about me to each and every one of them. "This is my nephew. He works at MTV and he runs a group called Men's Empowerment." I was sad when Aunt Priscilla and Tiffany left New York, but I got a bigger gift than I expected—I had reconnected with my family.

But I was still dealing with my sexuality. I refused to address it. I was so scared of people finding out and that they would abandon me. You would have thought with all the empowerment and inspiration I received I would have been liberated. I would have been one big ole happy gay man. But I wasn't. I couldn't let go of what I thought people would think of me, especially within the black community. I didn't want to be rejected by my own people, by my family.

I had to admit to myself that I was gay. I could no longer play the bisexual or down low role. I wasn't having sex with any women. Even though I rarely went to gay clubs or socialized with gay men, I was still a gay man. I preferred men and I wanted to be in a relationship with a man.

The word *gay* was hard to swallow. It was even more difficult trying to live that life. Why couldn't this all be so simple? Why did I have to deal with this? I wanted to be free. To live life on my terms and not worry about what people thought.

Maybe Landmark hadn't worked for me. Allen suggested that maybe this wasn't the time for me to focus on my sexuality. "You're just not ready to deal with it. You keep hiding and when you're comfortable and ready to deal with it, then you will."

Allen knew me too well.

Despite my inability to come to terms with my sexuality and free myself, I did start to rebuild a relationship with my family and realized how important they were. I saw them for the people they were, with feelings and emotions of their own. They hurt, cried, laughed, and experienced pain too. They might have their flaws—and hell, we all have flaws—but I learned that it's the ability to look beyond those flaws and see them for the human beings they are that's important. It was while I was at Landmark Education that I started communicating with my family. I let everything go. Everything I blamed my family for, I simply let go because I wanted to be connected to the people who knew me best, my family.

33. I THINK THEY LIKE ME

THE WORK I WAS DOING with Men's Empowerment was liberating. It was stress free, and I loved it.

One evening, I was fed up when I got off the train in Harlem. Young people were on the street corners, walking aimlessly through the neighborhood. It seemed like there was nothing for them to do.

I called and made an appointment to meet with the youth program director of the Harlem YMCA on 135th Street. I decided to create Young Men's Empowerment and Young Women's Empowerment, the adolescent versions of my Men's Empowerment group. I knew that young people, especially males, were interested in Hip Hop. Many wanted to be artists themselves. I figured if I combined Hip Hop with education, young people would get the best of both worlds.

The program was geared to help provide young men with alternative career choices in Hip Hop and to emphasize the importance of education. The plan was perfect. I would have the men in Men's Empowerment volunteer and mentor the young men. The Harlem YMCA loved it.

There were over thirty boys and girls in the program. They were the smartest and brightest group of kids I had ever met, and they were very respectful. They never complained and were thirsty for information.

I called upon my entertainment friends to speak with the kids, and those appearances made all the difference in those young people's lives.

My friends in the entertainment industry allowed the kids to tour their workplaces. The kids got a chance to see people like them working in a professional environment and being successful. They got to interact with these executives and to question what was necessary to do their jobs. The executives made sure to emphasize the importance of an education when they spoke to the young people.

On a trip to *VIBE* magazine, one of the young girls in the group asked me, "Why are you doing this?"

I looked at her quizzically. "Doing what?" I responded.

"Why are you doing this for us? Is this some part of a community service project?"

I smiled and said, "No, I just wish that when I was your age someone would have taken the time and helped me."

That moment allowed me to become clear about the fact that it really does take only one person to make a difference in someone's life. So many young people, especially young men, do not have fathers at home. Many come from single-parent homes or are raised by their grandparents. I knew that life. I could relate. I was one of those kids.

Soon after I created Young Men's Empowerment and Young Women's Empowerment, other community organizations and leaders started reaching out to me. They wanted to do tie-ins and collaborations with me, and I was excited to do something positive for the community. It was always something I desired, but I felt my sexuality limited me in doing a lot of things. I looked at it like a handicap. It stifled me. I figured if they knew I was gay, they wouldn't want me to be involved with the community. I was less than. I was somehow inadequate. When the community leaders contacted me, I was thrilled. I felt like I finally belonged. I became a leader and a voice in the community.

Working with the Harlem YMCA allowed me to work with their staff to create a children's literacy program. At the time, Harlem had some of the lowest reading scores in the city. We figured if we engaged the parents to become actively involved in reading with their children, we could change those scores.

The responsibility I was being given made me even more skeptical about my associations and affiliations with anything gay. I had to keep up the persona of being a heterosexual man. In my mind, I knew most of these organizations and leaders reached out to me because they saw me as a straight man who cared about his community. They saw me as an articulate, masculine man who was not afraid to go out in the streets and empower the young men and women.

I was fortunate to enlist some powerful people in the community of Harlem. One Hip Hop pioneer was instrumental in the inner workings of one of my programs. We formed a friendship and would often talk about getting more artists involved in the programs and the state of Hip Hop.

"Juice" was very involved in helping the young kids know how important Hip Hop was to the world and that it's not always about the bling and money. He stressed the importance of leaving a legacy, something you could be proud of. He never flaunted his legendary status, but he made sure those of us in the community knew of his group's role in Hip Hop.

Juice was smart and great to be around. However, he would often mention his "partner" or "significant other." When I asked him about this, his response was, "Me and my significant other live uptown" or "me and my partner did this." Initially I didn't make much of it, but then I knew something was up.

Most men, when they have a girl, wife, or lady friend, will refer to them as such. However, when a man keeps referring to someone he is in a relationship with as his "partner" or "significant other," it usually means he's in a relationship with another man. It neither confirms nor denies that the person referred to is a man or a woman.

Juice was letting me know that he was a down low man and didn't want to put his business out in the streets. We were friends, but it took a while before I'd meet his partner. In situations like this, it could take weeks, months, or even years before a down low man is ready to let you inside his world. When a down low man doesn't know you or isn't comfortable with you knowing his business, he will keep you at arm's length. You will never get close enough to know much about him. There will be no invitations to his home or any intimate gathering where he needs to bring a date. His world is only himself and his down low lover. Only those who know of his relationship are truly a part of his world.

I could only imagine the ridicule he would face if anyone found out about his lifestyle. Juice was in one of the most preeminent, old-school rap groups in Hip Hop. They had a wicked stage performance, which made them a great threat in rap circles. Even though it would have been groundbreaking if he had come out, it would have been more difficult in the late seventies and eighties. The black community was still recovering from the civil rights movement and the devastating era of Vietnam Veterans returning home, and the heroin epidemic. Hip Hop became a refuge and voice for young people. And being gay or involved in the gay movement was not one of the black community's priorities. We were fighting for jobs, housing, and equality in schools.

Even today being gay is not one of the black community's priorities. A female journalist from the *Amsterdam News* interviewed me and asked, "Since you have created Men's Empowerment it has done some amazing things for black men. Do you think it would benefit or help gay black men?"

I wasn't surprised by her question, because most people think gay black men are not masculine men. Many think being gay means you are less than a man. You are not macho or hard. Gay men are soft and weak. When in actuality being macho or hard doesn't make you a man. It's being responsible, having integrity, and being a man of your word. It's being a part of your community, giving back, and helping those in need. Being a man is not about how much pussy you can get and how many women you womanize, it's about respect and support. It's about loving one another and loving yourself.

In the black community, we host panel discussions, town hall meetings, and forums about acquiring wealth, politics, and community service, but we never openly discuss sex, sexuality, or HIV/AIDS. We live by the "Don't air your dirty laundry in the street" code. It permeates our communities so deeply that we'd rather let members of our family and friends die than confront it. We're afraid to ask real questions and be open to the truth.

I watched my mother and two brothers die from AIDS. No one openly talked about it. I never understood why we were so afraid to have a discussion about it since we had an ample amount of experience in dealing with the disease. When my mother was diagnosed, it was a blow to the family, devastating news, and we should have asked questions. We should have educated ourselves about the disease. But we didn't. We sat and watched them all die. That is complete and utter ignorance. The guilt of not stepping in and doing something gripped my family. I was mortified by the experiences. My family was wiped out by a single disease, and there I was, a young boy dealing with death and my sexuality. I should have immediately been schooled by an adult about sex.

When my family refused to talk about me being molested at thirteen, that was a problem. When my mother discovered I was having sex with the girl in my neighborhood, that was the perfect opportunity to have a dialogue. But my mother only cursed me out.

In the black church, pastors have yet to preach tolerance and acceptance of homosexuality. They never facilitate a dialogue with members of the black gay community, and no one would dare challenge the pastor. If black gay men are not willing to stand together and make a stand for ourselves, who will?

Because I understood this, it only made me want to hide my sexuality even more. I worked hard to keep my sexuality from being discovered. I made sure that people only saw me as a heterosexual man. I was the guy who worked at MTV, and the guy who headed up the Men's Empowerment Group. I couldn't possibly be gay.

My phone never stopped ringing, e-mails poured in, everyone asked for help in getting a job.

People I had never met or seen were coming out of the woodwork, handing me their CDs. Lunch and dinner offers poured in. Late-night meetings and invitations to events came along. They figured if I came to their events, I would bring one of my celebrity or entertainment friends with me.

"Trevor," a strikingly handsome video model, was persistent. I didn't really see how I could help him because he'd already appeared in a few female R&B singers' videos. He was well on his way.

His light skin, muscular body, and brown eyes were very appealing. I didn't see him having any problems getting any woman or man he wanted.

I ran into him on the street as I was leaving Interscope Records. He stopped me and we chatted for a few minutes. "Let me get your number," he asked as he pulled his backpack from his shoulder. His white T-shirt was clinging to his perfectly formed body.

"We have to get together," he said. "I want to talk with you about some things I'm doing."

"No problem," I said as I punched my number into his cell phone. I really didn't think much about it. I often ran into men I knew in the industry who wanted to give me updates or share some information about the projects they were working on. But when he called, he expressed a romantic interest in me. I was thrown off because I had never thought of him in a sexual way. "Terrance, I think you're a really cool brother. Don't you think we would be good together?"

"What gives you that idea?" I asked. "Don't we have to get to know each other first?"

"Well, I'm willing if you are."

Trevor and I went out a few times and continued talking on the phone. I discovered he had a desire to pursue a career in acting. Because he knew of my background in film, Trevor was willing to give himself to me. "I'm really feeling you. When are you going to invite me over to stay the night with you?" he asked one night we were on the phone.

"I don't think that's a good idea."

"Why not? Aren't you feeling me?"

"I am, and you're an attractive brother," I said. "Let's just keep it as it is for right now."

Trevor confessed to me that he'd already slept with a well-known

video director turned filmmaker, "Clark," who put him in a few videos. Clark promised Trevor that he would give him a part in his next
film.

As time went on Trevor became more and more adamant about us
sleeping together. "Why you playing hard to get?" he asked. "You know
you want me just as much as I want you."

I kept putting him off. I became agitated with his constant advances.
If a relationship was going to happen between us, I wanted it to occur
naturally. But Trevor was hopeful of a romantic relationship between
us, and as beautiful as he was and as tempting the offer, his pushi-
ness turned me off. I knew he was only using me to get something he
wanted.

There were times when I used people as well, when I took some
women up on their offers. I needed to make sure I was seen with
women. I knew how to play my cards for those who were watching, and
if I was out with a woman, then no one would think I was gay. But if
I didn't respond to their advances, they would think something was up
and the gossip would start.

So I accepted dates for lunch and dinner. If I had been a music
producer, an A&R type, or even a filmmaker, I could have had any of
those women at any time. I knew men who used women who wanted to
be a part of their world. I was now in that world, and the women were
everywhere.

I met Charlotte, a beautiful aspiring actress while I was hosting an
event at the Harlem YMCA on 135th Street. She had attended a few of
my workshops, and we would often make small talk and flirt with each
other. I thought it was innocent, but it was something different for her.
Charlotte pursued me. She called, e-mailed, and even showed up at
various events where I was. After much pursuing on her part, I made
a date with her. I thought it wouldn't do any harm going out on a date.
We had a lot of fun and we subsequently dated for a few months. It felt
good being with her. I missed this type of connection with a woman. It
was comfortable, and we had easy conversations. It was freeing being
with a woman with no one questioning me, wondering why I wasn't

dating. We could have public displays of affection. We could hold hands, kiss, and hug while we walked down the street.

Many of the women I was with became friends. We developed a relationship beyond sex. I got to know them, and they got to know me. I met their families.

Dating Charlotte, however, I saw once again that I had a much stronger attraction for men. Although I enjoyed her company, I yearned for the touch of a man. I desired to lay with a man and feel his body next to mine. As much as I wanted to hold on to being down low and sexing women, it wasn't me any longer. I only held on to the idea of being with a woman because I wanted a family. As I continued to grow and learn about myself, I realized it was time to accept who I was. I had to stop playing games and be truthful with myself.

Being in a down low relationship, I never really knew the other men. The introductions to their families were all lies. I was the friend or the cousin of a friend. His wife or girlfriend had no idea who I was. Hell, he didn't even know who I was. I didn't want to be vulnerable to a man and express any emotions. I didn't want to open up for him to then abandon me with a part of me and my history. The less he knew, the better.

Also at this time, I met a young woman, a publicist, who offered to work with me. Susan said she could help get me more exposure. I had heard of her and knew she had worked with a few other celebrities. She represented a friend of mine and was able to get him a lot of press. Susan said she wasn't going to charge me, so I jumped at the opportunity. What did I have to lose? She was looking to create a name for herself and I was too.

One thing about publicists is that they can be very aggressive. Susan was just that. She worked every angle to generate stories for all her clients. I liked her style. She wasn't afraid to go after the big name papers and magazines. She was becoming a true player in the game.

After a few phone conversations, she suggested I come to her place for a sit-down meeting. When I arrived, she was wearing a pair of short shorts and a sports bra. I thought it was odd, but I didn't make anything of it. We were meeting at her place, and I chalked it up to her just be-ing comfortable in her own environment.

Susan was quite the looker. She was a young woman and her body was ripe for the picking. I glanced at her body a few times, and thought if it had been a year or so earlier, I would have made sure not to leave there without tasting her.

She smiled as she ushered me inside. I sat on the sofa and noticed the pictures of her with celebrities hanging on the wall.

She offered me something to drink and disappeared into her kitchen. I put my folder on the table and sat back on the sofa. When she returned we discussed Susan's other accomplishments with her clients. I listened intently. I wondered if she was ever going to change clothes, but it was obvious she wasn't.

Susan was selling me her pitch. It was strong. "Terrance, you really need someone who can work you and get your name out there," she said, staring into my eyes. "I love the work you're doing. It's good to see a black man doing something in his community."

"Thank you," I said. I was becoming nervous. I had never been ner-vous around a woman before. Something in the way she looked at me caused my heart to race.

"You need me." She smiled as she placed her hand on my knee. I almost jumped. "I can make things happen for you."

I was now uncomfortable. I knew I could take advantage of this opportunity, but it's not what I wanted. I searched my head for some words to express what I was feeling.

Susan stood up, and it seemed her shorts were even shorter. Her ass cheeks were peeking through. Her nipples were erect. She stepped across me and went into the kitchen again.

I took a sip of my water. I needed to clear my head. This could not possibly be happening. *Doesn't she know I'm gay?* I said to myself. I felt a little perspiration forming under my arms. My heart was pounding and my palms started to sweat. I didn't like this feeling.

She returned from the kitchen and damn near straddled me as she crossed to take her seat next to me.

"You know," I said, "I don't think it's a good idea to mix business with pleasure. Let's keep it professional." I picked up my folder and stood up. She seemed taken aback at first, but quickly attempted to redeem herself. "Terrance, I would never cross the line with any of my clients."

I smiled and left. Susan saw me as part of a way to help her build her name and reputation. If sex was involved, I was not going to be a part of her plan.

I prided myself on not using my power to get sex. I knew many down low brothers in the industry who used their entertainment connections and power to get men to have sex with them, but I wasn't going to be one of them.

Creating Men's Empowerment was one of my greatest accomplishments, yet I inadvertently created more pressure and stress for myself. Just as I was rebuilding, empowering, and getting inspired, a new issue arose concerning the down low brothers in the group. One of the brothers warned me that too many gay men were attending the meetings and that I should be careful.

I wasn't concerned with anyone's sexuality in the group, but now that it was brought to my attention, I hated it. I didn't want to be bothered with it, so I ignored it.

Yet, the down low brothers were powerful voices inside of Hip Hop, and they had to keep their cover.

They had entrusted me with their secrets and warned me about socializing with openly gay men. They knew the dangers of being affiliated with the gay lifestyle. The down low brothers in Hip Hop had become my new best friends.

Although I was used to traveling in down low circles, they made me feel privileged. The down low brothers led me to think and feel as if they were in my corner, that I was now included in a prestigious circle. That in itself made me feel even more powerful and reluctant to out myself to anyone. As I've stated, I knew gay people, but I never was like them or socialized with them. And now, more than ever, I refused to be seen out in public with them. I did not want to jeopardize my newfound relationships.

Hell, I had become a king of hiding. I was so damaged emotionally and mentally that the thought of having a discussion about my sexuality was out of the question. Whenever the topic was brought up, I avoided it like the plague. It made me extremely uncomfortable.

The issue kept being brought up, however, so something had to be done, and I made a choice. I called an emergency meeting. The topic on the floor was "Gay Men and Straight Men—Can They Get Along?"

It took a lot for me to host the dialogue between the men. I wondered if the straight men would attack me, or if the gay men would publicly out me. I know I hated standing alone in front of the men as the martyr.

The topic sparked a heavy debate. Many thought I shouldn't have done it. Others encouraged the dialogue. It was a tug-of-war, and I knew no one would win if we skirted the issue.

In the meeting, there were a lot of profound statements and discoveries made. Many gay men didn't feel comfortable in the room with straight men because they thought they couldn't openly discuss relationships and other challenges they faced. They felt the heterosexual men couldn't relate to their issues. The gay men also felt that they were being judged and criticized by the straight men. There were also those men present who I knew were gay or down low and who didn't say anything, who just sat and listened.

The straight men responded by saying that they didn't care about the gay brother's sexuality. They made it known that they were fully aware that gay men were attending the meetings, and that they were not concerned or bothered by the presence of these gay men. The heterosexual men only wanted to bond and unite with like-minded men who were seeking empowerment and inspiration. They were there to network just like everyone else, unconcerned with sexuality.

I hoped the conversation would create understanding and tolerance and that afterward we would all be singing "Kumbaya." So many things could have occurred in that moment between the men, but didn't. It could have been a great dialogue to build relationships and understanding between gay and heterosexual men. Some light could have been shed on our commonalities instead of our differences. But I know as men we have our pride and ego. Despite us being gay or straight, we refuse to bow down and have to defend who we are. No one in that room wanted to be the first to admit we all shared something in common. We all were men seeking to be better men, and human beings. What could have taken place didn't. We were still afraid of one another.

I understood that as black gay men we have so many layers that sometimes it prevents us from opening up and sharing with others. Some of us have been conditioned for so long to hide our sexuality that we tend to mentally and emotionally disappear. We detach ourselves from others and escape into our own worlds—worlds built and surrounded by pain, hurt, and anger.

34. 1999

IT WAS BREAKING NEWS. Everyone in the industry was buzzing about Quincy Jones's protégé Tevin Campbell's arrest for soliciting sex from an undercover male police officer.

It was out in the public. I had met him on one occasion and seen him a few times in Los Angeles outside the gay club The Catch.

I thought, *Finally. Now someone will come forward and discuss gay men in the entertainment industry.* So I, along with many of the down low men and gay men, waited and waited and waited.

Nothing happened. It was hushed up and swept under the rug. Tevin never commented on the incident.

I'm sure if it had been a major, black male celebrity that no one had ever suspected of being gay, it would have made headline news. Tevin's sexuality had always been questioned. He wasn't a hard-core thug. He didn't boast and brag about the many women he was screwing. He was a timid R&B singer with a soprano voice. I would have to wait for my dream of a famous, black male celebrity to come out of the closet. It would have to be someone who was at the height of his career, someone the fans and the entertainment business were completely unaware of. A man like this could change the way the world views black gay men. Yet, many of them were too afraid and would stay hidden in the closet.

One of the biggest events of our time was about to occur. The new millennium was approaching, and MTV was preparing for the New Year's Eve bash.

The anticipation of ending 1999 had the entire world on pins and needles based on dire predictions as we approached the year 2000.

People were in a panic, stocking up on water, nonperishables, flashlights, batteries, and other emergency-kit items.

I was concerned with my own emergency. Damn near every twenty minutes I was getting calls from the Marriott Marquis, the hotel next door to MTV on Forty-fifth Street, regarding the talent and their entourages. Apparently they were causing a ruckus in the hotel rooms, and with the city already on edge, the hotel managers were not too thrilled with their outlandish antics.

After making several trips back and forth to the hotel to speak with various managers about their artists, I was fed up.

"Look, it's New Year's Eve. The hotel is sick and tired of the ruckus you all are keeping up. It has to stop now! Tell them pipe down or they will be put out of the hotel," I practically yelled.

"No problem, Terrance," the manager said. "We'll talk to them, and make sure they keep it down."

When I made it back to MTV, it was almost midnight. I rushed upstairs to the twenty-fifth floor. From there I could get a full view of the thousands of party revelers crammed into the streets around Times Square, and could hear them yelling. Everyone was excited. 1999 was ending. We were heading into the new millennium. New beginnings.

I looked out onto the vast hordes and thought about everything. Where I had been, where I was going, and what I needed to do.

Midnight. The ball dropped. Everyone was screaming. Everyone was celebrating. There were no computer glitches. No bombs. No nothing. Just everyone partying like it was 1999.

Behind me was one of our larger conference rooms. We had converted the space into a dressing room for one of the artists. "Carlos's" crew needed the space. He was notorious for his large entourages. There were well over twenty of them. His flashy and flamboyant style was a force to be reckoned with. Carlos often made the fashion A-list with his snazzy attire. He had a steady flow of women, and he's never seen without one gracing his side. Carlos is a true legend in Hip Hop and he helped to create some of the biggest acts, names, and styles.

I heard someone in the room so I went to check it out. Everyone should have been downstairs in the studio. That's where the megacelebrity brought in the New Year.

"Oh, my bad," I said as I came upon a very good-looking guy who was part of Carlos's entourage. "I thought everyone was downstairs."

"What up, man? I forgot something." His alcohol-tinged voice slurred his words.

He sat in the chair. He was definitely drunk and high. "Fuck," he said. "My man, you know where the bathroom is?"

"Yeah, follow me."

I lead him down the dark corridor, and he stumbled into the bathroom, pulling out his dick and practically pissing on the floor before he made it to the stall.

I closed the door and waited in the hall. And I waited. And I waited. *What the hell is this fool doing?* I asked myself. Nearly ten minutes had passed and he had not come out of the bathroom.

I went inside to check on him and he was leaning over the stall with his dick in his hand.

"You all right?" I asked, approaching him.

"Yeah I'm good," he mumbled. And just as I was about to turn around and leave, he stepped away from the stall, looked at me, looked at his dick, which was hard as a rock, and looked back.

I knew that look. Without him saying anything I knew what he was asking. He just stood there pointing his hard dick at me. I thought for a quick second how we might get caught. How someone might come inside the bathroom and see us. But no one was upstairs except for the two of us. He and I. It was New Year's Eve, and everybody else was celebrating downstairs. So I took advantage of the moment and enjoyed the beginning of the year 2000.

35. HYPNOTIZE

AS MUCH AS I LOVED WORKING in entertainment, my job became a chore. I no longer had the passion and drive I did when I first got in the business. I'd had enough. I'd had enough of the drama and egotistical artists. I'd had enough of worrying about an artist's seat on a plane or the hotel suite they didn't like and the constant demands of needing at least twenty tickets so the people in their crew could attend the show. I got sick of high maintenance artists, as well as many of their high-maintenance stylists, managers, publicists, or boys. "It's only an award show, people," I wanted to yell. "We're not saving the world."

But it was when I looked at the programming of the network that I realized that I was not in the demographics. The shows were not catered to me. Here I was, a gay thirty-something-year-old black man, trying to relate to thirteen, fifteen, eighteen, and twenty-one-year-olds. Something was wrong with this picture.

So I left. Many of my friends applauded me, but most in the business thought I had lost my mind.

It felt great not having to get up each morning and rush to the office for the daily dose of high drama at *As the World Turns Around MTV*.

I created several entities under the Men's Empowerment name. First was The Education Source. I wanted people in the community to have access to information. They wanted to go to the big conventions and workshops in the city with the big-named presenters, but most could not afford the enormous fees. So I thought of a way to educate and provide community members with resources for advancement and inspiration as it related to their careers, communities, and individual lives.

The Harlem YMCA gave me a classroom-size space and I only charged between twenty and forty dollars for a two-hour course. I called upon all my entertainment, corporate, and political friends to come in and lead the seminars.

I then decided to do panel discussions. People were fascinated with how to break into the music business. Everyone wanted to get in and get a piece of the pie. I had over ten years of experience in the business and I knew what it took to break in. Thus, the idea for Powerful Women in Business and Powerful Men in Business was created.

I was well on my way to branding Men's Empowerment, as well as my own name.

I then came up with another innovative idea. The Chat 'n Chew Power Brunch. This venture allowed guests to dine and have an exclusive interaction with a well-known celebrity in their respective fields.

One Saturday a month, people had the opportunity to sit and converse with personalities such as author and fashion guru Lloyd Boston; best-selling author E. Lynn Harris; film producer Lee Daniels of *Monster's Ball*; and actor Rockmond Dunbar, who appeared in *Soul Food* and *Prison Break*.

Nothing could compare with the rush I received from all the work I was doing in the community. All the resources, contacts, and experiences I had garnered from my years working in the business were now paying off for me.

I also started attending the Abyssinian Baptist Church, where the Reverend Dr. Calvin O. Butts, III, is a no-nonsense pastor. The fiery sermons he delivers feed my soul.

A fellow church member passed along some information about motivational speaker Les Brown, who was speaking at a center in Lower

Manhattan. I had heard of Les Brown growing up as a kid. He was a positive black man doing it and giving back to the community, so I went to hear what he had to say.

I was captivated from the moment he graced the stage. His words spoke to me. Les spoke of his background and how he came to be a motivational speaker.

After listening to him, I knew that was what I wanted to do. I wanted to travel across the country speaking to audiences, encouraging and inspiring them. As much as I thought no one shared my unique experiences, I realized that there were many who did. We just didn't talk about it openly. I felt that by sharing my story others would be inspired. I wanted to tell people that no matter what obstacles or challenges they faced, they should never give up or doubt themselves. I wanted to tell them to keep going and keep moving.

I began attending speaking engagements of other motivational speakers. It was imperative that I study their delivery and message. In order for me to make it a reality, I needed to study those who were out there doing it. I became a student once again. To become a motivational speaker was my goal.

I called my family and told them what I was up to. I was afraid they wouldn't be supportive. I thought they would shoot down my dream and try to convince me not to share my story. In order for me to heal, I had to release all my baggage. My aunts Lisa and Priscilla were very encouraging. They kept me uplifted with their endearing words of love. I was thrilled when they showed their support. They called to check up on me and see where I was speaking and if they could attend. That was extremely gratifying.

Grandma Pearl couldn't have been any prouder. She was elated with the news. Every time I spoke with her, she told me that no matter where she went—grocery store, restaurant, her apartment complex, church—she told everyone about her grandson who was a motivational speaker.

Hearing Grandma Pearl boast about me was an exhilarating

feeling. But more important, I made her happy. I could honestly say that I was doing something she could be proud of.

I was pursuing this new dream with a passion. I was determined to help others. I then began searching online for speaker's bureaus. A few people signed me to their agencies. I didn't have much to work with but I convinced them to take a chance on me. I explained to them that they were making an investment in me. I was not going to fail, it was not an option. They liked my delivery and approach. Hell, if I could motivate and inspire them, then just imagine what I would do to others.

Things were moving slow, very slow, at first. I would call to check in with the agents, but they didn't have anything. I started to think that maybe this wasn't what I was supposed to be doing. Maybe I should reconsider and refocus my ideas. But then the calls started to come in. The agents had engagements for me to speak at colleges and universities. The downhill slope I was sliding down was now becoming an easy uphill climb.

It was an awesome feeling when I spoke with the young kids about my life. I spoke candidly about my past and my family life. For the first time in my life, I openly discussed my past. It was freeing and rejuvenating. To see crying faces in the audience relating to me was my confirmation, especially when people lined up afterward to thank me for sharing my story.

It was amazing to share my story with others and to discover that there were many others like me going through what I had gone through. I discovered that my journey was not unique.

36. I NEED YOU NOW

I DROVE HOME TO DETROIT. It would be the first time in years my family and I had the chance to see one another face-to-face. They had not seen me since I buried my brother George in 1994. I had spent all those years running away and denying them access to my life, but after reconciling, we spent a lot of time on the phone, and now it was time for a good ole family reunion.

It was wonderful seeing my sister, Sheritta, and all my aunts, uncles, cousins, and Grandma Pearl. Our emotions were extremely high, with everyone hugging and crying. It felt good to be home again.

Every relative wanted to cook for me. They laid the food out. I swore I gained at least fifteen pounds. But it felt good. They loved me. I was proud of our reconnection. I had missed out on so much, and this trip was all about catching up.

The long, late-night conversations were plentiful. Grandma Pearl and I would talk about everything. No matter the topic, we conversed. And on one occasion, I was so caught up in one of our conversations, I accidentally came out of the closet. I was updating her on my life and said, "It gets hard sometimes being a black gay man." And once I said it, I couldn't take it back.

When I realized what I said I had an out-of-body experience, looking at myself sitting in the chair, waiting for a reaction from Grandma Pearl. But she just smiled at me and said, "Baby, I already knew. I love you just the same. Nothing has changed. I am proud of you and you have made me very happy. You're still a man, so hold your head up high and be proud of yourself." I knew then that it was all right in my world because Grandma Pearl said so.

After the many cook-outs at my aunt's homes, I begrudged the return to New York. I missed being a child in my old room. A few remnants from high school were still cluttered in drawers. Pictures of me and high school friends, along with programs I had participated in and my prom book. My homecoming king sash was on my wall, and my trophy for winning was displayed on my dresser.

The room seemed a lot smaller than I remembered. My full-size bed still had the neatly tucked colorful blanket as if it had never been slept in.

I drove through my old neighborhood smiling as I reflected on being a young, carefree boy who grew up to be a man in spite of what anyone thought of me. The neighborhood looked different. New residents had moved in. The playground was almost desolate. There were now vacant lots where buildings once stood. It's the cycle of life—things change, grow, and become old.

But as much as it was exhilarating being in Detroit again and reminiscing about old days, I had to get back to my own home, my own world. The trip home was complete for me. I got my family.

Since I'd already come out to Grandma Pearl, it was now time for the rest of the family. I decided to write letters to my aunts Lisa and Priscilla. I figured once they knew, they would tell the rest of the family. They'd spread this news quickly. They couldn't hold water. It would save me the agony of trying to face my uncles and telling them. I didn't worry so much about them finding out from family members, it's just I couldn't be the one to do it. Coming out to Grandma Pearl had been an accident, so I knew I wasn't really ready.

Aunt Lisa was very supportive. She, too, like my grandmother, said she already knew. "Boy, I knew you was gay. I knew it when you were little." I laughed when she said it.

Saved and sanctified Aunt Priscilla, however, didn't take it so well.

She cried and cried and cried. "You're like one of my boys," she told me. "I practically raised you." I knew her religious beliefs wouldn't allow her to embrace my sexuality, but she told me, "I love you no matter what. You're still my nephew." However, after that conversation we never discussed it again. Having gotten that obstacle off my chest, I was filled with an exuberant amount of love, joy, and support, and nothing could get in my way.

37. MAN IN THE MIRROR

I BEGAN MEETING more and more powerful men who were openly gay. I still had my hang-ups, but I was learning to look beyond outer appearances and at the person on the inside. A man was a man, but it was these men who were responsible, accountable, and integral with their lives. These men were not hung up on what others thought of them. They were proud black gay men who lived their lives without fear or shame. No matter what people may say about a man who is effeminate, or dresses or acts differently, or may not be what society deems as hard or rough, gay men refuse to be discounted. They refuse to be unheard, and there wouldn't be many companies, communities, or organizations that would exist without them.

I gained respect for the effeminate men, drag queens, transsexuals, transvestites, and lesbians. They were bold enough to take the brunt of the anger and spiteful words fired at gay people daily. They braved the cold world each day and stood up for all gay men and women without being asked. These individuals had more balls than most men I knew, even myself.

Slowly but surely I confided in more people about my sexuality. I walked with my head held high like Grandma Pearl taught me. It was a relief to let go of the armor I was hiding behind.

I was simply tired of pretending. I hated that I constantly monitored myself in conversations, was careful not to slip up and say *he* when I meant *she*. I made sure I didn't comment on an obviously handsome or good-looking man. I reserved those thoughts for myself.

Allen was right, I had to be comfortable with myself in order to have the breakthrough in my life with my sexuality. Though I thought I was okay in my own skin, I found myself reluctant to tell women who still flirted with me endlessly at speaking engagements that I was gay. After a speech, the women would slide up next to me slightly putting their hands on my chest or arm. They would laugh and toss their hair, inching closer and closer, letting me know they were available.

I had now stepped into another zone most down low gay men fall under. "I'm out, but if you don't ask, I won't tell." This is a still a dangerous place to be. When people discussed gay issues I didn't say anything. If a woman flirted and wanted to have sex, I didn't stop her. I liked the fact that people still saw me as a heterosexual man.

People are accustomed to hearing the word gay and seeing flamboyant men. I was not a representation of that. If I told someone I was gay, they didn't believe it. "You don't look gay," they would say. "You don't act like them." I hated hearing that. I hated that people had only a one-dimensional view when they imagined gay men.

I also would neither confirm nor deny my sexuality unless asked because, like most of us, I thought, "It's nobody's business who I sleep with." So technically, I still was not out. And some would say that we are out to those we care about. Did I care for no one?

However, I had not let some of my down low friends know I was coming out and I still got invitations to private parties. I was still part of a group of men who remained in secrecy. In some ways, I still needed a part of me not to be exposed. I still wanted some part of me for myself.

The lure of creeping and sneaking around was my high. The adrenaline would rush through my blood and every erogenous zone in my body would respond. As much as I wanted to walk away from the lifestyle, men seemed to show up at my most vulnerable moments. It is said that what you resist will persist.

If I went to a regular event, someone would introduce me to a man. "This is Terrance Dean, the founder of Men's Empowerment. He's been in the entertainment business for many years and he has created some powerful and amazing programs for the youth up in Harlem. You really got to know this man. He's a visionary and a leader." And before I knew it we were exchanging numbers for a date. That was how I was introduced to people all the time.

When someone heard all of that, their ears perked up. Their minds raced. Their body language let me know they were ready to receive me. All of their defenses dropped, and they were no longer the antelope in the Sahara Desert afraid of the lion who was lying in wait, ready to pounce. They *wanted* me to devour them.

Many down low men tried to stop me from coming out. "Why do you want to do that? You have everything. People are not going to accept you if you come out."

I heard it all. And the temptation to remain a part of the secret society of brothers was enticing. The invite-only parties. The networking and access to resources. The exclusivity of being a part of and befriending some of the most powerful circles of men in the business.

And the sex. The enormous amount of available, unemotional, no-strings-attached sex with men. Why would anyone in their right mind want to give up a good thing? All the pleasures I could imagine. And here I was walking away from it all. But I needed to. Sex for me was love. I had equated it with men liking me. I needed to be with someone who liked me for me. It was important for a man to get to know who I was. Sex was not who I was. I do enjoy it and love when someone's sexual appetite is as insatiable as mine, but I know it is not love.

As tempting as it all sounded, I was tired of being with down low men who only wanted sex. It was time to grow up, move on, and do for self. It was time for me.

I met a really cool brother, Kenny Greene, the lead singer of the group Intro. A down low friend introduced us at a party. When my friend introduced us, I was gushing over Kenny's accomplishments. He had written many hit songs for Mary J. Blige's album, *What's the 411?*

We talked practically the entire night. He was extremely nice and I found him to be one of the most genuine people.

Shortly after our introduction, I heard that Kenny was sick. He was in the hospital with AIDS. I was completely blown away when I heard the news. This scared me even more about the down low life. Many men thought that if another man on the down low appeared healthy, it was okay not to use a condom when having sex. Many men thought if they were a top and not a bottom that they were safe from getting HIV. When my friend Dirk died, I knew not to play that dangerous game with my life. I treated every man like he was HIV positive and made sure we wore condoms.

Kenny did a courageous thing. He broke his silence and did an interview with *Sister 2 Sister Magazine,* where he admitted to being bisexual and having full-blown AIDS.

The article sent shockwaves throughout the industry. People in the business were on the phone calling one another, and the e-mails were nonstop. Everyone wanted to know if it was true.

It was another opportunity for people in the industry to discuss homosexuality in the business. I knew for certain this was going to blow the lid off the down low brothers hiding in Hip Hop.

Many of my down low friends were scared. They feared they were going to be outed. People were going to start telling on one another. Our secret world would no longer be a secret. Men who were not afraid would stand up and admit their homosexual desires. They would no longer hide in the closet. Openly gay rap artists, singers, and record label executives would become a voice and a face for gay men and women in the entertainment industry.

As much as I hoped a celebrity would step out and proudly discuss his sexuality, it didn't happen. Nothing happened. Kenny Greene died, and the entertainment industry went on like business as usual.

I hated it that nothing occurred within the industry. There had been nothing to acknowledge that not only were there gay men in Hip Hop, but that a brother had just died from AIDS.

For once I let go of my shame and embarrassment about my sexuality. I called up a friend at Lincoln Center. "I want to put on a panel discussion. Do you think I can put it on there?"

"No problem," Claude said. "I'll make it happen."

I wanted the entertainment industry to acknowledge gay black men. I wanted to let Hip Hop know we were just as much a part of it as anyone. The panel, Young, Black, Gifted and Gay . . . Powerful Men in the Entertainment Industry, was one of the most talked-about and anticipated events to hit New York City at that time.

Lincoln Center's Kaplan Penthouse was jam-packed. Men from all aspects of the entertainment industry came out. Brothers who were openly gay, down low, and straight filled the auditorium. Women came. There wasn't an empty seat in the house. The theater had to pull out an additional hundred chairs.

I was thrilled to see such a huge turnout, but I thought I was in over my head. I felt flustered. I thought this would surely blackball me and my friends. I started to reconsider what I was doing. But then all the panelists started arriving: Quohnos Mitchell, former director of PR for Tommy Hilfiger USA; Timothy Benson, former HIV prevention coordinator, Gay Men's Health Crisis; Emil Wilbekin, former editor in chief, *VIBE* magazine; Andre Lee, former director of marketing, Urbanworld Films; James Saunders, U-Men Entertainment; a former entertainment executive with Arista Records; Byl Thompson, public relations consultant in fashion and entertainment; and Caushun, the Gay Rapper.

They all praised me for putting together the panel and inviting them. "It's about time something like is happening," Emil said. "This is long overdue."

After that panel discussion, I received so many e-mails from men and women praising me for being brave. I wasn't sure if it was brave or not, but I do know it felt like a ton of bricks were lifted off my shoulders. I also learned that it takes small steps to accomplish anything, and I had just taken mine.

38. MISSING YOU

AUNT LISA CALLED ME in late June with the news that my grand-mother was extremely ill. The doctors had discovered a blood clot near her heart. They feared giving her an operation because she was too old and they didn't want to send her body into shock.

They didn't know how much longer she had. She was going to die soon. When I heard those words they traveled through my body and the shock hit my system like an earthquake. The thought of not hav-ing Grandma Pearl around didn't register. It never crossed my mind. I always thought she would be around. She was only eighty-two. She had more time. I knew many elderly people who lived into their nine-ties. I always figured she would be one of them. Grandma Pearl was invincible. She taught me how to be strong and a fighter.

I hated seeing her in the hospital. She was frail. Her body was thin-ner, and she was not her lively self. The tubes going in and out of her body seemed to keep her more in pain than relieve it.

The entire family was in and out of the hospital room. Each one of us took turns sitting with Grandma Pearl. I was nervous and waited to be the last person. I couldn't handle seeing her lying in the hospital bed. The tubes in her nose caused her to whisper when she spoke. I sat in the chair next to her bed and occasionally glanced at the television. Her favorite soap opera, *All My Children*, was on. It was ironic that all of her children, grandchildren, and great-grandchildren were at the hospital.

I talked with her and thanked her once again for all she had done. I thanked her for the insights on how to handle the world. I thanked her for being my rock, my mother, and my father. I tried to hold back the tears, but they fell on my face. I had to excuse myself and went into the bathroom to wash up. I stood looking into the mirror, hoping this wasn't it. That this wasn't the last time I would see my grandmother alive.

After a week, Grandma Pearl's health improved, and I made it back to New York with high hopes of her recovering. I knew she would bounce back and defeat the illness in her body.

Then on September 1, seven days before my birthday, Grandma Pearl passed. She was gone.

I was glad that Grandma Pearl got a chance to see me make something out of myself. I am so proud she got a chance to read my first published book, *Reclaim Your Power!: A 30-Day Guide to Hope, Healing, and Inspiration for Men of Color.* I dedicated the book to her, my mother, brothers, and sister.

For a long time after she died, I couldn't seem to pull it together. I had not prepared myself for that moment. It was hard for me to go out on speaking engagements. I would break down and cry in the middle of the speeches. I just couldn't seem to focus on anything other than my loss.

One night I had a dream about Grandma Pearl, and in the dream, I was in the house I grew up in in Detroit. Everyone was in the house— my sister, aunts, uncles, and cousins, everyone except my grandmother. I was in my old bedroom upstairs watching television. I wasn't a child, I saw myself as an adult.

Grandma Pearl was walking by on a street paved with gold. She looked absolutely stunning. Her face was younger, and she looked healthy and happy. She was smiling and was dressed to the nines in an all-white business suit. It looked like she was on her way somewhere very important.

"Grandma, grandma," I called out to her. "I can't change the channel. I don't have the remote control." She smiled at me and reached out her hand. In it was a remote control. My grandmother handed it to me. She then turned and continued walking down the golden streets.

I woke up crying. I was really missing my grandmother.

I realized she had given me the remote control so I could be in control of my own destiny. It was now time for me to live for me. I could no longer be concerned with what others thought about me or my sexuality. I didn't need validation from a community of people who insisted on ignoring my presence. I no longer needed to justify being black, male, and gay. I was now in control.

39. QUIET STORM

AFTER SIX YEARS of traveling on the road speaking at colleges and universities, book signings, a fellowship at Vanderbilt University, and cleansing myself of the down low life in the entertainment industry, something inside me was yearning. I knew what it was and I kept trying to ignore it. The itch had returned.

I figured I'd keep myself busy and return to work. I had not had a nine-to-five job all this time and the only thing I loved doing other than writing was working in entertainment.

Since I had dropped out of the entertainment scene I knew it would be difficult getting back into the game. The players had changed dramatically. Only a few of my friends had remained and moved up the ladder. Others had gotten completely out of the business and were doing new things.

One of my down low friends in the business had moved up the ladder. He gave me a call. There was an opportunity at MTV, my old stomping grounds. "Terrance, just so you know, this job isn't what you're used to. Things have really changed at MTV, and it's going to be hard trying to come in as a coordinator or manager. You've been gone for too long."

He was right. I had been gone for too long. Six years away from the entertainment industry is a lifetime. This business has a high turnover rate, and people never stay in one place for too long.

"Man, you know me. All I need to do is get my foot in the door," I said. "I can handle the rest from there."

MTV is known for hiring freelancers and temps. It helps them to cut costs on many of the projects they do and payout for health insurance and other employee benefits. In order for me to get back inside, I had to be hired as a temporary employee. I was going to be in production events as an assistant.

It would have been a major blow to my ego, but this wasn't a career move for me. It was something to do just so I could get out of the house. I knew how crazy the business was. Besides I had already hung out with the celebrities, partied with the best of them, and slept with some. I had been there and done that.

At MTV, many of my friends had moved on. Only a handful of familiar faces were there. The place had completely changed. MTV had gone corporate. It was no longer the fun and carefree place it had been. It was serious business.

Production events was the hot ticket at MTV, the place where many people wanted to work, in and out of the business. Everybody wanted to be in my spot because our department handled the greenroom for the celebrities, the gift bags, red carpet arrivals, seating, and tickets. We were the pulse for every show.

I came in during the 2006 Movie Awards. Before I could get settled, my phone started ringing off the hook. Everybody was calling for tickets—publicists, managers, and sometimes the celebrities themselves. They had to be at the show. It was imperative they got tickets. "Terrance, you do know who my client is? How can we assure that they will get tickets?"

My boss, Kathy, had already schooled me on the many calls we were going to receive. She let it be my job to screen and handle all the ticket requests. If it was someone important, someone who was relevant to the show, or someone who was relevant at the time, then we took the request seriously. They were given top priority. If it was some random call, or a publicist with a B- or C-list actor, then we put them on a waiting list.

I was back in the groove, back in my element. It felt good to have my stride back. I thought I would have a difficult time adjusting to the new MTV, but I didn't. It was a very familiar place for me.

My down low friends discovered I was back. I had not communicated with many of them in years, others in months. They knew I was back in the game. I should have known it would only be a matter of time before I was back in the circle. I started receiving e-mails to down low parties. This time around however, the parties were more private. They were extremely discreet. The down low scene had become national news. It made it to Oprah. The world knew about the secret lives of down low men having sex with men.

Many of the down low men I knew had gone deeper into the closet. Those in the entertainment industry thought the plague hit us, especially the artists and executives. Many people in the business began speculating who was on the down low. Women started becoming more watchful of men they suspected. They watched his movements, who he hung out with, and who he was dating. Down low men knew they were being watched, so they covered their tracks with even more careful tactics. They monitored everything they did all the way down to the secret parties, which became more secretive. The new artists who came in the business were much harder and meaner. Their exteriors were rugged, dirty, and gritty, and nothing about them gave any indication if they were gay or had any desires for a man. Even members of their crews were wannabe gangsters and thugs.

The few down low friends I had in the industry kept me updated and abreast of the artists who were part of the family. It no longer thrilled me, like it used to, to hear the news about a new member of the down low family. I had come to the conclusion that most men were suspect and many men, if given the opportunity, would have sex with another man, whether it had anything to do with helping their career or not.

Even though I had not been part of the entertainment world for six years, I still continued to meet down low men while I traveled on the road and some in my neighborhood of Harlem. Once I met one down low brother, I was introduced to several of his friends. Each circle had their own private entrée with intense background checks. The cycle never ended. Down low men are simply everywhere.

I told myself I was going to be very low-key this time. I wasn't going to get caught up in the down low scene again. I had come out of the closet. I was no longer down low. I couldn't get back into the scene if I wanted to. Anyone seen with me people would know.

There was one thing I didn't do, however. Even though I came out to my family and some of my close friends, I had yet to live a gay lifestyle. I still did not socialize with a lot of gay men. I still did not go out to the gay clubs frequently. I would still get uncomfortable when I was around a bunch of gay men. Even though I thought I was out, I was still technically in the closet. If someone asked if I was gay, I would avoid the question or simply say, "Naw, I'm not gay." There was something about that word that still stung me in my chest. I hated hearing it, especially if it was directed toward me.

I asked many of my down low friends if they still struggled with their sexuality and if they thought of themselves as gay men. "Terrance, I am gay, but I'm not like those other gay guys. I don't go to the club or lead a gay lifestyle," one of my friends told me.

"But what if someone asks if you're gay. Would you tell them yes?"

"Nope. It's nobody's business who I sleep with."

With all of my down low friends that was their sentiment. Even though they knew they liked men and preferred to be with men, they would never admit to being gay. They were like me and still struggling with their sexuality. Even though their families and close friends knew, they wouldn't dare tell anyone else, or be open about their lifestyle.

When I got back to MTV, I noticed there were quite a few openly gay black men, who I stayed clear of because I still wasn't comfortable being around obviously gay men. If people were to find out about me, I wanted to be the one to tell them.

My first e-mail to a down low party came by way of a very good friend who was tied to the scene. "Greg" knew about every party happening in the city. He was the "go to" man for any information related to the down low scene.

"Terrance, you got to come to this party," he said. "It's going to be some *fine* men there!" I knew there would be. Greg was attractive, with his pretty-boy light skin, curly hair, and beautiful, dark eyes. Greg had a Rolodex of fine men in the entertainment industry.

I couldn't resist the temptation from Greg. I had to go and check it out for myself.

You would have thought it was a family reunion when I walked through the door. Everyone was happy to see me. There was a sea of familiar faces. It seemed like the entire night I was hugging and catching up with someone. Brothers I hadn't seen in years were coming up to me. It felt great being back in the mix. Once I told people I was back at MTV, they gave me the rundown of the newest members of the down low clique in the entertainment industry.

"Have you met so and so at BET yet? What about the new guy at Sony? I know you know my boy at J Records?" All night I was given new names to remember as well as new faces to meet. These brothers were fine. No, they were gorgeous. I don't know where I had been to miss out on a new crop of beautiful, black down low men.

I'm glad I resisted my body's reaction to want to take someone home. It wouldn't have been good for either of us. I had not been sexual with a man in over six months. If I had taken a brother home, I definitely would have put a hurting on him. The sexual tension would have proved too much for any man I came in contact with.

Greg continued to fill me in on all the down low functions. After the first party, I knew it would be wise to pace myself. I didn't want to jump back into the scene. I wanted to take it nice and slow. I didn't want to relive what I already had been through.

After our department finished the Movie Awards and the Video Music Awards, we started prepping for VH1's Hip Hop Honors. It was a star-studded event honoring MC Lyte, Rakim, Eazy E, Russell Simmons, Afrikka Bambaataa, and The Wu-Tang Clan.

I knew I was going to run into a lot of familiar down low faces at this event. Many of the men I had partied and sexed with were going to be there. I knew because of the influx of calls our department got from artists and their publicists wanting tickets.

My phone never stopped ringing. From the moment I walked in the office to the end of day, I got at least a hundred calls about tickets. "What do I need to do to get tickets? Who can I talk to? Can you hook me up? Can I hook you up?"

Some artists were persistent. They themselves would call two and three times a day. They desperately wanted to be at the biggest event in town.

I received one call from an old-school Hip Hop legend. I was smiling from ear to ear. I couldn't believe I was actually on the phone speaking with "Ezekial." I grew up listening to his group's music. They made history with their music, and many rap artists tried to emulate his style, but none could match his lyrical wit.

"Listen, Terrance," Ezekial said. "You know I need to be there, but more important, my group needs to be there. We are Hip Hop trailblazers."

"I know and I understand, but tickets are tight," I said. "If something comes up and we get more tickets I'll let you know."

"Let me give you my numbers to reach me." He provided me with every number from his home, cell, and his studio. From that day forward we spoke nearly twice every day. Sometimes he called just to say what's up. Ezekial was really cool and on one occasion he played some music over the phone for me.

My mind started to race. I knew I shouldn't make anything of it. He was probably running game. I had something he wanted. He wanted tickets to the show and if he played me close he could get them. I knew it was game, until he said, "I want to meet you, Terrance. You sound like a real cool dude. I'm serious. I really want to meet you and hook up."

I had to keep it professional. No matter how intrigued I was, this was crossing the line. I shouldn't have engaged him in conversation when he called. I shouldn't have taken his numbers and called him after hours. I knew it would be wrong to meet up with him. I still wasn't sure what his intentions were. But the only way to know for sure was to accept the invitation he extended to his studio. Ezekial wanted me to hear the group he was managing sing live. There was no harm in that. I mean for real now, how could I turn down a Hip Hop legend?

ACKNOWLEDGMENTS

I would first like to give thanks to God for this amazing experience called life in the human form. I've been truly blessed beyond measure. It's been an amazing journey, and each step of the way I have been reminded of who I am and why I am here by a host of wonderful guides.

Thanks to my aunt Prisicilla Bradford, and uncles John Williams and Andrew Dean, the most amazing support system and lovable people I could ever dream of having. As well as to my aunt by marriage, Amanda Williams; and my uncle by marriage, Eddie Bradford; my sister, Sheritta Gerald; and nephew, Mitchell—thanks for the love. To my huge, extended family of cousins and in-laws, and especially to my cousin Alfreda Dean-Taylor—thanks for taking my calls and listening while I was writing this book. You provided great feedback.

In memory of Grandma Pearl; my mother, Blanche Gerald; and brothers George and Jevonte Gerald. I always feel their presence.

There are some agents who are great, and then there are those who are exceptional. My agent, Karen E. Quinones Miller, is exceptional. You get it, got it, and have it. Ever so gracious and a visionary, you helped me to see beyond my wildest dreams. Thank you from the bottom of my heart. The Mojitos are on me!

To my editor, Krishan Trotman—thank you, thank you, thank you! You are so smart, talented, and a writer's dream. You got me to dig deeper, go where I was afraid to look, and pushed me to write as if my life depended on it. I only wish every editor were as excellent, thorough, and patient as you. My deepest gratitude to my publisher, Judith Curr. Thank you for believing in this book. To Malaika Adero for getting it and finding a home for it at Atria, and to Christine Saunders—you so understand it all. Also, to the rest of the Atria/Simon & Schuster family, who cheered and anticipated this book.

To my best friend, Gordon Chambers, who told me to "write the damn book." Thank you for all the years of listening, pushing, encouraging, and believing in me. To Imamu A.M. Baraka. You listened ever so intently and allowed me to "check-out" without ever forcing me to "check-in." Thank you to my suave frat brother Larry (PhD) Johnson; his wife, Monique; and their triplets, Kennedy, Kyler, and Chase, who have been my surrogate family. I'm so glad we've reconnected and I love you all so much. Also, to my extended surrogate family Lakey the Kid (your book is next), Mia Graham, Eliakim O. Johnson, Jr., and Terrina Johnson. Thank you to the baddest and smartest lawyer and frat brother, Marc Metze and the Metze family—Samantha, Miriam, Lawrence, and Marc Jr.

Special thank-yous to: Tara Powell; Phedra Price; Marlynn Snyder (it's all about the pesos); Marlon Gregory; Sean Brown; Eric Peace; Yarnell McCollum; Lloyd Boston; Derrick Thompson; Emil Wilbekin; Kevin E. Taylor; Iyanla Vanzant and Adeyemi Bandele; Margaret Pazant; Derek Luke and his wife, Sophia; Ernest Montgomery (my D.R. partner in crime); Jose Borrero; Anthony Montgomery (Monaga); Derrick Toliver (two hearts are always better together); Phil Wilson and The Black AIDS Institute; Keith Boykin; Nathan Hale; Nathan Scott; Karu Daniels; Patrick Riley; Dwayne Jenkins; Patrick Ian-Polk; *Bleu Magazine; Clik Magazine;* Doron Lee; Desiree Cooper; Charles Pugh; Darrien Trotter; Peter Holoman; William A. Allen; Chris Montgomery; Ron Jackson; Malik Simmonds; Paul Butler, Esq.; Sean Johnson, Esq.; Ivan Matias; Victor DeJesus; Dr. Alton Byrd; Tarya Lewis; Keelon Hawkins; Wayman; Dawn Daniels; Candace Sandy; Merrick Buckingham; Pam Patino; Sabrina Lamb; Mondella Jones; Stacey Adams; Fred Jackson; James Staten; Leslie "Buttaflysoul" Taylor; Dion

Vines; Maurice Williams; Nahshon Anderson; Cord (you better sing, damn it!); Malaku; Jeff Johnson; The Permel family—Chris Beal, Ron, and Jenai Beal; Georgette Hayden; Felisha Booker and the Dynamic Producer family; Larry & Sabir; Ron Rodgers; Louis Brown; William DuBose; Michael Scott Jones; Winsome Sinclair; Tracey Hinds; Andre Peterson; Ailene Torres (we did it!); and Robbie Morganfield (thank you for saving me in Nashville).

If I forgot anyone, please forgive me. You know how you have touched my life.

To my wonderful speaking agent, Bob Klages, and The Klages Agency. To my editors at the *Tennessean,* the *New York Sun,* and All The Rage, who allowed me to write and taught me how to be a better writer.

To the Blow-Up Kids, Tamara Francois, Sydney Margetson, Lydia Andrews, Brian St. John, and Adolfo and Sara Vasquez. (Y'all still my family).

To all the men in Men's Empowerment. You are all so dear to me, and I thank you for your patience and encouragement.

To my MTV family, Dawn Kinard (we got another book to write), Kathy Flynn, Dara Rothenbiller, Marisa Pena, Martha Rubiano, Suz-Anna DeLaRosa, and Christina Norman. Thank you all for letting me write during my "down" time.

To two wonderful ladies and editors who have also been extremely supportive, Melody Guy and Glenda Howard.

To all the bookstores who supported my first book, and especially Our Story Books, Afrocentric Bookstore, A&B Books, Brownstone Books, Hue-Man Bookstore, Alkebu-Lan Images, Howard University Bookstore, Shrine of the Black Madonna, The Truth Bookstore, Karibu Bookstore, and Black Expressions Book Club.

To the Queen of all Media, Wendy Williams.

To my Los Angeles family of friends, actors, producers, directors, and exes. To my New York family of friends, singers, rappers, music executives, and exes. Lastly, to all those who are Hiding in Hip Hop and who encouraged me to tell my story.